SPANISH 2
for Christian Schools®

Bob Jones University Press, Greenville, SC 29614

Beulah E. Hager
with
Kenneth G. Casillas
María Isabel Ruiz Bell
Ivonne B. Gardner

SPANISH 2
for Christian Schools®

Bob Jones University Press, Greenville, SC 29614

Beulah E. Hager
with
Kenneth G. Casillas
María Isabel Ruiz Bell
Ivonne B. Gardner

LAS ÁREAS DE HABLA ESPAÑOLA

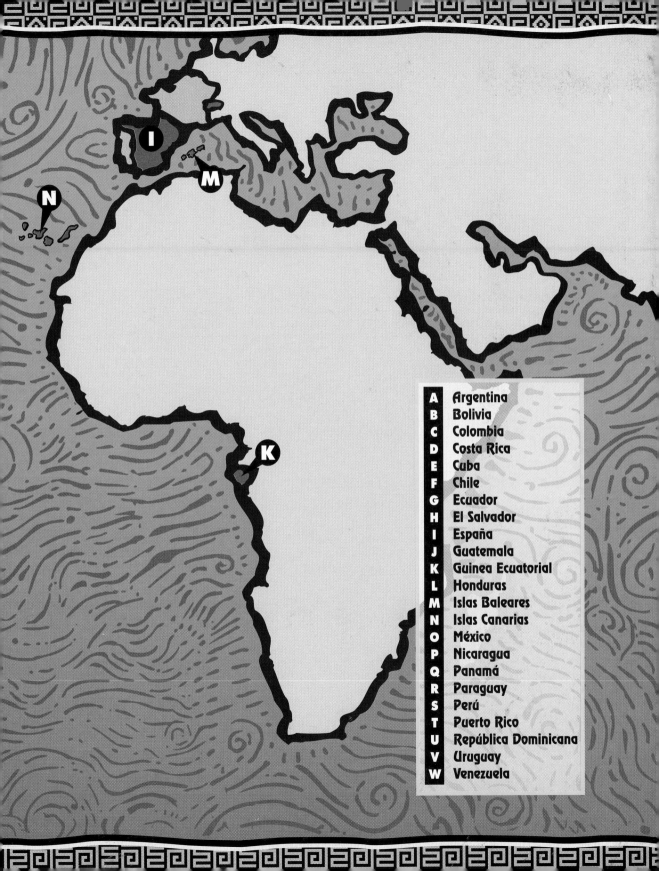

A	Argentina
B	Bolivia
C	Colombia
D	Costa Rica
E	Cuba
F	Chile
G	Ecuador
H	El Salvador
I	España
J	Guatemala
K	Guinea Ecuatorial
L	Honduras
M	Islas Baleares
N	Islas Canarias
O	México
P	Nicaragua
Q	Panamá
R	Paraguay
S	Perú
T	Puerto Rico
U	República Dominicana
V	Uruguay
W	Venezuela

NOTE:
The fact that materials produced by other publishers are referred to in this volume does not constitute an endorsement by Bob Jones University Press of the content or theological position of materials produced by such publishers. The position of Bob Jones University Press, and the University itself, is well known. Any references and ancillary materials are listed as an aid to the student or the teacher and in an attempt to maintain the accepted academic standards of the publishing industry.

SPANISH 2 for Christian Schools®

Beulah E. Hager, M.A.
Kenneth G. Casillas, M.A.
María Isabel Ruiz Bell, M.Ed.
Ivonne B. Gardner, M.Ed.

Produced in cooperation with the Bob Jones University Department of Modern Languages of the College of Arts and Science, the School of Religion, and Bob Jones Academy.

for Christian Schools is a registered trademark of Bob Jones University Press.

ISBN 0-89084-873-4

15   14   13   12   11   10   9   8   7   6   5   4   3   2   1

TABLE OF CONTENTS

Capítulo Uno

Capítulo Dos

Capítulo Tres

Capítulo Cuatro

Capítulo Cinco

Capítulo Seis

Capítulo Siete

Capítulo Ocho

Capítulo Nueve

Capítulo Diez

Capítulo Once

Capítulo Doce

Introduction

¡Bienvenidos al estudio del español!

Throughout this second year of study, you will learn more about the Spanish language itself *and* about the Hispanic world—its fascinating history, rich culture, and, above all, its great need for the gospel of Christ. Perhaps some day you will have the privilege of sharing the message of God's great love with Spanish-speaking people in their own language.

As you continue to develop your skills in reading, writing, speaking, and listening to Spanish, keep in mind the admonition of Colossians 3:23-24:

> And whatsoever ye do, do it heartily as to the Lord, and not unto men; knowing that of the Lord ye shall receive the reward of the inheritance: for ye serve the Lord Christ.

¡Disfruten el año! ¡Que Dios les bendiga ricamente!

En todo tiempo ama el amigo,
y es como un hermano en tiempo
de angustia. **Proverbios 17:17**

CAPÍTULO UNO

1-1 ¡BIENVENIDOS A LA ESCUELA!

Diálogo ▲▲

Raúl: Hola, Pedro. ¿Qué tal?

Pedro: Bien, gracias. ¿En qué clase de español estás ahora?

Raúl: Estoy en la clase del señor García. Él es muy inteligente. Habla cuatro *idiomas:* inglés, español, portugués y francés.

languages

Pedro: ¿Hay chicas en la clase?

Raúl: Sí, hay diez chicas y son muy simpáticas. Estudian mucho y cantan en el coro de español.

Pedro: ¿Cantan en español?

is looking for / people

Raúl: Sí. El señor García *está buscando* más *gente* para cantar en el coro.

So

Pedro: *Así que* tú cantas en el coro, ¿no?

no way

Raúl: No, *qué va.* Yo nunca canto.

Pedro: Pues, yo sí. Voy a hablar con el señor García para cantar con ellos. ¿Dónde está su oficina?

next to
only

Raúl: Está *junto a* la clase de ciencias. Pero, Pedro, ¡el coro es *sólo* para chicas!

◆ **Conversación**

1. ¿Quién enseña la clase de español de Raúl?

2. ¿Qué idiomas habla el profesor?

3. ¿Cuántas chicas hay en la clase?

4. ¿Qué necesita el coro?

5. ¿Quiere cantar Pedro en el coro? ¿y Raúl?

6. ¿Cantas tú en un coro? ¿Cantas en español?

Vocabulario

Las muchachas **andan** por el campo de fútbol.

Los estudiantes **aman** su patria.

Carmen y Mirna **cantan** en el coro.

Javier **trabaja** en el laboratorio de computadoras.

Ella **mira** la tarea de matemáticas en la pizarra.

Pablo **busca** un libro en la biblioteca.

El estudiante **lleva** sus libros en la mochila.

Ella **compra** una pluma en la librería.

Pedro **llega** tarde a la parada de autobús.

*Pedro **toma** un taxi.*   *Pedro **paga** al taxista.*

Gramática ▲▲▲

El presente: los verbos regulares *-ar*

Verbs in Spanish are grouped according to their infinitive ending: *-ar* (called the first conjugation), *-er* (the second conjugation), or *-ir* (the third conjugation). In this section we review the present tense of the regular *-ar* verbs along with the subject pronouns. Note carefully the conjugated endings of the verb *hablar* (to speak).

Hablar			
yo	hablo inglés.	*nosotros(as)*	hablamos alemán.
tú	hablas español.	*vosotros(as)*	habláis portugués.
Ud., él, ella	habla francés.	*Uds., ellos(as)*	hablan ruso.
Present Participle:	hablando		

Subject pronouns (*yo, tú, él, nosotros, etc.*) may be omitted in Spanish sentences because the verb ending indentifies the subject.

Estudio español.

Subject pronouns, however, are used for emphasis or for clarification if the subject is not clear.

El señor García habla portugués, pero **ella** habla ruso.

The pronoun *tú* is called the *familiar you* because it is used to refer to people you would normally address by first name. The pronoun *Ud. (usted),* on the other hand, is considered the *formal you* because it is used to refer to people you would address only by last name.

In Latin America, the pronoun *vosotros* and its corresponding verb form are rarely used. The pronoun *Uds. (ustedes)* is the equivalent to the plural *you* in English. Note, however, that even though *Ud.* and *Uds.* are second-person pronouns, they always take the third-person form of the verb. (For a review of the subject pronouns, see Reference Tables, p. 337.)

◆ **Actividad 1**

For each sentence, choose an appropriate verb from the list below and then provide its correct form.

andar	buscar	entrar	escuchar	llegar
llevar	mirar	pagar	tomar	trabajar

1. Carmen busca su libro de biología que está perdido (*lost*).
2. Los estudiantes llegan temprano a la clase.
3. Nosotros miramos las fotos de las vacaciones.
4. Tú tomas mucho café.
5. Yo trabajo los sábados.
6. Juan paga la cuenta del restaurante.
7. Los chicos llevan los libros de las chicas.
8. Tú andas en el centro comercial con tus compañeros (*classmates*).
9. Yo escucho las noticias (*the news*) a las seis de la tarde.
10. Ustedes entran en la clase con todos sus libros.

La negación

Raúl **nunca** canta.   *Raúl never sings.*

To make sentences negative in Spanish, use the following word order: **negative word + verb.**

Hablo español.	**No hablo** español.
Hablas inglés en la clase.	**Nunca hablas** inglés en la clase.
Ellas hablan muy bien.	Ellas **no hablan** muy bien.

The adverb *nunca* (never) may also follow the verb if the word *no* precedes the verb.

Raúl **nunca** canta.   Raúl **no** canta **nunca.**

◆ **Actividad 2**

Form new sentences by using each new subject given in parentheses and by making each verb negative. You may use *no* or *nunca.*

Modelo: Mis compañeros caminan a la escuela. (yo)
　　　　Yo no camino a la escuela.

1. Yo estudio español. (mi madre)
2. Nosotros practicamos los verbos. (los niños)
3. El maestro enseña la lección. (el director)
4. Manuel saca fotos para la clase de fotografía. (tú)
5. Ellos necesitan plumas y papel. (yo)
6. Tú terminas la tarea a tiempo. (ellos)
7. Mi compañera olvida la lección del día. (nosotros)

Artículos, sustantivos y adjetivos

Unos muchachos simpáticos están en **la** clase de español.

An **article** precedes a noun and indicates the noun's *gender* (masculine or feminine) and *number* (singular or plural). Can you determine the gender and number of the articles in the sentence above? (For a review of the indefinite and definite articles, see Reference Tables, p. 335.)

In Spanish, all **nouns** (*sustantivos*) are either masculine or feminine, whether the noun designates a person, animal, place, thing, or idea. The chart below reviews some common masculine and feminine noun endings.

Masculine Noun Endings	o, l, n, r	*un libro, un pastel, el avión, el marcador* **Exceptions:** *la foto, la mano*
Feminine Noun Endings	a, d, -ción, -sión	*una tiza, una pared, la nación, la expresión* **Exceptions:** *el día, el mapa,* and words ending in *-ama* or *-ema: el programa, el problema*

Nouns ending in *e* or *z* may be either masculine or feminine: *el sobre, la fuente; el lápiz, la cruz.*

◆ **Actividad 3**

Pedro is looking for various objects but cannot find them because his desk is such a mess! Provide the correct indefinite article with each object he looks for.

Modelo: revista
　　　　Pedro busca una revista.

1. pluma
2. cuaderno
3. borrador
4. papel
5. regla
6. canción

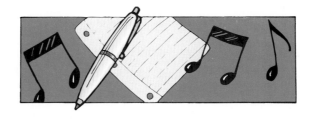

An **adjective** is a word that modifies a noun or pronoun. Adjectives must agree in gender and number with the noun or pronoun they modify. Note the four different forms of the adjective *pequeño*.

el cuaderno **pequeño**   los cuadernos **pequeños**
la clase **pequeña**   las clases **pequeñas**

Las formas de adjetivos masculinos y femeninos:

Adjectives that end in *o* in the masculine singular usually end in *a* in the feminine singular.

el perro **blanco**
    the white (male) dog
el papel **amarillo**
    the yellow paper
el bolígrafo **caro**
    the expensive pen

la perra **blanca**
    the white (female) dog
la pared **amarilla**
    the yellow wall
la pluma **cara**
    the expensive pen

◆ **Actividad 4**

For each of the following nouns, give the correct form of the adjective provided in parentheses.

Modelo: la Biblia (nuevo)
     la Biblia nueva

1. la casa (grande)
2. la sala (pequeño)
3. el automóvil (viejo)
4. la bicicleta (rojo)
5. el sombrero (bonito)
6. la bolsa (nuevo)
7. la gata (mimoso)

Some adjectives end in a letter other than *o* in the masculine singular. The masculine and feminine forms of these adjectives are usually the same.

el carro **grande**	la casa **grande**
el hombre **tenaz** (*tenacious*)	la mujer **tenaz**
el vestido **azul**	la falda **azul**

Exception: Some masculine adjectives end in a consonant but take an *a* ending in the feminine: adjectives ending in *-dor, -án,* and *-ín,* and certain adjectives of nationality.

el niño **hablador**	la niña **habladora**
el señor **alemán**	la señora **alemana**
el joven **francés**	la joven **francesa**

♦ **Actividad 5**

Complete each sentence by giving the correct form of the adjective in parentheses.

1. Cristina es una princesa (español) _____ .

2. La reina Sofía es (feliz) _____ .

3. El rey de España tiene una mansión (elegante) _____ .

4. El príncipe Felipe tiene un automóvil (francés) _____ .

5. La princesa Elena compra ropa (italiano) _____ .

Las formas del plural de sustantivos y adjetivos:

If the noun or adjective ends in a vowel, add *s.*

Ellas son buena**s** chica**s.**

If the noun or adjective ends in a consonant, add *es.*

Ellos son doctor**es** intelectual**es.**

Los chicos español**es** estudian con los frances**es.**

If the noun or adjective ends in *z,* change the *z* to *c* and add *es.*

Ellas son feli**ces.**

María tiene dos lápi**ces.**

La posición de los adjetivos

Descriptive adjectives usually follow the nouns they modify, but certain common adjectives, such as *bueno* and *malo,* may sometimes precede the noun.

Las **chicas simpáticas** cantan en el coro.

Es una **escuela buena.** No tenemos **malos estudiantes.**

Note: The shortened forms *buen* and *mal* precede a singular masculine noun.

Roberto es un **buen** estudiante, pero es **mal** deportista.

◆ **Actividad 6**

Supply the correct plural form of the word(s) given in parentheses.

Modelo: (La novela) _____ de misterio son (interesante) _____ .
Las novelas de misterio son interesantes.

1. (La muchacha) _____ de la clase son (bonita) _____ .

2. (El carro) _____ de (el profesor) _____ son (grande) _____ .

3. Tengo (la mano) _____ muy (frío) _____ .

4. (El señor) _____ donan (nuevo) _____ (escritorio) _____ para la clase.

5. (El estudiante) _____ están (feliz) _____ con los escritorios.

6. (El video) _____ de español son muy (informativo) _____ .

7. (El lápiz) _____ de mi compañero son (azul) _____ .

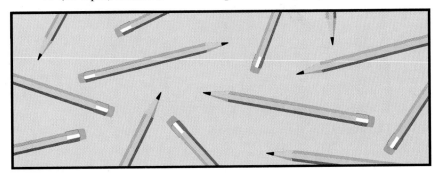

◆ **Actividad 7**

Supply the appropriate form of the words in parentheses. All verbs should be in the present tense.

Hoy es el primer día de clase. Yo (entrar) _____ a la escuela a las ocho de la mañana. (Comprar) _____ un cuaderno y dos (lápiz) _____ en la librería. A las ocho y cuarto (estudiar) _____ geometría. Es mi clase (favorito) _____ . A las nueve (trabajar) _____ en el laboratorio de computadoras. A las diez (llegar) _____ a la capilla. Todos los estudiantes (cantar) _____ himnos y (escuchar) _____ al director. Después yo (tomar) _____ leche y como en la cafetería. Las (clase) _____ en la tarde no son (aburrido) _____ . ¡Son (fascinante) _____ ! Pero cuando (acabar) _____ las clases, estoy (cansado) _____ .

Estar

The verb *estar* (to be) is used with adjectives to describe a condition or a state (physical, mental, or emotional) that may be subject to change.

Estar			
yo	estoy contento.	nosotros(as)	estamos enfermos.
tú	estás cansado.	vosotros(as)	estáis alegres.
Ud., él, ella	está triste.	Uds., ellos(as)	están enojados.

◆ **Actividad 8**

Describe how the following people feel by providing the correct form of *estar* and by choosing an adjective from the list below.

alegre	cansado	contento	de mal humor	enfermo
enojado	nervioso	satisfecho	tranquilo	triste

Modelo: En la clase, Lisa . . .
   En la clase, Lisa está contenta.

1. En casa, Antonio . . .

2. En la escuela, los estudiantes . . .

3. Los viernes, Sonia y Carmen . . .

4. Después de (*after*) comer mucho, tú . . .

5. Durante el concierto, el pianista . . .

6. Cuando tengo que limpiar la casa, yo . . .

7. Cuando mis amigos no llaman por teléfono, yo . . .

8. Cuando papá nos regaña (*scolds us*), nosotros . . .

9. Usted no va a la escuela hoy porque . . .

The verb *estar* + a prepositional phrase indicates location.

¿Dónde está el reloj?   El reloj **está en la pared**.
¿Dónde están los libros?   Los libros **están encima de la mesa.**

(For a review of prepositions see Reference Tables, p. 339.)

Hay

The verb form *hay* means "there is" or "there are."

Hay un reloj en la pared.   *There is a clock on the wall.*
Hay diez chicas en la clase.   *There are ten girls in the class.*

◆ **Actividad 9**

Answer the following questions.

1. ¿Cuántas chicas hay en tu clase de español?

2. ¿Cuántas personas hay en tu familia?

3. ¿Hay muchos estudiantes en tu escuela?

◆ **Actividad 10**

Write a paragraph of at least six sentences telling where things are located in your classroom. Use both *hay* and *estar.*

Modelo: *Hay un reloj en la pared. El escritorio de la maestra está delante de la clase.*

Vocabulario adicional ▲▲▲▲▲▲▲▲▲▲▲▲▲▲▲▲▲▲▲▲▲▲▲▲▲▲▲▲▲▲▲▲

You may already be familiar with these verbs. Can you guess what the nouns derived from the verbs mean?

Verbo	Sustantivo
amar	amante
cantar	cantante
estudiar	estudiante
participar	participante
practicar	practicante
entrar	entrada
llamar	llamada
llegar	llegada
mirar	mirada

La Cordillera de los Andes se extiende a lo largo del continente sudamericano desde Venezuela hasta Chile.

CHILE

- **AREA:** *292,300 sq. mi.*
  (approximately twice
  the size of California)

- **POPULATION:** *13.9 million*

- **GOVERNMENT:** *Republic*

- **CAPITAL:** *Santiago*

hile consists of a narrow stretch of land extending 2,650 miles down the Pacific coast of South America. Chileans grow wheat, barley, and tropical fruit in the central valley lying between the Andes Mountains on the east and a coastal mountain range on the west. The country is best known, however, as the world's leading producer of copper.

Due to its unusual geographic location, Chile's climate ranges from arid in the north to polar in the south, with tropical in the center. At the northern extreme, the Atacama Desert is not only one of the world's driest spots but also the world's only natural source of the mineral sodium nitrate, which is used to make gunpowder. At the opposite end of the country, Chile shares Tierra del Fuego with Argentina. Searching for a route to the Pacific, Magellan discovered this group of islands in 1520 and named it "Land of Fire" because of the many Indian bonfires along the shore.

1-2 HACIENDO AMIGOS

Diálogo ▲▲

Los jóvenes de varias iglesias están en la Iglesia Evangélica Bautista para un día de actividades. Pedro encuentra a una chica y habla con ella.

Pedro: Hola. Soy Pedro. ¿Cómo te llamas?

Maritza: Me llamo Maritza. Mucho gusto. ¿De dónde eres?

Pedro: Soy de Linares, pero vivo en Santiago.

Maritza: ¿De veras? ¿Estudias en Santiago?

high school   **Pedro:** Sí. Estoy en la *escuela superior.*

Maritza: Y, ¿cuántos años tienes?

Pedro: Tengo dieciséis. Y tú, ¿dónde estudias?

Maritza: Estudio en una escuela de comercio. Estoy aprendiendo a usar computadoras.

here   **Pedro:** ¡Qué bien! ¿Cuántos están *aquí* de tu iglesia?

By the way   **Maritza:** Somos doce, con el pastor. *Por cierto,* tengo dos amigas aquí. Debes hablar con ellas también. Se llaman Maribel y Susana.

like   **Pedro:** ¿Son bonitas *como* tú . . . ?

◆ Conversación

1. ¿Por qué están los jóvenes en la Iglesia Evangélica Bautista?

2. ¿Dónde vive Pedro?

3. ¿Cuántos años tiene Pedro?

4. ¿Dónde estudia Maritza?

5. Y tú, ¿dónde vives y estudias?

Gramática ▲▲

Preguntas y respuestas

Notice the position of the subject and verb in each of the following sentences.

Los estudiantes viajan a Chile.　　¿Adónde **viajan los estudiantes**?
Tú bebes café con leche.　　　　　¿Qué **bebes tú**?
Pedro tiene tres clases por la　　　¿Cuántas clases **tiene Pedro** por
　　tarde.　　　　　　　　　　　　　　la tarde?

In statements, the subject usually precedes the verb. The pattern is **subject + verb.** When forming a question using an interrogative word, however, the subject usually follows the verb. The pattern is **¿interrogative word + verb + subject?**

　　When the subject is understood, it may be omitted from a question.
　　　¿Adónde viajan?
　　　¿Qué bebes?
　　　¿Cuántas clases tiene por la tarde?

¿Recuerdan las palabras interrogativas? *(Do you remember the interrogative words?)*

¿Adónde?	¿Adónde vas para las vacaciones? —Yo voy a Miami para las vacaciones.
¿Cómo?	¿Cómo estás? —Yo estoy muy bien.
¿Cuál?	¿Cuál es tu color favorito? —Mi color favorito es el verde.
¿Cuándo?	¿Cuándo estudian los alumnos? —Estudian por la tarde.
¿Cuánto?	¿Cuánto cuesta? —Cuesta cinco pesos. ¿Cuántas clases tienes? —Yo tengo seis clases.
¿De dónde?	¿De dónde es María? —María es de Santiago.
¿Dónde?	¿Dónde trabajas? —Yo trabajo en el banco.
¿Por qué?	¿Por qué estudias español? —Yo estudio español porque *(because)* quiero hablar español.
¿Qué?	¿Qué tienes en la bolsa? —Yo tengo un lápiz en la bolsa.
¿Quién?	¿Quién es tu mejor amigo? —Manuel es mi mejor amigo.

◆ **Actividad 1**

Déborah is a student from Santiago, Chile. What questions would you ask her to find out the following information about her?

1. her name

2. her age

3. where she is from

4. what her phone number is

5. how much it costs to travel to Santiago

6. what her favorite class is

◆ **Actividad 2**

Using the interrogative words, write a question for each statement below.

Modelo: Margarita estudia biología.
    ¿Qué estudia Margarita? or *¿Quién estudia biología?*

1. La familia González vive en Puerto Rico.

2. Mario tiene un carro nuevo.

3. Pablo y Eduardo estudian francés.

4. La profesora llega a las ocho de la mañana.

5. Compramos cuadernos en la tienda.

6. Ana y Maribel escuchan música religiosa.

7. Miro la televisión por la noche.

8. El Sr. González está enfermo.

9. Mi dirección es: 1009 Avenida Metropolitana.

10. Mi amigo Roberto es de Santiago, Chile.

El presente: los verbos regulares *-er / -ir*

In this section you will review the present tense of the regular *-er* and *-ir* verbs (or verbs of the second and third conjugations, respectively). Most verbs that end in *-er* are conjugated like *deber* (to owe), and most verbs that end in *-ir* are conjugated like *vivir* (to live).

Deber			
yo	debo 6 pesos.	*nosotros(as)*	debemos 8 soles.
tú	debes 7 colones.	*vosotros(as)*	debéis 15 pesetas.
Ud., él, ella	debe 5 córdobas.	*Uds., ellos(as)*	deben 3 dólares.
Present Participle:	debiendo		

Vivir				
yo	vivo en Perú.	nosotros(as)	vivimos en Miami.
tú	vives en México.	vosotros(as)	vivís en Ecuador.
Ud., él, ella	vive en Cuba.	Uds., ellos(as)	viven en Chicago.
Present Participle:	viviendo		

Vocabulario ▲▲▲▲▲▲▲▲▲▲▲▲▲▲▲▲▲▲▲▲▲▲▲▲▲▲▲▲▲▲▲▲▲▲▲▲▲▲▲

Verbos regulares *-er / -ir*

aprender	**Aprendo** español.
beber	La niña **bebe** un vaso de leche.
comer	Tomás y yo **comemos** en la cafetería.
correr	Anita no **corre** rápidamente.
creer	**Creo** en Dios.
deber	**Debemos** orar todos los días.
leer	Margarita **lee** un libro cada semana.
abrir	La profesora **abre** la ventana.
escribir	**Escribimos** cartas a nuestros amigos en España.
recibir	**Recibimos** cartas de ellos también.
repartir	Los jóvenes **reparten** tratados los sábados.
vivir	**Vives** en una casa grande y bonita.

The verb *aprender* followed by *a* + an infinitive means "to learn to do something."

Aprendo a hablar español.   *I learn to speak Spanish.*

The verb *deber* followed by an infinitive means "to ought to."

Debemos leer la Biblia todos los   *We ought to read the Bible every*
   días.   *day.*

If *deber* is followed by a noun, it means "to owe."

Juan me debe cinco dólares.   *Juan owes me five dollars.*

◆ **Actividad 3**

Change the sentences according to the new subjects given in parentheses.

Modelo: Marta vive en San Francisco. (Tomás y Pablo)
   Tomás y Pablo viven en San Francisco.

1. Mario debe mucho dinero. (yo)

2. Nunca bebo chocolate caliente por la noche. (nosotros)

3. Aprendemos un himno nuevo cada domingo. (el coro)

4. Papá lee el periódico todos los días. (los profesores)

5. Yo creo la Palabra de Dios. (tú)

6. Los atletas corren rápidamente. (usted)

7. Recibimos correspondencia de los misioneros en Chile. (ellos)

8. Tú abres las cartas ahora. (ella)

9. Enrique escribe la tarea en el cuaderno. (nosotros)

10. La profesora reparte los libros a los estudiantes. (Ana y Pedro)

◆ **Actividad 4**

Write five complete sentences using words from each column as shown in the model. You may write statements or questions.

Modelo: *Yo (no) leo el periódico en la biblioteca.*

A	B	C	D
yo	escribir	los libros	en casa
ellos	repartir	Juan 3:16	en la clase
nosotros	aprender	pizza	en la biblioteca
Ud.	leer	la tarea	en el restaurante
tú	abrir	el español	en la escuela
él	comer	el periódico	en la iglesia
ella	recibir	los tratados	en la calle

Gramática ▲▲▲

Ser

Ser			
yo	**soy** chilena.	*nosotros(as)*	**somos** delgados(as).
tú	**eres** simpático.	*vosotros(as)*	**sois** inteligentes.
Ud., él, ella	**es** grande.	*Uds., ellos(as)*	**son** leales.

When *ser* is followed by an adjective, the adjective must agree with the noun it modifies in number and gender. The adjectives used with *ser* describe basic traits and inherent characteristics such as size, shape, color, or personality.

Los sombreros son **grandes** y **negros.**

María es **bonita** y **amable.**

¿Cómo es tu mejor amigo(a)?		
amable (kind)	o	maleducado(a) (rude)
chistoso(a)/gracioso(a) (funny)	o	serio(a)
fiel (faithful)	o	infiel
generoso(a)	o	tacaño(a)
honesto(a)	o	deshonesto(a)/mentiroso(a)
leal (loyal)	o	desleal
paciente	o	impaciente
delgado(a)	o	gordo(a)
guapo/bonita	o	feo(a)
moreno(a)	o	rubio(a)

When *ser* is followed by the preposition *de* plus a noun, it may be used to indicate substance, origin, or possession.

¿De qué es la bolsa?	Es **de cuero** (*leather*).
¿De dónde es su padre?	Es **de San Juan.**
¿De quién es el libro?	Es **del profesor.**

The verb *ser* is used to indicate nationality, profession, religion, or political affiliation.

La Srta. López es **española**.

El señor Blanco es **dentista**.

Marta González es **bautista**, pero su hermano es **católico**.

Mi padre es **demócrata**, pero mi abuelo es **republicano**.

Note: After *ser,* the article is usually omitted with a noun indicating profession, unless that noun is modified by an adjective.

El hermano de Carlos es médico.

Es **un** médico famoso.

◆ **Actividad 5**

Replace the words in italics with the words in parentheses. Be sure to make any other necessary changes.

Modelo: *Los hermanos* son simpáticos. (Ella)
　　　　Ella es simpática también.

1. *Nosotros* somos americanos. (ellas)

2. *El señor Méndez* es republicano. (La señora de Méndez)

3. *Pedrito* es gracioso. (Juan y Carlos)

4. *Los profesores* son inteligentes. (la profesora)

5. *Rubén* es guapo. (yo)

6. *Mi amigo* es rico. (nosotros)

7. *El profesor Sánchez* es cristiano. (tú)

8. *El pastor Suárez* es joven. (ustedes)

9. *Ellos* son amables. (ella)

10. *Mi vecino* es honesto. (nosotras)

◆ **Actividad 6**

At a missions conference, each missionary quotes John 3:16 in the language of his country. Tell where each missionary is from:

Alemania	Canadá	la China
España	Francia	Italia
el Japón	Portugal	Rusia

Modelo: El Sr. Martin dice el versículo en chino.
       Es de la China.

1. Ted y Catherine Perry lo dicen en ruso.

2. Fred y Rachel Whitman lo dicen en italiano.

3. La familia Bixby lo dice en francés.

4. Bill y Karen Lowry lo dicen en alemán.

5. Dick y Pam Baker lo dicen en inglés.

6. Lynn Porter y yo lo decimos en español.

7. Joyce Oshiro lo dice en japonés.

8. Tú lo dices en portugués.

Ser vs. estar

1. *Ser* + an adjective describes a basic trait or inherent characteristic.
   Estar + an adjective describes a temporary state or condition.

Paco es guapo.	Paco está guapo.
(*He is a handsome fellow.*)	(*He looks handsome today.*)
Ana es mala.	Rosita está mala.
(*She is a bad girl.*)	(*She is sick.*)
El tomate es rojo.	Sus ojos están rojos.
(*The tomato is red.*)	(*His eyes are [look] red.*)

2. *Ser* + *de* gives origin.
   Estar + a preposition gives location.

Marcos es de Los Angeles.	*Marcos is from Los Angeles.*
Hoy está en Quito, Ecuador.	*Today he is in Quito, Ecuador.*

◆ **Actividad 7**

Provide the correct form of *ser* or *estar.*

1. Mariano _____ de Caracas.

2. Los estudiantes _____ en la clase de español.

3. El reloj _____ de oro.

4. El libro de historia _____ en el portafolio del profesor.

5. Los ojos de María _____ azules.

6. Paco y Tomás _____ mexicanos.

7. La madre de Rosita _____ profesora.

8. Rosita _____ enferma.

9. Ella _____ en el hospital.

10. El padre de Rosita _____ médico.

◆ **Actividad 8**

Interview one of your classmates. Ask all questions in Spanish.

What is his or her name? How old is he or she? Where is he or she from? Where does he or she live?

What does he or she prefer to eat? What are his or her favorite classes?

Describe his or her best friend. Who is his or her best friend? What is his or her best quality (*mejor cualidad*)?

Refrán ▲▲▲

Are you careful in choosing your friends? This proverb emphasizes the influence friends have upon you.

Dime con quien andas y te diré quien eres.

1-3 Reunión Familiar

Diálogo ▲▲▲▲▲▲▲▲▲▲▲▲▲▲▲▲▲▲▲▲▲▲▲▲▲▲▲▲▲▲▲▲▲▲▲▲▲▲

celebrating the golden wedding anniversary

Hoy tenemos una reunión familiar en casa porque estamos *celebrando las bodas de oro* de mis abuelitos. Mi abuelo Víctor tiene 73 años y mi abuela Rosa tiene 71.

just had / as you can imagine / proud great-grandchild fiancé or boyfriend

Mi tía Lorena y su esposo Adolfo están aquí también. Nuestro primo Jorge y su esposa Rut *acaban de tener* una niña. Se llama Cristina. *Como ya pueden imaginarse*, mis tíos están muy *orgullosos* de su nueva nieta, pero mis abuelos están más orgullosos que ellos. Cristina es su primera *bisnieta*.

Mi hermana Margarita está con su *novio*, Javier. Ellos se van a casar en noviembre.

—¡Sonrían, chicos!

Ahora, enfrente de la cámara de video están mis padres y mi hermana menor.

so

—Papá, ¿qué palabras tienes para nuestra familia en este día *tan* especial?

—¡Muchas felicidades a los abuelos y que cumplan 50 años más de casados!

◆ Conversación

1. ¿Qué celebra la familia?

2. ¿Cuántos años cumplen de casados los abuelos?

3. ¿Quiénes son los abuelos de Cristina?

4. ¿Por qué está orgullosa la abuela Rosa?

5. ¿Puedes adivinar (*guess*) quién saca el video?

Vocabulario ▲▲

Los parientes

bisabuelo (*great-grandfather*)	bisabuela (*great-grandmother*)
abuelo	abuela
nieto (*grandson*)	nieta (*granddaughter*)
esposo (*husband*)	esposa (*wife*)
padre	madre
hijo	hija
tío	tía
sobrino (*nephew*)	sobrina (*niece*)
primo	prima
hermano	hermana
cuñado (*brother-in-law*)	cuñada (*sister-in-law*)
suegro (*father-in-law*)	suegra (*mother-in-law*)
yerno (*son-in-law*)	nuera (*daughter-in-law*)

La Familia López

◆ **Actividad 1**

Supply the correct term by referring to the family tree illustration.

1. Lucía es _____ de Adolfo.

2. Margarita, Lucía y Paola son _____ de Jorge y Rut.

3. Jorge es _____ de Víctor y Rosa.

4. Roberto es _____ de Yolanda.

5. Víctor es _____ de Cristina.

6. Lorena es _____ de Yolanda.

7. Adolfo es _____ de Rut.

Gramática ▲▲▲

Los adjetivos posesivos

We have studied one way to indicate possession:

el sombrero **de** Margarita (*Margarita's hat*)

Another way to indicate possession is to use the possessive adjectives.

Possessor	Possessive Adjectives
yo	mi familia (*my family*)
tú	tu amiga (*your friend*)
Ud., él, ella	su clase (*his/her/your class*)
nosotros(as)	nuestro tío (*our uncle*) nuestra tía (*our aunt*)
vosotros(as)	vuestro abuelo (*your grandfather*) vuestra abuela (*your grandmother*)
Uds., ellos(as)	su pariente (*your/their relative*)

In Spanish, possessive adjectives must agree in number with the thing possessed (the noun that follows them). Thus, all possessive adjectives have both a singular and a plural form: *tu cámara/tus cámaras, su tía/sus tías*. The plural possessive adjectives are formed by adding an *s* to the singular endings.

The possessive adjectives *nuestro* and *vuestro* must also agree in gender: *nuestro abuelo/nuestra abuela, nuestros abuelos/nuestras abuelas*.

The possessive adjectives *su* and *sus* have several equivalents in English.

la nuera de Adolfo	su nuera	*his daughter-in-law*
el cuñado de Lorena	su cuñado	*her brother-in-law*
la suegra de usted	su suegra	*your mother-in-law*
el yerno de mis padres	su yerno	*their son-in-law*
las primas de ustedes	sus primas	*your cousins*
las amigas de ellos	sus amigas	*their friends*

When it is necessary to clarify to whom the possessive adjective *su* or *sus* is referring, the expression **de + a pronoun** (*de él, de ella, de Ud., de ellos, de ellas, de Uds.*) is used.

El padre **de él** es pastor.

◆ **Actividad 2**

Supply the correct possessive adjectives. The possessors are given in parentheses.

Modelo: El otoño es _____ estación favorita. (yo)
   El otoño es mi estación favorita.

1. _____ aniversario es el 20 de octubre. (él)

2. ¿Cuándo es _____ cumpleaños? (tú)

3. _____ abuela está en el hospital. (María y Ana)

4. ¿Dónde viven _____ abuelos? (María y Ana)

5. Tengo _____ libros en la mochila. (yo)

6. _____ maestro de historia es el señor Blanco. (nosotros)

7. Rebeca y María son _____ primas. (Rafael)

8. _____ tía Margarita es soltera. (nosotros)

9. _____ padres están de viaje. (nosotros)

10. _____ madres están en la oficina del director. (nosotros)

El comparativo de los adjetivos

Pedro es más simpático que Pablo.   *Pedro is nicer than Pablo.*
Tu bicicleta es menos cara que mi   *Your bike is less expensive*
  bicicleta.   *than my bike.*

In each sentence above, two people or things are being compared. To make unequal comparisons in English, adjectives may take *-er, more,* or *less.* In Spanish, adjectives take *más* (more) or *menos* (less).

más nuevo (que)	más antiguo (que)
newer (than)	*older (than)*
más largo (que)	más corto (que)
longer (than)	*shorter (than)*
más fácil (que)	más difícil (que)
easier (than)	*more difficult (than)*
menos aburrido (que)	menos divertido (que)
less boring (than)	*less amusing (than)*

The following adjectives of quality, quantity, and age have irregular comparative forms.

bueno	*good*	→	mejor (que)	*better (than)*
malo	*bad*	→	peor (que)	*worse (than)*
mucho	*much*	→	más (que)	*more (than)*
poco	*little*	→	menos (que)	*less (than)*
viejo	*old*	→	mayor (que)	*older (than)*
joven	*young*	→	menor (que)	*younger (than)*

◆ Actividad 3

Compare the following nouns by using a form of *mejor* or *peor.* These adjectives must agree in number with the nouns they modify.

Modelo: las frutas / los dulces
> *Las frutas son mejores que los dulces.*
> *Las frutas son peores que los dulces.*

1. las piñas / los mangos
2. los perros / los gatos
3. el frío / el calor
4. el café / el té
5. las flores / los chocolates

◆ Actividad 4

Compare the following people or objects using the adjectives in parentheses. Be sure to make the adjectives agree with the nouns they modify in gender and number.

Modelo: tu prima / tu primo (honesto)
> *Mi prima es más honesta que mi primo.*
> *Mi primo es menos honesto que mi prima.*

1. tu padre / tu madre (generoso)
2. tu padre / tu tío(a) (rico)
3. las matemáticas / el inglés (fácil)
4. la pizza / los tacos (delicioso)
5. tu libro de español / tu libro de historia (largo)
6. tu hermano(a) / tu amigo(a) (cómico)
7. tus padres / tus abuelos (viejo)

El comparativo de los adverbios

The comparative of adverbs is formed in the same way as that of adjectives. Note, however, that while adjectives must agree in number and gender with the nouns they modify, adverbs are invariable.

Carmen corre **más rápido que** su prima.	*Carmen runs faster than her cousin.*
Jorge habla **más rápido que** su hermano.	*Jorge speaks faster than his brother.*

The following common adverbs have irregular comparative forms.

bien	→	mejor (que)
mal	→	peor (que)
mucho/muy	→	más (que)
poco	→	menos (que)

◆ **Actividad 5**

For each sentence, use the word in parentheses to make a comparison. Be sure to use the comparative form of the adverb in italics.

Modelo: Mamá cocina *bien*. (papá)
   Sí, mamá cocina mejor que papá.

1. María llega *temprano*. (Mario)

2. Manuel estudia *poco*. (Manuela)

3. Los muchachos hablan *muy* fuerte en la clase. (las muchachas)

4. Pablo debe *mucho* dinero. (Paulina)

5. Los niños escriben *claramente*. (los jóvenes)

The construction **as** (easy) **as** indicates an equal comparison. The Spanish counterpart is **tan** (fácil) **como.**

◆ **Actividad 6**

Compare the two items given by giving your opinion.

Modelo: el fútbol / el béisbol (popular)
   El fútbol es más popular que el béisbol.
   El fútbol es menos popular que el béisbol.
   El fútbol es tan popular como el béisbol.

1. una hamburguesa / un filete de pescado (delicioso)

2. el negro / el azul (oscuro)

3. los deportes / los estudios (importante)

4. Andrés (5'7") / Carlos (6'1") (alto)

5. un Ford / un Chevrolet (bueno)

6. un Lear jet / un Concord (rápido)

7. una ópera / una comedia musical (cómico)

8. un metro / un kilómetro (corto)

9. tus primos(as) / tus hermanos(as) (atlético)

10. la escuela / la universidad (difícil)

Tener (to have)

> **Tengo** tres hermanas.
> Mi hermana mayor **tiene** 25 años.

In the second sentence above, *tener* is used to indicate age. Do you remember some of the other idiomatic expressions we use with the verb *tener?*

Tengo calor (frío / hambre / sed).	*I'm hot (cold / hungry / thirsty).*
Tienes razón.	*You are right.*
Tiene miedo.	*He is scared.*
Tenemos ganas de comer.	*We feel like eating.*
Tenéis sueño.	*You are sleepy.*
Tienen que estudiar para el examen.	*They have to study for the exam.*

◆ **Actividad 7**

Supply the correct form of *tener.*

1. Mi tío _____ dos carros.

2. ¿Qué libro de la Biblia (contener) _____ la historia de David y Goliat?

3. A las dos de la tarde yo _____ mi clase de piano.

4. Nosotros _____ tres días de vacaciones.

5. Ustedes _____ tres días para terminar el trabajo.

◆ **Actividad 8**

What would you say in the following situations? Use idiomatic expressions with *tener.*

Modelo: It is hot outside, and you have not had anything to drink all day.
¡Tengo sed!

1. You skipped breakfast and lunch today.

2. You got only five hours of sleep last night.

3. You feel like reading a book.

4. A classmate asks you, "¿Cuántos años tienes?"

5. The temperature is 100° F.

6. You are riding the highest roller coaster in the world.

7. It is snowing outside.

8. Your friend says that 2 plus 2 equals 4.

◆ **Actividad 9**

Supply the correct form of *tener que* + an infinitive. You may use an appropriate infinitive of your choice.

Modelo: Mañana mis padres _____ un carro nuevo.
Mañana mis padres tienen que comprar un carro nuevo.

1. El/la profesor(a) de español _____ en su casa.

2. Yo _____ mañana.

3. Tú _____ esta noche.

4. Nosotros _____ para nuestra clase de español.

5. Mi madre _____ en la iglesia el domingo.

◆ **Actividad 10 Repaso**

Act out the following situation: Pretend that your brother or sister is lost in the mall. You find a police officer and describe your brother or sister to him. (You may compare your lost sibling to yourself in order to give the officer more clues.)

Lectura bíblica ▲▲▲▲▲▲▲▲▲▲▲▲▲▲▲▲▲▲▲▲▲▲▲▲▲▲▲▲▲▲▲▲▲▲▲▲▲

Proverbios 15:1, 3, 16, 20

La blanda respuesta quita la ira; mas la palabra áspera hace subir el furor.
Los ojos de Jehová están en todo lugar, mirando a los malos y a los buenos.
Mejor es lo poco con el temor de Jehová, que el gran tesoro donde hay turbación.
El hijo sabio alegra al padre; mas el hombre necio menosprecia a su madre.

Si, pues, coméis o bebéis,
o hacéis otra cosa, hacedlo
todo para la gloria de Dios.
I Corintios 10:31

CAPÍTULO DOS

2-1 ¡A COMER!

Diálogo ▲▲

half way
to stop

El grupo de jóvenes va hacia un campamento. Están *a medio camino* y es la hora del almuerzo. El pastor decide *parar* en un restaurante.

what you want
the order

Pastor: Jóvenes, somos muchos. ¿Por qué no me dicen *lo que quieren* y yo hago *el pedido*?

same

Paco: Pastor, pienso que es mejor si pedimos todos la *misma* comida.

thing

Susana: Pero no todos quieren la misma *cosa*, Paco.

Pastor: Está bien. Podemos tener tres opciones; despúes todos pueden *escoger*.

to choose

Camarera: Buenas tardes, ¿están listos para pedir?

Pastor: Bueno, quisiéramos saber cuáles son las especialidades del día.

the cut / tender

Camarera: Pues, el mejor plato de hoy es el churrasco. Usamos *el corte* de carne más *tierno* y lo servimos con arroz blanco y verduras.

Sounds delicious to me!

Pastor: *¡Me parece muy rico!*

oysters

Camarera: También recomiendo el pollo asado; es una de las especialidades de la casa. Además tenemos sopa de *ostras*, para los que prefieren marisco.

Pastor: Paco, por favor, dime cuántos quieren churrasco, pollo asado o sopa de ostras.

Paco: ¿Cuántos quieren churrasco? . . . nueve.
¿Cuántos prefieren pollo asado? . . . ocho.
¿Cuántos quieren la sopa de ostras? . . . nadie.
Somos 18 y sólo hay 17 pedidos.

Susana:	*Si no les importa,* prefiero comer un sandwich de *pavo.*	If you don't mind / turkey
Camarera:	*Lo siento,* señorita, no servimos sandwiches de pavo aquí.	I'm sorry
Paco:	La señorita va a querer la sopa de ostras. ¿Verdad, Susana?	

◆ **Conversación**

1. ¿Adónde van los jóvenes?
2. ¿Cuántas personas hay?
3. ¿Cuáles son las tres opciones de comida?
4. ¿Cuál es la opción menos favorita?
5. ¿Cuál es el mejor plato del restaurante?
6. ¿Qué plato prefieres tú?

Vocabulario ▲▲▲▲▲▲▲▲▲▲▲▲▲▲▲▲▲▲▲▲▲▲▲▲▲▲▲▲▲▲▲▲▲▲▲▲▲

EL MENÚ

el desayuno
huevos fritos (*fried*)
huevos revueltos (*scrambled*)
tocino (*bacon*)
jamón
pan tostado con mantequilla
   (*butter*) y mermelada
pan dulce (*sweet bread*)

bebidas
jugo de naranja
jugo de piña (*pineapple juice*)
café negro
café con leche
chocolate caliente
refrescos (*soft drinks*)
agua mineral

sopas (soups)
de vegetales
de ostras (*oysters*)

ensaladas
de lechuga (*lettuce*) y tomate
con aceite (*oil*) y vinagre
   (*lettuce and tomato salad with a
   vinaigrette dressing*)
de papas
de repollo (*coleslaw*)
de frutas

sandwiches y bocadillos
de jamón y queso (*cheese*)
de atún (*tuna*)
hamburguesa con papas fritas

carnes
ternera asada (*roast beef*)
churrasco (*tenderloin steak*)
chuletas de cerdo
pollo (*chicken*) asado
pollo frito

pescado y mariscos (seafood)
filete de pescado
langosta (*lobster*)
camarones (*shrimp*)
sopa de ostras

las verduras (vegetables)
puré de papas (*mashed potatoes*)
frijoles negros (*black beans*)
habichuelas verdes (*green beans*)
zanahorias (*carrots*)
maíz (choclo) (*corn*)
espinacas (*spinach*)
brécol (*broccoli*)
lentejas (*lentils*)

los postres (desserts)
arroz con leche (*rice pudding*)
flan
pastel de manzana
pastel de cereza (*cherry*)

el desayuno	*breakfast*
el almuerzo	*lunch*
la comida	*dinner*
la cena	*supper*
la cuenta	*the bill*
la propina	*the tip*

◆ **Actividad 1**

You may refer to the menu and the dialogue to comply with the following situations.

1. Tell the waiter that you wish to order ham and eggs and hot chocolate for breakfast. (*Quisiera pedir . . .*)

2. Ask the waiter what the house specialty is.

3. Play the role of the waiter and state that the specialty is baked chicken served with carrots and corn.

4. Tell the waiter that your mother prefers to have just a fruit salad for lunch. (*Mi madre prefiere . . .*)

5. Order dessert for yourself and two of your classmates.

6. Tell the waiter that you wish to order two mineral waters and one coke.

7. Ask the waiter to bring you the bill.

◆ **Actividad 2**

Help the kitchen staff at camp by creating a menu for one day of the week. Make sure you include plans for *el desayuno, el almuerzo,* and *la cena.*

Gramática ▲▲▲

El presente: los verbos con cambios *e → ie*

The following verbs have regular endings, but a change occurs in their stem. The last **e** in the stem changes to **ie** in all conjugated forms of the present tense except in the *nosotros* and *vosotros* forms.

	pensar to think	querer to want	preferir to prefer
yo	pienso	quiero	prefiero
tú	piensas	quieres	prefieres
Ud., él, ella	piensa	quiere	prefiere
nosotros(as)	pensamos	queremos	preferimos
vosotros(as)	pensáis	queréis	preferís
Uds., ellos(as)	piensan	quieren	prefieren
Present Participle:	pensando	queriendo	prefiriendo

Notice that *-ar* and *-er* verbs do not undergo the *e → ie* stem change in the present participle. However, the stem of *-ir* verbs changes from *e → i* in the present participle.

The verbs *pensar, querer,* and *preferir* may be used to express an opinion, desire, or preference.

pensar + que + a statement	Yo **pienso que** el pollo es mejor que el pavo.
querer + infinitive . . .	Nosotros **queremos pedir** huevos fritos.
preferir + infinitive . . .	Ellos **prefieren comer** pescado.

◆ **Actividad 3**

Your parents have taken you to a Hispanic restaurant for your birthday. After reading the menu, you are trying to make your choice. For each blank below, supply the correct present tense form of the verb in parentheses, or supply a vocabulary word from the menu in the vocabulary section.

¡Mmmmm! Yo (pensar) _____ que la comida hispana es deliciosa, pero

no (querer) _____ comer _____ . (Preferir) _____ comer _____ ,

pues me gustan los mariscos. Mis padres (pensar) _____ que voy a pedir

_____ , pues siempre pido verduras también. Ellos (preferir) _____

probar el menú ligero *(light)*. (Ellos/ querer) _____ comer la sopa de

_____ y una ensalada de _____ .

Otros verbos con el cambio *e → ie:*

-ar verbs

cerrar	C**ie**rro la ventana y la puerta cuando hay mucho viento.
comenzar	La historia misionera com**ie**nza a las nueve.
confesar	Si conf**ie**so mis pecados, Dios me perdona.
despertar(se)	Me desp**ie**rto a las siete.
empezar	Los cultos especiales emp**ie**zan el domingo.
recomendar	El pastor recom**ie**nda el libro devocional *Manantiales en el desierto*.

-er/-ir verbs

entender	Repite, por favor. No ent**ie**ndo tu pregunta.
perder	Yo nunca p**ie**rdo mis llaves.
sentir	¡Lo s**ie**nto mucho!

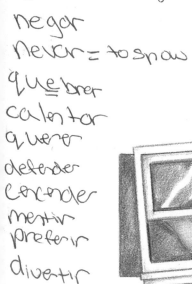

Pensar
Senterse
gobernar = to govern
negar
nevar = to snow
quebrer
calentar
querer
defender
encender
mentir
preferir
divetir

◆ **Actividad 4**

Write as many sentences as you can using one element from each column. You may make the sentences affirmative or negative, questions or statements.

yo	cerrar	la lección
tú	comenzar	el churrasco
el camarero	empezar	la tarea
nosotros	entender	las preparaciones para la cena
el muchacho	perder	la ventana
mi hermano	querer	el plato del día
ellos	recomendar	el dinero

El superlativo de los adjetivos

El edificio más alto de México es la Torre Latinoamericana.
Silvia es **la muchacha más inteligente de** la clase.

In the sentences above, a thing or person was compared to a group. To form the regular superlative of adjectives, use the following construction: **a definite article + a noun + *más/menos* + an adjective + *de*.**

La Pasiva es **el restaurante más popular de** Montevideo.

The irregular superlative adjectives *el mejor* and *el peor* (the best/the worst) precede the noun they modify.

Carmen es **la mejor chica** del campamento.
La sopa de ostras es **el peor plato** del restaurante.

The irregular superlative adjectives *(el) mayor* and *(el) menor* (the oldest/the youngest) follow the noun they modify.

Yo soy **el hijo mayor** de mi familia.
Raquel y Reina son **las hijas menores** de la familia.

Note: In the superlative, the noun is often omitted altogether.

Dorcas es **la menor** de la casa.
El doctor Rodríguez es un buen médico. Es **el mejor** de Puerto Rico.

◆ **Actividad 5**

Conteste las preguntas.

1. ¿Cuál es el país (*country*) más grande de América del Norte?
2. ¿Cuál es el río (*river*) más largo de los Estados Unidos?
3. ¿Cuál es el estado más pequeño de los Estados Unidos?
4. ¿Quién es el/la mejor estudiante de tu escuela?
5. ¿Quién es el/la peor estudiante de tu familia?
6. ¿Cuál es el mejor restaurante de la ciudad?
7. ¿Cuál es el mejor libro que conoces?
8. ¿Quién es el/la menor de tu casa?

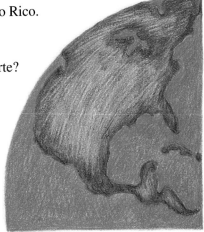

El presente: los verbos *-ir* con cambios e → i

The verb *pedir* (to ask for, to request) has regular *-ir* endings, but a change occurs in its stem. The last **e** in the stem changes to **i** in all the conjugated forms of the present tense except in the *nosotros* and *vosotros* forms.

Pedir			
yo	pido	nosotros(as)	pedimos
tú	pides	vosotros(as)	pedís
Ud., él, ella	pide	Uds., ellos(as)	piden
Present Participle:	pidiendo		

Notice that the present participle also undergoes the stem change.

Otros verbos con el cambio e → i:

conseguir (*to get*)

reír(se) (*to laugh*)

repetir (*to repeat*)

seguir (*to follow*)

seguir + present participle (*to keep on doing something*)

servir (*to serve, to function*)

sonreír(se) (*to smile*)

Note:

1. The verbs *reír* and *sonreír* have an accent mark in all forms of the present:

   río, ríes, ríe, reímos, reís, ríen.

2. In the verbs *conseguir* and *seguir*, the **gu** changes to **g** before **o:**

   Sigo las instrucciones de la maestra.

◆ **Actividad 6**

Complete la historia usando la forma correcta de cada verbo entre paréntesis.

1. La familia González está en el Restaurante Lina. El señor González (pedir) _____ una mesa al lado de una ventana. La camarera les (conseguir) _____ una mesa para seis personas. La familia González (seguir) _____ a la señorita.

2. En la mesa, todos (comenzar) _____ a hablar mientras miran el menú. Llega el camarero y (recomendar) _____ la especialidad del día. Cada uno (pedir) _____ un plato diferente. Rosita y su hermana (querer) _____ la especialidad del día; Roberto y Manuel (pedir) _____ carne asada; el señor González (querer) _____ pollo asado; y su esposa (pedir) _____ jamón.

3. Tienen que esperar media hora. Los hijos (hablar) _____ y
   (reírse) _____ . Por fin el camarero les (servir) _____ los
   platos. La comida es deliciosa y todos están satisfechos.

Los verbos *ir* y *venir*

The verb *ir* (to go) + *a* is used to indicate a destination.

ir + a + destination

The verb *venir* (to come) + *de* is used to indicate origin.

venir + de + origin

Notice how the verbs are used in the following examples:

Yo **vengo del** gimnasio y **voy a** la cocina.

Ellos **vienen de la** cocina y **van al** comedor.

Nosotros **venimos de** la cabaña y **vamos a** la capilla (*chapel*).

(For the full conjugation of these verbs see Reference Tables, pp. 329 and 333.)

The construction *ir + a* + infinitive is used to express an action that is going to
happen in the near future. This form occurs frequently in Spanish.

Ella **va a ir** a la montaña.

Tú **vas a cantar** esta noche.

◆ **Actividad 7**

The staff members at camp are very busy cleaning the campground. Use
the elements given to make sentences that tell where they are coming from
and where they are going.

Modelo: Noemí / el mercado / la cocina
Noemí viene del mercado y va a la cocina.

1. Vanesa / los baños / las cabañas (*the cabins*)

2. Gustavo y Mateo / el pueblo / el gimnasio

3. Tomás / la cocina / el comedor

4. Lorena / las cabañas / las duchas (*the showers*)

5. Teresa y Carlos / la capilla / el comedor

◆ **Actividad 8**

Answer the questions below using the construction *ir + a + infinitive.* Finish your answers with some type of food item from the menu in the vocabulary section.

Modelo: La Señora Blanco quiere hacer una ensalada. ¿Qué va a comprar?
La Señora Blanco va a comprar lechuga y tomates.

1. Tú estás en el restaurante. Tienes hambre. ¿Qué vas a pedir?

2. Nosotros estamos en la cafetería. ¿Qué vamos a beber?

3. El pastor y su señora están en el mercado y quieren mariscos. ¿Qué van a comprar?

4. Ustedes no quieren verduras. ¿Qué no van a comer?

5. Mis padres están en el restaurante. Quieren comer postre. ¿Qué van a pedir?

6. Yo estoy en casa. ¿Qué voy a desayunar?

7. Las cocineras están en la cocina. ¿Qué van a preparar para la cena?

Vocabulario adicional ▲▲▲▲▲▲▲▲▲▲▲▲▲▲▲▲▲▲▲▲▲▲▲▲▲▲▲▲▲▲▲▲

Endings such as *-eza* and *-ura* are used to change an adjective to a noun. Can you determine the meaning of the following nouns from the adjectives given?

Adjetivos	**Sustantivos**
bello (*beautiful*)	belleza
grande	grandeza
natural	naturaleza
pobre	pobreza
puro	pureza
rico	riqueza
triste	tristeza
hermoso	hermosura
largo	largura
loco	locura

2-2 ¡A JUGAR!

Diálogo ▲▲

Todos en el campamento duermen, *menos* David y Paco. Ellos hablan *acerca*   **except / about**
del partido de mañana.

David: Paco . . . Paco, ¡escucha!

Paco: *¿Qué pasa?*   **What's up?**

David: Hablemos del partido que vamos a jugar mañana.

Paco: ¿Qué partido?

David: ¡El partido de fútbol! Hablemos de *la alineación*.   **the alignment**

Paco: ¡Ah, sí! Yo quiero ser el portero.

David: Pongamos a Tomás y a Juan de delanteros.

Paco: No, no pongas a Tomás; pon a Antonio de delantero y a Tomás de defensa contigo.

David: Bueno, bueno, pero no hables tan fuerte. Todos están durmiendo.

Paco: David, salgamos *afuera* y practiquemos ahora.   **outside**

David: No. Esperemos hasta mañana. Tengo sueño. Vamos a ver, Pedro puede jugar de lateral y . . .

A la mañana siguiente todos los jugadores están en el campo de fútbol . . . menos David y Paco. ¡Ellos duermen!

◆ **Conversación**

1. ¿Quién quiere ser el portero?
2. ¿Quiénes van a formar parte de la defensa?
3. ¿Por qué no están David y Paco en el campo de fútbol al día siguiente?
4. ¿Juegas al fútbol? ¿Cuál es tu posición?
5. ¿Cuál es tu opinión acerca del fútbol en los Estados Unidos? ¿Piensas que es un deporte popular?

URUGUAY

- **AREA:** 68,500 sq. mi.
  (approximately the size
  of Washington State)

- **POPULATION:** 3.2 million

- **GOVERNMENT:** Republic

- **CAPITAL:** Montevideo

Uruguay, south of Brazil and east of Argentina, displays a European flavor unique in South America. There are German, Swiss, and Russian colonies in the southwest of the country, but most Uruguayans are of Spanish and Italian descent. The Indian population (the *charrúas*) disappeared more than a century ago.

Over a third of the population of Uruguay lives in Montevideo, a port city at the mouth of the Río de la Plata. Approximately 85 percent of Uruguayans live in urban areas, and there is a large middle class. Rural areas are dominated by *estancias,* cattle ranches where cowboys known as *gauchos* inspire Uruguayan folk culture by their hard work and free spirit.

Gauchos uruguayos durante un momento de descanso

In Uruguay soccer is not a mere pastime; it is a passion which drives both the players and the general public. Uruguay hosted and won the first World Cup competition in 1930 and the commemorative fiftieth anniversary Copa de Oro in 1980. Other countries often recruit Uruguayan soccer players because of their fine style—a fact which has led to the Uruguayans' popular saying that their number one export is soccer players!

El equipo uruguayo, ganador de la Copa de Oro en 1980

Los deportes

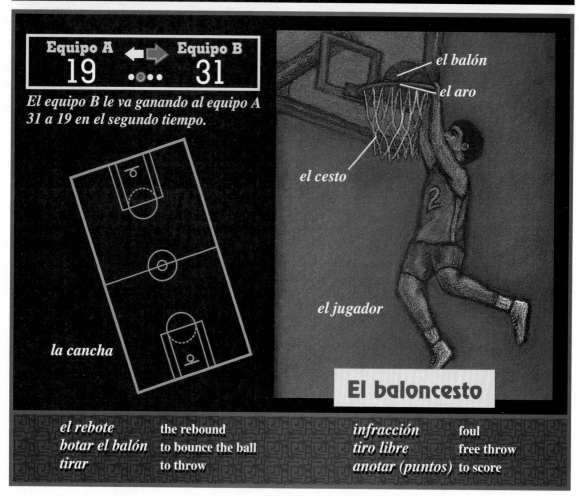

Equipo A ⬅➡ **Equipo B**

19 •••• **31**

El equipo B le va ganando al equipo A 31 a 19 en el segundo tiempo.

el balón

el aro

el cesto

el jugador

la cancha

El baloncesto

el rebote	the rebound	*infracción*	foul
botar el balón	to bounce the ball	*tiro libre*	free throw
tirar	to throw	*anotar (puntos)*	to score

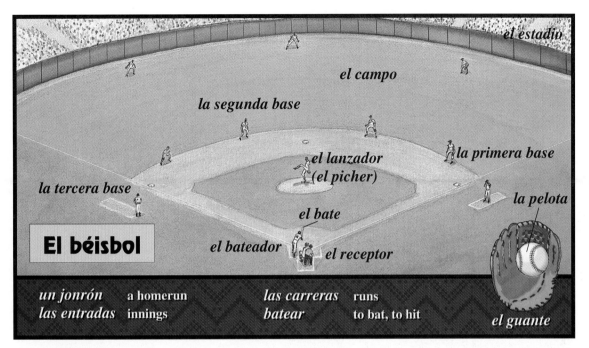

El béisbol

el estadio

el campo

la segunda base

el lanzador (el picher)

la primera base

la tercera base

la pelota

el bate

el bateador

el receptor

| un jonrón | a homerun | las carreras | runs |
| las entradas | innings | batear | to bat, to hit |

el guante

◆ **Actividad 1**

Supply the correct vocabulary words. Each answer may be used only once.

el baloncesto

1. El jugador tira _____ .

2. El balón no entra en _____ .

3. Otro jugador toma _____ .

4. El balón entra en el cesto sin tocar _____ .

5. Yo puedo _____ el balón con los ojos cerrados.

el béisbol

6. _____ tira la pelota al bateador.

7. _____ batea la pelota con el bate.

8. _____ está detrás del bateador.

9. El jugador batea un _____ . ¡La pelota sale fuera del campo!

10. Hay cuatro _____ en el campo de béisbol.

11. Hay nueve _____ en un juego de béisbol.

12. El lanzador tiene una pelota y _____ en la mano.

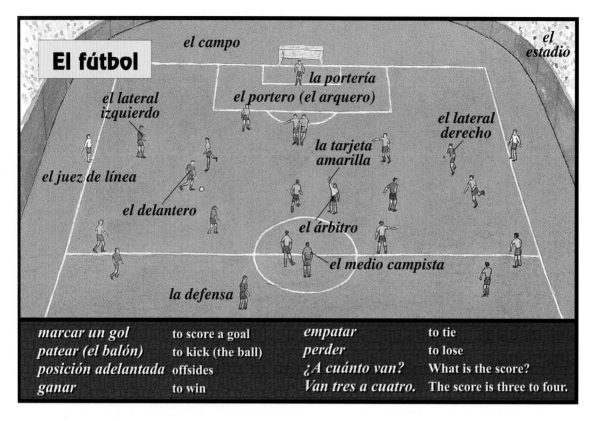

El fútbol

el campo

el estadio

la portería

el portero (el arquero)

el lateral izquierdo

el lateral derecho

la tarjeta amarilla

el juez de línea

el delantero

el árbitro

el medio campista

la defensa

marcar un gol	to score a goal	*empatar*	to tie
patear (el balón)	to kick (the ball)	*perder*	to lose
posición adelantada	offsides	*¿A cuánto van?*	What is the score?
ganar	to win	*Van tres a cuatro.*	The score is three to four.

◆ **Actividad 2**

Supply the correct vocabulary words. Each answer may be used only once.

1. Los jugadores están en _____ de fútbol.

2. Hay muchos aficionados uruguayos en _____ .

3. El arquero está en frente de _____ . Está nervioso.

4. _____ ejecuta (*enforces*) las reglas del juego.

5. Hay infracción (*foul*). El árbitro le da _____ al delantero.

6. _____ ayuda al árbitro. Un jugador está en posición adelantada.

7. ¡El medio campista patea el balón y el delantero marca _____ !

8. En el segundo tiempo, _____ Uruguay. Ahora van uno a uno.

9. Ambos equipos quieren _____ la Copa de América.

10. Termina el partido. Gana Uruguay; _____ Brasil.
   ¡Uruguay es Campeón de América!

Gramática ▲▲▲

El presente: los verbos con cambios *o→ue*

Todos en el campamento **duermen.**   *Everyone at camp is sleeping.*
In some verbs like *dormir*, the **o** in the stem changes to **ue** in all the conjugated forms of the present tense except in the *nosotros* and *vosotros* forms.

| | contar | volver | dormir |
	to count / to tell	*to return*	*to sleep*
yo	cuento	vuelvo	duermo
tú	cuentas	vuelves	duermes
Ud., él, ella	cuenta	vuelve	duerme
nosotros(as)	contamos	volvemos	dormimos
vosotros(as)	contáis	volvéis	dormís
Uds., ellos(as)	cuentan	vuelven	duermen
Present Participle:	contando	volviendo	durmiendo

Notice that *-ar* and *-er* verbs do not undergo the *o→ue* stem change in the present participle. However, the stem of *-ir* verbs changes from *o→u* in the present participle.

Otros verbos con el cambio *o→ue:*

-ar verbs

acostar(se)	Durante el año escolar me ac**ue**sto temprano.
almorzar	Los estudiantes alm**ue**rzan en la cafetería a las doce.
costar	Los zapatos c**ue**stan cuarenta dólares.
encontrar	Mario enc**ue**ntra los versículos en la Biblia rápidamente.
recordar	Roberto y su hermano nunca rec**ue**rdan los versículos.

-er verbs

devolver	La profesora dev**ue**lve los cuadernos a los estudiantes.
poder	"Los que viven según la carne no p**ue**den agradar a Dios." (Romanos 8:8)

-ir verb

morir	Muchas personas m**ue**ren sin Cristo.

Jugar

The verb *jugar* (to play) is the only *u→ue* stem-changing verb in Spanish. It conjugates like the verbs in the preceding section. Note the following sentences:

David **jue**ga al béisbol.   David y yo jugamos juntos.

Note: The verbs *tocar* and *poner* also mean "to play" in English, but note the differences.

David **toca** el piano.   *David plays the piano.*
David **pone** el radio.   *David turns on (or plays) the radio.*

◆ **Actividad 3**

Supply the correct form of the verb in parentheses.

1. El viernes nosotros (jugar) _____ al fútbol con la escuela de Uruguay.

2. Nuestro maestro nos (contar) _____ que los jóvenes de Montevideo (jugar) _____ muy bien.

3. Marcos, ¿cuánto (costar) _____ tu guante de béisbol?

4. En el centro, tú (poder) _____ encontrar los guantes a $45.

5. Entonces, yo (devolver) _____ mis guantes y (comprar) _____ otros.

6. Cuando yo (jugar) _____ al baloncesto, (acostarse) _____ temprano pero no (dormir) _____ bien. ¿Y tú, (dormir) _____ bien antes de un partido?

◆ **Actividad 4**

Arrange the words to construct complete sentences. Be sure to use the correct form of the verb.

1. dormir / las / yo / a / diez

2. volver / la / a / él / cancha / volibol / de

3. recordar / jonrón / Mario / su / ayer / de

4. almorzar / a / nosotros / doce / las

5. morir / muchos / accidentes / en / automóvil / de

6. devolver / receptor / el / pelota / la / lanzador / al

7. jugar / el viernes / nosotros / al baloncesto

◆ **Actividad 5**

For each sentence, supply the correct form of the appropriate verb: *jugar, tocar,* or *poner.*

1. Tú _____ la guitarra muy bien.

2. Antes de acostarme, _____ el radio para escuchar música.

3. Los jóvenes no _____ la televisión durante la siesta.

4. Yo voy a _____ el violín en la orquesta.

5. Los jóvenes del campamento _____ en el lodo (*mud*).

El presente: los verbos con cambios en la primera persona

Some verbs in the present tense are irregular only in the singular first person. The other forms are regular.

• Verbs that end in **-go,** like the verb *hacer* (to make, to do):

Hacer			
yo	**hago**	nosotros(as)	hacemos
tú	haces	vosotros(as)	hacéis
Ud., él, ella	hace	Uds., ellos(as)	hacen

Other verbs like *hacer:*

poner   **Pongo** mi ropa en la cama.
salir   **Salgo** de la escuela a las tres.

• Verbs that end in **-zco,** like the verb *conocer* (to know):

Conocer			
yo	**conozco**	*nosotros(as)*	conocemos
tú	conoces	*vosotros(as)*	conocéis
Ud., él, ella	conoce	*Uds., ellos(as)*	conocen

Other verbs like *conocer:*

obedecer	Siempre **obedezco** a mis padres.
pertenecer	Yo **pertenezco** a Dios.
conducir	Tengo dieciséis años y ahora **conduzco** un auto.
traducir	A veces **traduzco** para mi amigo mexicano.

◆ **Actividad 6**

After reading each statement, say whether you do likewise.

Modelo: Felipe pone sus libros en la cama.
Yo pongo mis libros en la cama también.
(Yo no pongo mis libros en la cama.)

1. Carmen pone sus pies en el sofá.

2. Rebeca hace sandwiches de jamón.

3. Tomás obedece a sus padres.

4. Carlos traduce cartas del inglés al español.

5. Gonzalo sale para la escuela a las ocho.

6. Isabel conoce al presidente de los Estados Unidos.

7. Alberto conduce el automóvil de su padre.

El imperativo: las formas regulares

Imperative verbs are used to give commands or make requests. Most verbs derive their imperative, or command, forms from the stem of the singular first person (*yo*) of the present indicative. The endings below are added to this stem.

	-ar verbs hablar → hablo → habl-	*-er/-ir* verbs comer → como → com- venir → vengo → veng-
affirmative and negative *Ud.* commands	-e	-a
affirmative and negative *Uds.* commands	-en	-an
affirmative and negative *nosotros* commands	-emos	-amos
negative *tú* commands	-es	-as

When speaking to an adult or someone you address by last name, use the polite form *Ud.*

¡Habl**e**!	*Talk!*	¡No habl**e**!	*Don't talk!*
¡Com**a**!	*Eat!*	¡No com**a**!	*Don't eat!*
¡Veng**a**!	*Come!*	¡No veng**a**!	*Don't come!*

When speaking to a group of two or more, use the plural *you* form *Uds.*

¡Escuch**en**!	*Listen!*	¡No escuch**en**!	*Don't listen!*
¡Le**an**!	*Read!*	¡No le**an**!	*Don't read!*
¡Salg**an**!	*Leave!*	¡No salg**an**!	*Don't leave!*

When speaking to a group of two or more that includes you, use the *nosotros* form to suggest "Let's . . . ."

¡Cant**emos**!	*Let's sing!*	¡No cant**emos**!	*Let's not sing!*
¡Aprend**amos**!	*Let's learn!*	¡No aprend**amos**!	*Let's not learn!*
¡Escrib**amos**!	*Let's write!*	¡No escrib**amos**!	*Let's not write!*

When speaking to a friend, a family member, or someone you can address by first name, use the *tú* form.

¡Estudia!*	*Study!*	¡No estudi**es**!	*Don't study!*
¡Corre!	*Run!*	¡No corr**as**!	*Don't run!*
¡Repite!	*Repeat!*	¡No repit**as**!	*Don't repeat!*

*Affirmative *tú* command forms

For most verbs, the affirmative *tú* command uses the same form as the *él* form of the present indicative. The negative commands, however, are derived from the stem of the *yo* form of the present indicative, plus the added endings.

Stem-changing -ar and -er verbs

Stem-changing -ar and -er verbs have the same change patterns in the imperative forms that they have in the present indicative. Notice the verbs *cerrar* and *volver* in the table below.

Stem-changing -ir verbs

Verbs that have *e→ie* and *o→ue* stem changes in the present indicative have the same change patterns in the imperative forms. However, they also have an additional stem change in the *nosotros* imperative form. The changes are *e→i* and *o→u*. Notice the verbs *sentir* and *dormir* in the table below.

	cerrar *e → ie*	volver *o → ue*	sentir *e → ie*	dormir *o → ue*
Ud.	cierre no cierre	vuelva no vuelva	sienta no sienta	duerma no duerma
Uds.	cierren no cierren	vuelvan no vuelvan	sientan no sientan	duerman no duerman
nosotros	cerremos no cerremos	volvamos no volvamos	sintamos no sintamos	durmamos no durmamos
tú	cierra no cierres	vuelve no vuelvas	siente no sientas	duerme no duermas

Spelling changing verbs

Verbs that end in **-car, -gar,** and **-zar** have a spelling change when the vowel following the *c, g,* or *z* changes to *e*. This spelling change is necessary in order to retain correct pronunciation. Note the following examples:

    to**car** (c→qu): to**que**, to**quen**, to**quemos**, no to**ques**
    lle**gar** (g→gu): lle**gue**, lle**guen**, lle**guemos**, no lle**gues**
    empe**zar** (z→c): empie**ce**, empie**cen**, empe**cemos**, no empie**ces**

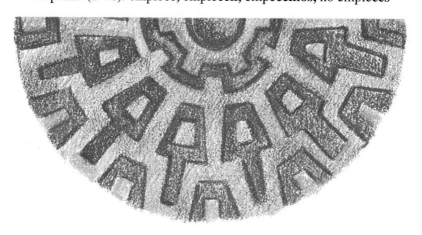

El imperativo: las formas irregulares

The following verbs do not derive their imperative forms from the stem of the *yo* present indicative.

	dar	estar	ir	saber	ser
Ud.	dé no dé	esté no esté	vaya no vaya	sepa no sepa	sea no sea
Uds.	den no den	estén no estén	vayan no vayan	sepan no sepan	sean no sean
nosotros	demos no demos	estemos no estemos	vayamos no vayamos	sepamos no sepamos	seamos no seamos

Eight verbs have an irregular form in the *tú* affirmative command, but most are regular in the negative.

	Affirmative Command	**Negative Command**
decir	di	no digas
hacer	haz	no hagas
ir	ve	no vayas
poner	pon	no pongas
salir	sal	no salgas
ser	sé	no seas
tener	ten	no tengas
venir	ven	no vengas

◆ **Actividad 7**

For each of the following situations, give an appropriate affirmative command form of the verb in parentheses.

Modelo: (hacer) Un jugador quiere hacer un gol. Su compañero dice . . .
   ¡Haz un gol!

1. (salir) Tu gato no quiere salir de la casa. Tú dices . . .

2. (decir) Un niño no le quiere decir la verdad a su padre. El padre dice . . .

3. (comer) Dos jóvenes no quieren comer verduras. Sus padres les dicen . . .

4. (ir) Fifí, la perra de Elena, tiene que ir a buscar el periódico. Elena dice . . .

5. (escribir) La Sra. Gómez tiene que escribir los nombres de los jugadores. El director dice . . .

6. (sacar) Un padre manda a su hijo a sacar la basura. El padre dice . . .

Tell the following people not to do what they want to do.

Modelo: Maribel quiere salir.
    ¡No salgas!

1. Teresa quiere jugar al tenis.

2. Pedro quiere tocar el piano.

3. Tu profesor(a) quiere venir a tu casa.

4. Tus amigos quieren ver el partido.

5. El director quiere marcar un gol.

6. El jugador del otro equipo quiere tirar un jonrón.

7. El árbitro quiere terminar el partido.

Refrán ▲▲

Are you frequently late? Well, you should change that, but here are some words of encouragement.

    Más vale tarde que nunca.

2-3 ¡A Cantar!

Diálogo ▲▲

Pedro y Tomás están tocando la guitarra. Dos muchachas vienen para hablar con ellos.

Luisa: ¡Hola! Tocan muy bien la guitarra.

Pedro: Gracias.

Teresa: ¿Cuánto tiempo hace que tocan la guitarra?

Tomás: Hace 3 años que yo toco; Pedro hace 12 años.

Pedro: Sí, cada año aprendo algo nuevo *acerca de* la guitarra.　　about

Teresa: ¿Pueden tocar *otros* instrumentos también?　　other

Tomás: Yo puedo tocar la trompeta. La toco en la banda de mi colegio.

Pedro: Yo sé tocar el arpa un poco. ¿Y ustedes?

Luisa: Yo toco el piano desde los 10 años.

Teresa: Sí, Luisa toca muy bien. A veces toca en la iglesia.

Luisa: ¿Por qué no tocan la guitarra y todos cantamos?

Tomás: Bueno, practiquemos el canto otra vez. ¡Toque, maestro!

◆ **Conversación**
1. ¿Cuántos años hace que Tomás toca la guitarra?
2. ¿Qué otro instrumento sabe tocar Pedro?
3. ¿Toca Tomás la guitarra en la banda?
4. ¿Quién toca el piano en la iglesia?
5. ¿Sabes tocar algún instrumento?
6. ¿Qué instrumento te gustaría (*would you like to*) aprender a tocar?

Vocabulario ▲▲▲▲▲▲▲▲▲▲▲▲▲▲▲▲▲▲▲▲▲▲▲▲▲▲▲▲▲▲▲▲▲▲▲▲▲▲

Los eventos culturales

El concierto (*the concert*)

la orquesta
los instrumentos de cuerda
    el arpa
    el contrabajo
    la guitarra
    el violín
    el violoncelo
los instrumentos de percusión
    las castañuelas (*castanets*)
    el güiro
    las maracas
    la marimba
    los platillos (*cymbals*)
    el tambor (*drum*)

el/la cantante
el/la compositor(a) (*composer*)
el/la músico(a) (*musician*)
el/la director(a)

la banda
los instrumentos de metal
    el trombón
    la trompa (*French horn*)
    la trompeta
    la tuba

los instrumentos de viento
    el clarinete
    la flauta
    la gaita (*bagpipe*)
    el saxofón

la batuta (*baton*)
¡Bravo! (*Well done!*)
¡Otra! ¡Bis! ¡Que se repita!
    (*Encore!*)

El teatro

la comedia
el drama
la tragedia

el actor/la actriz
el/la protagonista (*lead character*)
el villano (*villain*)
el público
aplaudir (*to clap*)

la obra musical
la ópera
la zarzuela (*a traditional Spanish
    musical drama*)
el balcón (*the balcony*)
la plataforma
el telón (*the curtain*)
los boletos (*the tickets*)

Vocabulario adicional

a veces	*at times*
algunas veces	*sometimes*
cada vez	*each time*
otra vez	*one more time / again*
una vez	*once*
(dos) veces	*(two) times*

◆ **Actividad 1 Encuesta musical** (*musical survey*)

Conteste las preguntas.

1. ¿Cuántas veces al año asistes a un concierto de música clásica?

   a. una vez al año

   b. dos veces o más

   c. nunca

2. ¿Qué instrumento(s) sabes tocar?

3. Si tocas un instrumento, ¿lo tocas en la iglesia?

   a. sí

   b. no

   c. a veces

4. ¿Sabes quiénes son Plácido Domingo y José Carreras?

   a. Son pianistas famosos.

   b. Son cantantes de ópera.

   c. Son músicos en una banda.

5. ¿Tiene tu escuela una banda?

6. ¿Tiene tu escuela un coro musical?

7. ¿Quién es tu compositor favorito?

8. Empareja (*match*) los siguientes instrumentos con las regiones.

la gaita	Andalucía, España
el güiro	Paraguay
las castañuelas	Asturias, España
el arpa paraguaya	el Caribe

Gramática ▲▲

Saber

The first-person singular form of *saber* is irregular in the present tense.

Saber	
yo	**Sé** que soy salvo.
tú	**Sabes** dónde está Miguel.
Ud., él, ella	**Sabe** que las clases comienzan el lunes.
nosotros(as)	**Sabemos** el Salmo 23 de memoria.
vosotros(as)	**Sabéis** mi dirección.
Uds., ellos(as)	**Saben** escribir en español.

Saber vs. conocer

The verb *saber* means to know information or to know facts.

- *Saber* can be followed by nouns, pronouns, or phrases that represent information or facts.

  El sabe **mi nombre.**

  Yo sé **donde él vive.**

  Ellos saben **quienes vienen a la fiesta.**

- When followed by an infinitive, it means *to know how to do something.*

  Tomás **sabe jugar** al fútbol.

The verb *conocer* means to be acquainted with someone or something.

- It can be followed by people or places.

  Conozco al nuevo vecino, pero no **sé** si tiene hijos.

  Pablo y Raúl **conocen** el Palacio Legislativo en Montevideo, pero no **saben** si está abierto hoy.

◆ **Actividad 2**

Supply the correct form of *saber* or *conocer.*

1. Nosotros _____ los nombres de los doce discípulos.

2. Roberto no _____ el campamento que está en Uruguay.

3. Él _____ a dos jóvenes que trabajan en el campamento.

4. Ellos no _____ si van a trabajar allí el año que viene.

5. Yo _____ tocar el piano.

6. Tú _____ que tienes que practicar todos los días.

7. Yo _____ a un pianista famoso.

8. Déborah _____ el Teatro Solís en Montevideo.

El presente progresivo

Pedro **toca** la guitarra.	*Pedro plays the guitar.*
Pedro no **toca** en la banda este año.	*Pedro is not playing in the band this year.*
Pedro **está tocando** la guitarra.	*Pedro is playing the guitar (right now).*

As shown in the first two sentences, the simple present tense in Spanish may refer to our simple present or our present progressive in English. The present progressive tense in Spanish, however, should be used to express events actually in progress at the moment.

Look at the following sentences to review the formation of the present progressive.

> **Estoy hablando** con María.
>
> ¿**Estás comiendo** ahora?
>
> Paco y Mateo **están leyendo** libros.
>
> Nosotros **estamos escribiendo** cartas.

The present progressive has two parts: the conjugated form of *estar* and the present participle. The -*ar* verbs form the present participle by replacing the infinitive ending with **-ando;** the -*er* and -*ir* verbs with **-iendo.** Note, however, the following -*er* verbs which end in **-yendo.**

> leer → leyendo
> caer → cayendo
> oír → oyendo

(See Reference Tables, pp. 321-322 for more review of the present participle.) The progressive tense is not used as frequently in Spanish as it is in English. Spanish speakers use it to emphasize that something is being done *right now.*

◆ **Actividad 3**

During free time at camp, people do different things. Relate what each person is doing at this moment.

Modelo: Pablo / lavar los platos
Pablo está lavando los platos.

1. Ana María / caminar en el bosque

2. Roberto y José / reparar el autobús

3. Carmen y yo / comer dulces

4. Carlos y Andrés / jugar al ping pong

5. tú / escribir cartas

6. Margarita / leer la Biblia

7. el director / preparar sus notas para la lección

8. yo / correr en el campo de fútbol

El objeto directo

The direct object is the recipient of the action of the verb. It answers the questions *whom?* or *what?* after the verb. The following sentences contain direct objects.

Juan busca **al director.**	Juan busca **la oficina.**
Yo espero **a Carolina.**	Yo espero **el autobús.**
Ana visita **a los jóvenes.**	Ana visita **el campamento.**

In the sentences above, the direct objects in the left column are *persons,* whereas the direct objects in the right column are *things.* Note that when the direct object refers to a person, the personal *a* precedes the direct object.

◆ **Actividad 4**

Paco is always waiting for something or someone. For each sentence below supply the personal *a* if necessary.

Modelo: Paco espera _____ su hermana.
　　　　Paco espera a su hermana.

1. Paco espera _____ el autobús.
2. Paco espera _____ la profesora.
3. Paco espera _____ los resultados del examen.
4. Paco espera _____ sus amigos.
5. Paco espera _____ su padre.
6. Paco espera _____ la Navidad.

Los pronombres del objeto directo

In Spanish, the following pronouns replace direct object nouns or noun phrases.

me	me		nos	us
te	you (fam.)		**os**	you (fam., —used in Spain)
lo	you (formal, m.), him, it		**los**	you (pl., m.), them (m.)
la	you (formal, f.), her, it		**las**	you (pl., f.), them (f.)

The pronouns *lo, la, los,* and *las* must agree in number and gender with the nouns they replace.

¿Compra Paco **una camisa**?	—Sí, **la** compra.
¿No **nos** conoces?	—Sí, **los** conozco, señores.
¿Jorge mira **el partido de béisbol**?	—No, no **lo** mira hoy.
¿**Nos** escucha Ud. bien?	—Sí, **las** escucho, señoritas.
¿Tiene Ramonita **los himnarios**?	—No, no **los** tiene.

La colocación (*placement*) del objeto directo

The placement of direct object pronouns is different from the placement of direct object nouns.

1. The direct object pronoun usually precedes a conjugated verb. In a negative sentence, the pronoun comes between the *no* (or other negative word) and the conjugated verb.
   Me miras.
   Ustedes no **nos** conocen bien.

2. In a sentence with an infinitive or progressive construction, the direct object pronoun may be attached to the end of either the infinitive or the present participle or may come before the conjugated verb.

¿Quiere leer **el periódico**?	No, no quiero leer**lo.**
	No, no **lo** quiero leer.
¿Vas a escribir **la carta**?	Sí, voy a escribir**la** hoy.
	Sí, **la** voy a escribir hoy.
¿Está Ud. cantando **el himno**?	Sí, estoy cantándo**lo.***
	Sí, **lo** estoy cantando.

*Note: When adding an object pronoun to the end of a present participle, place an accent mark over the next to the last syllable of the present participle to retain the correct stress.

3. Direct object pronouns follow and are attached to affirmative commands, but they precede negative commands.

¡Escucha **la radio**!	¡Escúcha**la*** en tu cuarto!
	No **la** pongas muy fuerte.

*Note: An accent mark is added to the next to the last syllable of an affirmative command before an object pronoun is attached.

◆ **Actividad 5**

Teresa asks Pedro if the following people play musical instruments. Answer each question using a third-person direct object pronoun.

Modelo: ¿Tocas la guitarra? —Sí, (yo) . . .
   Sí, la toco.

1. ¿Toca Manuela la flauta? —No, . . .
2. ¿Toca Tomás la trompeta? —Sí, . . .
3. ¿Toca Luis las maracas? —Sí, . . .
4. ¿Tocan Uds. los tambores? —No, (nosotros) . . .
5. ¿Toca Rita el clarinete? —Sí, . . .

◆ **Actividad 6**

Enriqueta and Enrique have gone to town to get some supplies for camp.
Enrique sees many things and wants Enriqueta to buy them. Pretend you
are Enriqueta and answer Enrique according to each model.

Modelo: Enrique: Enriqueta, mira las naranjas.
     Enriqueta: *¡Estoy mirándolas!*

1. Enriqueta, mira el pan.

2. Enriqueta, mira los refrescos.

3. Enriqueta, mira la carne.

4. Enriqueta, mira las tortas.

Modelo: Enrique: Enriqueta, ¿vas a comprar las naranjas?
     Enriqueta: *Sí, voy a comprarlas.*

5. Enriqueta, ¿vas a comprar el pan?

6. Enriqueta, ¿vas a comprar los refrescos?

7. Enriqueta ¿vas a comprar la carne?

8. Enriqueta, ¿vas a comprar las tortas?

◆ **Actividad 7**

The following young people have not yet met at camp. Answer each
question with a direct object pronoun.

Modelo: ¿Conoce Rolando a Rubén y a Rosana?
     No, Rolando no los conoce.

1. ¿Conoce Margarita a Sonia?

2. ¿Conoce Sandra a Carmen y a Victoria?

3. ¿Te conoce Roberto?

4. ¿Nos conoce Carlos?

5. ¿Conoce Felipe a Rafael?

6. ¿Me conoce Tito?

7. ¿Conocen Pedro y Antonio a Emilio?

8. ¿Conoce Marisol a ustedes?

9. ¿Conoce Carlos a Marisol?

10. ¿Conocen Uds. a Miguel?

◆ Actividad 8

Answer the following questions using the cues given in parentheses.

Modelo: ¿No nos conocen Uds.? (No, . . .)
No, no los conocemos.

1. ¿Nos busca Ud.? (Sí, . . .)
2. ¿Nos conoce Ud.? (No, . . .)
3. ¿Quién nos está mirando desde la ventana? ¿Susana? (Sí, . . .)
4. ¿Las conozco a Uds., señoritas? (Sí, . . .)
5. ¿Quiere Ud. esperarnos a nosotras en la esquina? (No, . . . en el restaurante.)
6. ¿A qué hora pasas a buscarnos? (. . . a las ocho . . .)
7. ¿Dónde podemos llamarlo, señor? ¿en casa? (Sí, . . .)

◆ Actividad 9

You are coordinating the preparation of the fellowship hall for the Thanksgiving banquet at school. Respond to the questions below in the form of commands and with the correct object pronouns.

Modelo: Marcos: ¿Abro las ventanas? (no)
No, no las abras.

1. Jaime: ¿Dónde pongo estas sillas? (junto a la pared)
2. Sra. Domínguez: ¿Cuándo preparo los refrescos? (a las siete)
3. Srta. Nogales: ¿Debo traer mis otros platos? (no)
4. Sr. Cortés y Sr. Silva: ¿Dónde ponemos las mesas largas? (en medio del salón)
5. Paco: ¿Cuándo empiezo a tocar el piano? (durante la comida)
6. Laura: ¿Saco los postres del refrigerador? (no ahora)

Oír

The verb *oír* (to hear) is irregular. Notice the way it is formed.

Oír			
yo	oigo	nosotros(as)	oímos
tú	oyes	vosotros(as)	oís
Ud., él, ella	oye	Uds., ellos(as)	oyen
Present Participle:	oyendo		

Note: Since the combination *oi* is a diphthong, *oír, oímos,* and *oís* have written accent marks on the *í* in order to divide the diphthong and thus retain the stress on the correct syllable.

Caer

The verb *caer* (to fall) is irregular only in the first-person singular form (*yo*) of the present tense.

Caer			
yo	**caigo**	nosotros(as)	caemos
tú	caes	vosotros(as)	caéis
Ud., él, ella	cae	Uds., ellos(as)	caen
Present Participle:	cayendo		

◆ **Actividad 10**

The campers are in bed with the lights out. They hear strange sounds. Complete the sentences using the correct forms of the verbs *oír* and *caer*.

1. Felipe _____ un ruido (*a noise*). Un vaso se _____ de la mesa.

2. Ramón y Santiago _____ el ruido también.

3. Muchachos—dice Santiago—(yo) _____ ruidos. —¿Qué hacen?— les dice el consejero.

4. —Estamos acostados, señor. Cosas se están _____ de la mesa. Creo que hay un oso (*bear*) por aquí.

5. Felipe dice—No es un oso; es Esteban, que está buscando su pasta de dientes. Cada cosa que toca se _____ al suelo (*ground*).

◆ **Actividad 11**

The campers are walking around the campsite. They can hear many sounds. Supply the correct form of *oír*:

Modelo: Pedro _____ una banda.
  Pedro oye una banda.

1. Santiago _____ un camión.

2. Felipe y yo _____ una trompeta.

3. Rosario y Carmen _____ un avión.

4. Tú _____ el viento (*the wind*).

5. Tomasina _____ un perro.

6. Yo _____ los pájaros (*the birds*).

7. Ustedes _____ al predicador.

8. Federico y su hermano _____ música.

Lectura bíblica ▲▲▲▲▲▲▲▲▲▲▲▲▲▲▲▲▲▲▲▲▲▲▲▲▲▲▲▲▲▲▲▲▲▲▲

Juan 10:7-11, 14-17

Volvió, pues, Jesús a decirles: De cierto, de cierto os digo: Yo soy la puerta de las ovejas. Todos los que antes de mí vinieron, ladrones son y salteadores; pero no los oyeron las ovejas. Yo soy la puerta; el que por mí entrare, será salvo; y entrará, y saldrá, y hallará pastos. El ladrón no viene sino para hurtar y matar y destruir; yo he venido para que tengan vida, y para que la tengan en abundancia. Yo soy el buen pastor; el buen pastor su vida da por las ovejas.

Yo soy el buen pastor; y conozco mis ovejas, y las mías me conocen, así como el Padre me conoce, y yo conozco al Padre; y pongo mi vida por las ovejas. También tengo otras ovejas que no son de este redil; aquéllas también debo traer, y oirán mi voz; y habrá un rebaño, y un pastor. Por eso me ama el Padre, porque yo pongo mi vida, para volverla a tomar.

PARAGUAY

- **AREA:** *157,000 sq. mi.*
  (approximately the
  size of California)

- **POPULATION:** *5.2 million*

- **GOVERNMENT:** *Republic*

- **CAPITAL:** *Asunción*

Located in the heart of South America, Paraguay has no seacoast. The Paraguay River flows through the center of the country dividing it into two distinct regions. To the west of the river lies the Chaco, a semi-jungle covering sixty percent of the country but containing less than five percent of the population. Most of the people live in eastern Paraguay, many of them working in agriculture and forestry. One of Paraguay's main exports is the *quebracho colorado*, a hard, red native wood.

The Guaraní Indians make up a large portion of the population, and thus Paraguay has two official languages: Spanish and Guaraní.

Nota cultural ▲▲

Las tunas

ensembles

its own

En muchos países, los estudiantes universitarios forman *conjuntos* musicales llamados tunas, y tocan y cantan música folklórica. En España, cada escuela de la universidad tiene *su propia* tuna. Los miembros se visten de trajes de colores que representan su escuela. De noche andan de plaza en plaza tocando para el público. También tocan para ocasiones especiales como banquetes de bodas o aniversarios. Después de escuchar la música, la gente les da dinero y

expenses

los estudiantes lo usan para pagar sus *gastos* en la universidad.

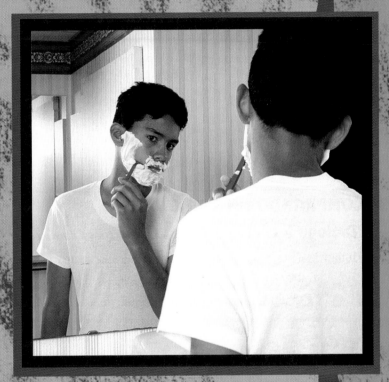

Mas buscad primeramente el reino de Dios y su justicia, y todas estas cosas os serán añadidas.

Mateo 6:33

Las modas

la chaqueta con botones

la camiseta rayada

la corbata

el pañuelo

el cinturón

la camisa de cuadros

la blusa de mangas cortas

el vestido de mangas largas

las sandalias de cuero

los pantalones

la falda plisada

el chaleco

las medias

los pantalones cortos

los zapatos de tacón alto

los zapatos deportivos (los tenis)	tennis shoes
los cordones	shoelaces
el abrigo	winter coat
el traje	suit
las botas	boots
el sombrero	hat
el gorro	cap
la bufanda	winter scarf

◆ **Actividad 1**

Answer the following questions using articles of clothing and jewelry.

Modelo: ¿Qué te vas a poner (*what are you going to wear*) para ir a la escuela?
Me voy a poner una falda plisada, una blusa blanca, una cadena, una pulsera de oro y unas sandalias negras.

1. ¿Qué te vas a poner para ir al estadio mañana?

2. ¿Qué tipo de zapatos usas para hacer deportes? ¿y para ir a la iglesia?

3. ¿Qué se ponen tus padres para ir a un concierto?

4. ¿Qué vas a llevar puesto (*what are you going to wear or have on*) para ir al programa de Navidad?

5. ¿Qué se pone tu hermano(a) para salir a cenar?

Gramática ▲▲

Decir

The verb decir (*to say, to tell*) is irregular. Notice how it is formed.

Decir			
yo	digo	nosotros(as)	decimos
tú	dices	vosotros(as)	decís
Ud., él, ella	dice	Uds., ellos(as)	dicen

To report what someone else says, use the following construction: **Subject + decir + que + the statement.**

Roberto: Quiero comprar esta corbata.

Roberto **dice que** él quiere comprar esa corbata.

◆ **Actividad 2**

The Fernández family has great plans for Saturday. Report what they say they are going to do.

Modelo: Jaime: Voy a trabajar.
Jaime dice que va a trabajar.

1. Lupita: Voy a jugar al tenis con las jóvenes de la iglesia.

2. los señores Fernández: Vamos a ir al centro comercial.

3. Tomás y yo: Vamos a lavar el auto de la abuela.

4. Margarita: Voy a probarme (*to try on*) unos vestidos nuevos.

5. tú: Voy a practicar un himno especial en la trompeta.

6. yo: Voy a dormir hasta las diez de la mañana.

◆ **Actividad 3**

Antonio and Rosana are upset with each other, and you are caught in the middle of their problem. Do your best in communicating their messages back and forth. (When their teacher intervenes, communicate her message to them.) Follow the models.

Modelos: Antonio: El vestido de Rosana es horrible.
Antonio dice que tu vestido es horrible, Rosana.
Rosana: Pues, los pantalones de Antonio están sucios.
Rosana dice que tus pantalones están sucios, Antonio.

1. Antonio: Su blusa tiene las mangas muy largas.

2. Rosana: Pero su camisa está arrugada (*wrinkled*).

3. Antonio: Sus zapatos son feos.

4. Rosana: Pues, sus zapatos están rotos.

5. Profesora: Antonio y Rosana deben decir cosas buenas.

6. Antonio: Lo siento mucho.

7. Rosana: Tiene razón. No quiero decir más cosas malas.

8. Antonio: Pues, su abrigo es muy bonito.

9. Rosana: Gracias. Su camisa es elegante.

Los adjetivos y los pronombres demostrativos

Demonstrative adjectives precede a noun. They must agree in gender and number with the nouns they modify. Review all the forms of the demonstrative adjectives:

este pantalón	**estos** pantalones
esta camiseta	**estas** camisetas
ese vestido	**esos** vestidos
esa cartera	**esas** carteras
aquel abrigo	**aquellos** abrigos
aquella bufanda	**aquellas** bufandas

Demonstrative pronouns take the place of nouns. They contain written accent marks on the stressed syllable in order to differentiate them from the demonstrative adjectives.

¿Cuál corbata prefieres, **ésta, ésa,** o **aquélla**?

◆ **Actividad 4**

Fill in the blanks with a demonstrative adjective or a demonstrative pronoun. Be sure to use the correct form.

En la tienda

Julia: Maritza, ¿qué te parece (this) _____ falda? Es como (that one over there) _____ que está al otro lado de los pantalones.

Maritza: No está mal, pero (this one) _____ es más cara. Yo prefiero (that one over there) _____ .

Julia: (This one) _____ va bien con (those) _____ zapatos que tengo en casa.

Maritza: Puedes comprarla si tienes dinero. Oye, ¿qué piensas de (this) _____ vestido?

Julia: (That) _____ vestido es más caro que mi falda.

Maritza: Bueno, sí, pero, ¿recuerdas (those over there) _____ zapatos que tienes en casa . . . ?

Julia: Eres muy graciosa, Maritza. Tú compras (that) _____ vestido y yo compro (this) _____ falda, ¿de acuerdo?

El pronombre relativo *que*

Tengo un amigo.	Tengo un amigo **que** vive en
Mi amigo vive en Guatemala.	Guatemala.
El señor se llama Marcos.	El señor **que** vende computadoras
El señor vende computadoras.	se llama Marcos.

Que (without an accent mark) is a relative pronoun. This word usually introduces a clause that refers or *relates* to some noun (*amigo, señor*) in the sentence. *Que* allows you to join two simple sentences into one complex sentence by turning one of the sentences into a dependent clause.

The relative pronoun *que* is equivalent to the English pronouns *that, who, whom,* and *which.* While these words may be omitted in English, *que* is necessary in Spanish.

Yo compro la camisa que	*I buy the shirt (that)*
Manuel quiere.	*Manuel wants.*

◆ Actividad 5

Combine las dos oraciones, usando el pronombre relativo *que*.

Modelo: La blusa es bonita. La blusa tiene mangas largas.
La blusa que tiene mangas largas es bonita.

1. La camisa es grande. La camisa tiene rayas rojas.
2. Esa chaqueta es mi favorita. La chaqueta tiene botones dorados.
3. La camisa combina con los pantalones. La camisa tiene el cuello blanco.
4. Me gustan esos zapatos. Los zapatos están a buen precio.
5. Voy a comprar el abrigo. El abrigo cuesta cincuenta dólares.
6. Esa bufanda es la más cara. Rosa compra la bufanda.
7. La corbata es roja y azul. La voy a comprar para David.
8. Los calcetines están rotos. Los uso para jugar al fútbol.
9. El cinturón es de cuero. Roberto quiere el cinturón.
10. Tú tienes la falda. Yo quiero la falda.

Adverbios

The following adverbs are often used to modify an adjective or another adverb. Remember that the ending of an adverb does not change like that of an adjective.

El precio de los tenis es **demasiado** alto.	*too*
Los precios suben **muy** rápido en esta tienda.	*very*
El precio de estos zapatos es **bastante** bueno.	*quite*
El precio de esta mochila es **algo** caro.	*somewhat*
El precio de los calcetines **no** es **nada** económico.	*not . . . at all*

♦ **Actividad 6**

For each sentence, modify the adjective in parentheses by using one of the following adverbs: *muy, bastante, algo, demasiado, no . . . nada.*

Modelo: Juan puede correr una milla en seis minutos. Juan es . . . (rápido)
   Juan es bastante rápido.

1. Margarita camina un kilómetro en veinte minutos. Margarita es . . . (lenta)

2. El abrigo cuesta 300 (trescientos) dólares. El abrigo es . . . (barato)

3. La camisa tiene nueve colores diferentes. La camisa es . . . (colorida)

4. Compro tres bufandas por el precio de una. Las bufandas están . . . (baratas)

5. La falda de María llega hasta los pies. La falda es . . . (larga)

6. Los zapatos me molestan. Los zapatos son . . . (pequeños)

7. Los pantalones necesitan un cinturón. Los pantalones son . . . (grandes)

8. Los zapatos tienen un tacón de 4" (pulgadas). El tacón es . . . (alto)

Usos del infinitivo

The following four points summarize four uses of the infinitive that you have already encountered.

1. An infinitive is used after a preposition.

Después de tomar café, ellos salen para el trabajo.	*After drinking coffee, they leave for work.*
Antes de comer, doy gracias a Dios.	*Before eating, I give thanks to God.*
No tengo tiempo **para hablar** ahora.	*I don't have time to talk now.*

2. An infinitive is often combined with certain verbs such as *deber, desear, esperar, necesitar, pensar, poder, querer,* and *saber.*

Deseo aprender mucho en la lección del día.	*I desire to learn much in the lesson of the day.*
Espero ser médico.	*I hope to become a doctor.*
¿**Puedes hacer** tortillas?	*Can you make tortillas?*
Quiero ayudar a los clientes.	*I want to help the clients.*

3. An infinitive may be used as a subject and has the equivalent use of the English *-ing* gerund.

Nadar es buen ejercicio.	*Swimming is good exercise.*

4. An infinitive follows certain impersonal expressions such as, *es bueno, es necesario, es importante,* and *hay que.*

Es bueno dormir ocho horas.	*It is good to sleep eight hours.*
Es importante estudiar todos los días.	*It is important to study every day.*
Es necesario hacer las tareas.	*It is necessary to do homework.*
Hay que llegar temprano.	*One ought to arrive early.*

◆ **Actividad 7**

Form original sentences using an infinitive with the following prepositions or verbs.

1. Después de . . .
2. Espero . . .
3. Necesito . . .
4. Deseo . . .
5. Antes de . . .
6. Debo . . .

◆ **Actividad 8**

Write five sentences using elements from each column.

Modelo: *Es importante estudiar las lecciones.*

Es bueno . . .	hacer	a las clases
Es importante . . .	comer	las lecciones
Es necesario . . .	llegar	al maestro
Hay que . . .	practicar	las tareas
	participar	por la noche
	estudiar	en las actividades
	estar	todas las comidas
	escuchar	a tiempo
	levantarse	los deportes
	dormir	en la capilla temprano

◆ **Actividad 9 ¿Eres buen estudiante?**

Do you do what you should do? Use the above expressions to describe the actions of the students in each of the following illustrations.

Modelo: Es bueno participar en la clase.

Modelo:

1.

2.

3.

4.

5.

Nota cultural ▲▲

La quinceañera

Para una señorita latinoamericana el día que cumple sus quince años es una de las fechas más importantes de su juventud. Muchos padres celebran la ocasión con un banquete al cual invitan a todos sus familiares y *amistades*. En muchos países la quinceañera se viste con un traje largo de vuelos, que usualmente es de color blanco o rosado, y con zapatos de tacón alto. Por lo general, la señorita recibe flores y muchas prendas *de regalo*—cadenas, pulseras o anillos de oro.

friends

as gifts

GUATEMALA

Aún quedan restos de la civilización maya.

Las plantaciones de Guatemala producen la exportación principal del país, el café.

GUATEMALA

- **AREA:** *42,000 sq. mi.*
  (approximately the
  size of Tennessee)

- **POPULATION:** *10.7 million*

- **GOVERNMENT:** *Republic*

- **CAPITAL:** *Guatemala*

GUATEMALA

uatemala is the most populous Central American country, and Guatemala City the largest Central American city. Most Guatemalans live in the mountainous region that traverses the country from east to west. The southern edge of these mountains produces most of Guatemala's chief export, coffee.

Before the Spanish conquest of the Americas, the Mayan civilization flourished throughout the territory that now includes Mexico's Yucatán Peninsula, Guatemala, and part of Honduras. The Petén region of northern Guatemala was the site of Uaxactún, the oldest known Mayan city. A monument dating back to the fourth century B.C. was discovered near Uaxactún. Today more than half the population of Guatemala are descendants of the Mayas, and many still speak their own native languages.

3-2 Una Visita al Barbero

Diálogo ▲▲▲

Marcos y su padre están hablando en casa.

Padre: Marcos, creo que debes ir a la barbería hoy. Tu pelo está demasiado largo.

this way

Marcos: Pero, papá, *así* me gusta.

Padre: ¿Me oyes, Marcos?

Marcos: Sí, papá.

Padre: Aquí tienes siete pesos para el corte de pelo.

Marcos: Sí, papá. ¿Y para el autobús?

in the back / at the sides

Padre: Y dos pesos más para el autobús. Pídele al barbero que te corte el pelo *atrás* y *a los lados.*

En la barbería . . .

Barbero: Buenas tardes, Marcos. ¿En qué puedo servirte?

Marcos: Mi padre dice que necesito un corte de pelo.

Shall I leave your hair short in the back?

Barbero: Ya veo. ¿Cómo quieres el corte? *¿Te dejo el pelo corto atrás?*

Marcos: Sí. Y me lo puede dejar corto a los lados también.

Barbero: Muy bien.

razor / the neck

El barbero toma un peine y las tijeras y comienza a cortar. Cuando termina con las tijeras, toma una *navaja* y corta el pelo en *el cuello.*

Marcos: Muchas gracias. Creo que mi padre tiene razón. Con el nuevo estilo, me veo mejor.

◆ **Conversación**

1. ¿Por qué necesita Marcos un corte de pelo?

2. ¿Adónde va Marcos?

3. ¿Cuánto cuesta un corte de pelo?

4. ¿Qué usa el barbero para cortarle el pelo a Marcos?

5. ¿Cómo es el corte?

el secador
de pelo

la navaja

la crema
de afeitar

el barbero

el pelo / el cabello

las tijeras

el bigote

el asiento

la barba

el cepillo

el peine

el corte de pelo

La barbería

el pelo rubio	blond hair	*el pelo liso*	straight hair
el pelo castaño	brown hair	*el pelo rizado*	curly hair
el pelo negro	black hair	*el pelo largo*	long hair
el pelo rojo	red hair	*el pelo corto*	short hair
las canas	gray hairs	*la peluquería, el salón de belleza*	the beauty parlor

Gramática ▲▲

Pedir vs. preguntar

Note the differences between these two verbs.

- The verb *pedir* means "to ask for" or "to request." A noun usually follows this verb.

    Rosa **pide un refresco** en el restaurante.

- The verb *preguntar* means "to ask" or "to inquire." It is usually followed by *si* (if) or an interrogative expression beginning with *dónde, cuándo, de quién, a qué hora,* and so on. Use this verb to report a question.

—¿Puedo llamar al barbero?	Rafael pregunta si puede llamar al barbero.
—¿Dónde está mi champú?	Rafael pregunta dónde está su champú.
—¿A qué hora es la cita?	Rafael pregunta a qué hora es la cita.

Los pronombres del objeto indirecto

In Chapter 2 you learned that the direct object receives the action of the verb. Note the direct object in each of the following sentences. (For a review of the direct object pronouns, see Reference Tables, pp. 337-338.)

¿Recomiendas **la peluquería** nueva? —Sí, **la** recomiendo.
El barbero vende **los peines. Los** vende a buen precio.
Usted escribe **una carta.** Usted **la** está escribiendo ahora.

The indirect object, however, tells *to whom* or *for whom* the action is performed.

¿**Nos** recomiendas esta peluquería? —Sí, **les** recomiedo esa peluquería.
El barbero **me** vende los peines a buen precio.
Usted **le** escribe una carta a Maritza.

The following chart lists the indirect object pronouns.

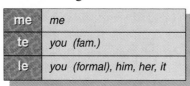
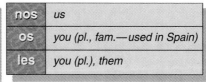

me	me		nos	us
te	you (fam.)		os	you (pl., fam.—used in Spain)
le	you (formal), him, her, it		les	you (pl.), them

- **Note:** The indirect object pronouns are the same as the direct object pronouns except in the third person.

- In addition to its third-person usage, *le* is used to refer to the formal second person (*usted*). When speaking to a teacher or to someone you must address by title (*Sr., Srta., Sra., Dr., Profesor*) and last name, *le* replaces *te* in your question. The person answering will respond using *me*.

    ¿**Le** explico el problema, Sr. Fuentes? —Sí, explíca**me** el problema.

- Like the direct object pronoun, the indirect object pronoun usually precedes a single conjugated verb. In a verb + infinitive or a present progressive construction, the indirect object pronoun may either precede the conjugated verb or be attached to the end of the infinitive or the present participle.

Le voy a escribir una carta esta noche.	Voy a escribir**le** una carta esta noche.
Le estoy escribiendo a Miguel ahora.	Estoy escribiéndo**le** a Miguel ahora.

- The indirect object pronouns are used for emphasis or clarification even when there may be an indirect object noun in the same clause.

Le digo la verdad **al profesor.**	Carlos **nos** habla **a nosotros**, no **te** habla **a ti**.
Les estoy escribiendo una carta **a las chicas** ahora.	Yo no **le** escribo cartas **a Teresa, le** escribo **a Ud.**

- The following verbs usually take indirect objects:
    Verbs of communication: *contar, decir, escribir, hablar, pedir, preguntar*
    Verbs of transmission: *dar, entregar, enviar, pagar, prestar, regalar*

◆ **Actividad 1**
Rewrite the sentences using the indirect objects given in parentheses.

Modelo: Adrián compra una revista. (me)
    Adrián me compra una revista.

1. Roberto regala sus discos viejos. (te)

2. Ana va a preparar una taza de café. (nos)

3. José está escribiendo una carta. (me)

4. Rafael envía las fotos. (nos)

5. Rosa María dice su número de teléfono. (me)

6. Merche corta el pelo. (le)

7. Luisa lava la cabeza. (te)

8. Marta cobra más barato. (nos)

◆ **Actividad 2**

Answer each of the following questions using an indirect object pronoun. Follow each model.

Modelo: ¿Les vas a escribir una carta a tus abuelos? —Sí, . . .
    —*Sí, voy a escribirles una carta.*

1. ¿Les vas a leer cuentos a tus hermanos? —No, . . .

2. ¿Le vas a comprar un regalo a tu madre? —Sí, . . .

3. ¿Le vas a dar consejos a tu amiga? —Sí, . . .

4. ¿Me vas a prestar tu cámara? —No, . . .

5. ¿Nos vas a decir la verdad? —Sí, . . .

Modelo: ¿Nos vas a escribir una carta a nosotros? —Sí, . . .
    Sí, les voy a escribir una carta a ustedes.

6. ¿Le vas a pedir permiso a tu padre? —Sí, . . .

7. ¿Me vas a pagar el dinero? —No, . . .

8. ¿Nos vas a llevar al parque? —No, . . .

9. ¿Les vas a preguntar a tus abuelos cuándo salen para Guatemala? —Sí, . . .

10. ¿Le vas a pagar al barbero por el corte de pelo? —Sí, . . .

◆ **Actividad 3**

Answer the questions. Remember to include the appropriate indirect object pronouns.

1. ¿Qué les das a tus padres para su aniversario?

2. ¿Me vendes tu bicicleta en $25.00?

3. ¿Le escribes cartas a tu abuela?

4. ¿Quién te escribe cartas a ti?

5. ¿Qué les pides a tus padres para tu cumpleaños?

6. ¿Qué le piden Uds. a su maestro(a) al final del semestre? ¿una buena nota?

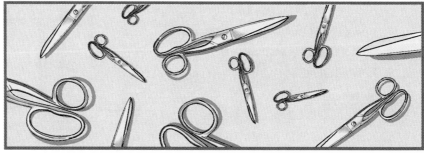

◆ **Actividad 4**

Decide whether the pronoun *le* in the questions below is second or third person; then answer accordingly.

Modelo: ¿Le ayudo con los libros, Sr. Pérez? —Sí, . . .
        (second person) —Sí, ayúdame con los libros.

  1. ¿Le doy los papeles, Sra. Sánchez? —No, . . .

  2. ¿Le entrego mi tarea al Sr. Ramos? —Sí, . . .

  3. ¿Le vendo mi bicicleta a Daniel, Srta. Lupe? —No, . . .

  4. ¿Le pido ayuda (*help*) al Dr. Gil? —Sí, . . .

  5. ¿Le doy la composición ahora, Srta. Oviedo? —No, . . .

Los pronombres objetivos múltiples

Sometimes we use a direct and an indirect object pronoun in the same sentence.
    ¿*Me* vas a dar **tu dirección**? —Sí, *te* **la** voy a dar.

1. When both the direct and indirect object pronouns occur in the sentence, the indirect object pronoun always precedes the direct object pronoun.
    ¿*Me* prestas **tu libro**? —Sí, *te* **lo** presto.
    ¿*Me* vas a comprar **la blusa**? —Sí, voy a comprár*te*la.
    ¿El señor *nos* está regalando **estos libros**? —Sí, *nos* **los** está
      regalando.

2. Both *le* and *les* become *se* when followed by another object pronoun that begins with *l* (*lo, la, los, las*).
    ¿*Le* pides **permiso** a *tu padre*? —Sí, *se* **lo** pido.

3. When two object pronouns occur in the same sentence, both pronouns precede a single conjugated verb. In a sentence containing a verb + infinitive or a progressive construction, the object pronouns may precede the conjugated verb or be attached to the end of the infinitive or present participle.
    ¿*Le* vas a vender **la bicicleta** a *Miguel*?
    —Sí, voy a vendér*se*la.
    —Sí, *se* **la** voy a vender.
    ¿*Les* están enviando **el dinero** a *ellos*?
    —No, no están enviándo*se*lo (*a ellos*).
    —No, no *se* **lo** están enviando (*a ellos*).

Notice that it is necessary to place an accent mark on the last syllable of the infinitive and on the next to the last syllable of the participle in order to retain the stress on the correct syllable.

4. When the direct object is a phrase, idea, or concept, the neuter object pronoun *lo* is used.

> ¿***Nos*** dijo la profesora **cuándo tenemos que entregar la tarea**?
> —Sí, ***nos* lo** dijo.

> Martín *te* pregunta **dónde está la barbería.** Martín *te* **lo** pregunta otra vez.

◆ **Actividad 5**

Carmen is very demanding of her brother Carlos. Play the role of Carlos as you answer Carmen's questions. Follow the model.

Modelo: Carmen: ¿Me vas a comprar el cuaderno?
Carlos: Sí, voy a comprártelo. / No, no te lo voy a comprar.

1. ¿Me vas a prestar tu cámara?
2. ¿Me vas a dar el libro?
3. ¿Nos vas a preparar dos refrescos?
4. ¿Le vas a decir la verdad a mamá?
5. ¿Le vas a llevar el periódico a papá?

◆ **Actividad 6**

In addition to being demanding, Carmen is also nosey. Play the role of Carlos and patiently answer her questions with the aid of the items in parentheses. Follow the model.

Modelo: Carmen: ¿Quién te va a prestar una cámara? (Luis)
Carlos: Luis me la va a prestar.

1. ¿Quién te va a vender una bicicleta? (Ramón)
2. ¿Cuándo te van a enviar el paquete? (la semana que viene)
3. ¿Te explica hoy la lección el profesor? (Sí . . .)
4. ¿Quién te está contando la historia de Jesús? (Miguel)
5. ¿Cuándo te va a pagar Daniel lo que te debe? (mañana)

◆ **Actividad 7**

Mr. Rojas is teaching a Sunday school class. Answer his questions politely as in the model.

Modelo: Sr. Rojas: ¿Quién me va a escribir el versículo en la pizarra? (yo)
Yo se lo voy a escribir, señor.

1. ¿Quién me trae un Nuevo Testamento? (José)
2. ¿Quiénes me van a repetir el versículo? (nosotros)
3. ¿Quiénes me van a prestar su atención? (todos)
4. ¿Quién me va a buscar los himnarios? (yo)

◆ **Actividad 8**

Conteste las preguntas.

1. ¿Cuándo les debo enviar las fotos a Uds.? (mañana)

2. ¿No te van a pagar el dinero los clientes? (sí)

3. ¿Cuándo nos vas a contar el cuento? (hoy en la noche)

4. ¿Le vas a decir al barbero cómo quieres el pelo? (¡Claro que sí!)

5. ¿Le pregunto a la peluquera cuánto cuesta un permanente? (no)

◆ **Actividad 9**

State your reactions to the following questions by using each verb in parentheses along with the appropriate object pronouns.

Modelo: ¿Qué haces cuando un compañero quiere usar tu diccionario? (prestar)
Se lo presto. / No se lo presto.

¿Qué haces cuando . . .

1. un amigo quiere usar tu cámara? (prestar)

2. tus hermanas quieren usar tu champú? (dar)

3. un amigo te pide el número de teléfono de tu prima? (dar)

4. una compañera de clase perezosa te pide tu tarea porque quiere copiarla? (prestar)

5. los estudiantes nuevos no entienden las reglas (*rules*) de tu escuela? (explicar)

6. tu hermano de cinco años quiere dulces? (comprar)

7. los libros de tu amigo David están en tu casa? (devolver)

8. tu amigo que está a dieta (*on a diet*) te pide cinco dólares para comprar un helado y un pastel? (prestar)

◆ **Actividad 10**

   Conteste las preguntas.

   1. ¿Qué nos está explicando Ud.? ¿la gramática? (Sí, . . .)

   2. ¿Les envío a Uds. el dinero por correo? (Sí, . . .)

   3. ¿Cuándo nos da Ud. el informe? (ahora)

   4. ¿Debemos traerles a Uds. los documentos mañana? (No, . . .)

   5. ¿Cómo van Uds. a pagarnos la cuenta? (al crédito)

Gustar (*to like*)

Nos gusta el corte de pelo.	*We like the haircut.*
Me gustan los niños.	*I like children.*

The literal translation of the verb *gustar* is "to be pleasing." In the above phrases, *gustar* agrees in number with its subject, which usually follows the verb (*el corte de pelo, los niños*). *Me* and *nos* are the indirect object pronouns that tell to whom the subject is pleasing.

   The haircut is pleasing **to us.**

   Children are pleasing **to me.**

Notice sentences with the other personal object pronouns:

   ¿**Te gusta** el pelo corto?

   A Víctor le gustan los deportes.

   A mis padres no **les gustan** los perros grandes.

Note: The indirect object pronoun must be used even though the noun to whom it refers might already be included in the same clause.

   A Víctor **le** . . . ; A mis padres no **les** . . .

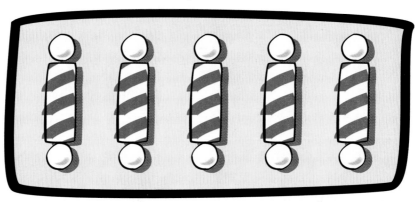

◆ **Actividad 11**

What do the following girls like? Form complete sentences using the following subjects and objects.

Modelo: los colores rojo y amarillo / Maribel y tú
A Maribel y a ti les gustan los colores rojo y amarillo.

1. el español / Elizabet
2. el francés / María y Ana
3. las hamburguesas / Rosita
4. los juegos olímpicos / Sara y Rut
5. el pelo largo / Beatriz
6. los niños / Catalina y Diana
7. los autos grandes / Rosalina
8. el fútbol / Déborah
9. la pizza / Carolina y yo
10. los chicos / Anita y Graciela

Otros verbos como *gustar*

Other verbs in Spanish pattern themselves after *gustar: interesar* (to interest), *importar* (to matter), *encantar* (to delight), *agradar* (to please), *preocupar* (to concern), and *faltar* (to lack).

¿No **te interesan** los programas culturales?

Me importan sus problemas.

A mi hermano **le encanta** esquiar en Colorado.

Me agrada la belleza del mar.

Al profesor **le preocupan** los alumnos ausentes.

Me falta dinero para comprar el automóvil.

◆ **Actividad 12**

Use the following words to make complete sentences. Follow the model.

Modelo: la profesora / encantar / las películas de vaqueros (*cowboys*)
   A la profesora le encantan las películas de vaqueros.

1. Jaime / gustar / el helado de mango

2. Federico / importar / la apariencia física

3. mis padres / preocupar / mis notas

4. tú / agradar / el calor

5. Pablo y Andrés / gustar / los autos deportivos

6. los estudiantes de francés / interesar / la vida en París

7. yo / faltar / tiempo

8. nosotros / encantar / la música de guitarra

◆ **Actividad 13**

Write a paragraph describing yourself. Tell about your likes and dislikes. Comment on what is interesting to you and what is important to you. Use as many vocabulary words as possible.

Refrán ▲▲▲

Using a humorous figure from the animal world, this proverb teaches that one cannot disguise his or her real self.

Aunque la mona se vista de seda, mona se queda.

HONDURAS

- **AREA:** *43,300 sq. mi.*
  (slightly larger
  than Tennessee)

- **POPULATION:** *5 million*

- **GOVERNMENT:** *Democratic constitutional republic*

- **CAPITAL:** *Tegucigalpa*

The history of Honduras, as in much of Central America, is the history of the Mayan civilization, as evidenced by the ancient ruins of Copán and the country's largely Indian population of today.

The most important agricultural product is the banana, but Honduras also produces coffee, cattle, sugar cane, and fine woods, as well as a number of manufactured goods, including clothing. It has vast deposits of precious metals, plus significant deposits of iron ore, but these deposits remain largely unutilized due to a lack of manpower and funds.

Earlier in this century an American company, the United Fruit Company, today called Standard Brands, was often at the center of political controversy in Honduras. This company's most positive and important contribution was the establishment in 1942 of an international center for agricultural research and education whose graduates are in great demand throughout the Americas.

3-3 Un Día Típico en el Campo Misionero

Lectura ▲▲

Daniel Salinas está en Honduras con un grupo de jóvenes de su iglesia para ayudar en la construcción de una iglesia. Daniel escribe lo siguiente en su diario.

even though

Me encanta la vida en el campo misionero *aunque* es mucho trabajo también. Todos los días nos levantamos a las seis de la mañana. Nos bañamos con agua fría—para despertarnos—y nos vestimos rápidamente. Después, cada uno tiene sus devociones personales. A las siete en punto la esposa del misionero nos tiene el desayuno preparado. Siempre sirve algo delicioso. ¡Pienso que es buena cocinera!

At least
hardware store

A las siete y media todos nos marchamos a trabajar. Yo, normalmente, acompaño al misionero. *Por lo menos* tres veces a la semana, tenemos que ir a la *ferretería* para comprar los materiales de la construcción.

custom

Todos trabajamos hasta el mediodía y después almorzamos en la casa de los misioneros. A veces, tomamos una siesta antes de volver al trabajo. ¡Me gusta esa *costumbre*!

Casi siempre trabajamos hasta las seis y media o las siete, y después jugamos un partido de volibol. Por eso, después de cenar, ¡me voy directo a la cama!

finished

La iglesia que estamos edificando va a ser grande. El misionero se pone contento cuando piensa que pronto va a estar *terminada*. Y yo me pongo triste cuando pienso que pronto tengo que irme.

◆ **Conversación**

1. ¿Por qué está Daniel Salinas en Honduras?

2. ¿Qué hace Daniel desde las seis hasta las siete de la mañana?

3. ¿Adónde van para comprar los materiales?

4. ¿Qué hace Daniel después del almuerzo?

5. ¿Cuándo se acuesta?

6. ¿Por qué se pone contento el misionero?

7. ¿Por qué se pone triste Daniel?

8. ¿Te gustaría (*would you like*) hacer un viaje misionero?

Gramática ▲▲▲

Los verbos reflexivos

Reflexive verbs are those verbs in which the action reflects back to the subject. They are used to indicate that the subject does something to itself (or a part of itself), for itself, or on its own. Verbs are made reflexive by conjugating them with reflexive pronouns. The reflexive pronoun is in the same grammatical person as the subject of the verb.

Review the reflexive pronouns in the chart below.

Mirarse		
yo	me miro	I am looking at myself
tú	te miras	you are looking at yourself
usted	se mira	you are looking at yourself
él, ella	se mira	he is looking at himself she is looking at herself
nosotros(as)	nos miramos	we are looking at ourselves
vosotros(as)	os miráis	you are looking at yourselves
ustedes	se miran	you are looking at yourselves
ellos(as)	se miran	they are looking at themselves
Present Participle:	mirándose	

Notice that **se** is the reflexive pronoun for *él, ella, Ud., ellos, ellas,* and *Uds.*

Reflexive verbs are used frequently in Spanish. On the contrary, reflexive pronouns are often implied rather than expressed in modern English.

Me baño. I am taking a bath.
 (I am bathing myself.)

Raúl se afeita. Raúl is shaving.
 (Raúl is shaving himself.)

Many verbs in Spanish can be used in either reflexive or nonreflexive constructions. Notice how the addition of the reflexive pronoun affects the meaning of the verbs below.

La niña **se acuesta** temprano.	*The little girl goes to bed early.*
La madre **acuesta** a la niña temprano.	*The mother puts the little girl to bed early.*
Raquel **se duerme** a las nueve.	*Raquel goes to sleep at nine.*
Raquel **duerme** toda la noche.	*Raquel sleeps all night.*
Paco **se baña** por la noche.	*Paco takes a bath at night.*
Paco **baña** a su perro con agua y jabón.	*Paco bathes his dog with water and soap.*

The following reflexive verbs deal with daily routine:

acostarse	Carlos **se acuesta** a las ocho.
despertarse	Cuando suena el reloj, **me despierto.**
dormirse	Yo me acuesto y **me duermo** rápidamente.
levantarse	Mamá siempre **se levanta** temprano.
ponerse	Pedro **se pone** los zapatos.
quitarse	Margarita **se quita** el abrigo.
vestirse	Tú **te vistes** por la mañana.

The following reflexive verbs deal with personal grooming:

afeitarse	Él **se afeita** todos los días.
bañarse	María **se baña** por la mañana.
cepillarse	**Me cepillo** los dientes después de comer.
ducharse (*to shower*)	Yo **me ducho** por la noche.
lavarse	Roberto **se lava** las manos y la cara.
peinarse	¡Anita **se peina** diez veces al día!
secarse	Ella **se seca** con una toalla (*towel*) grande.

Posición del pronombre reflexivo

Reflexive pronouns follow the same rules of placement that other object pronouns do. They usually precede the conjugated verb; however, in a verb + infinitive or progressive construction, they may either precede the conjugated verb or be attached to the end of the infinitive or present participle.

Usted **se** va a levantar a las ocho.	Usted va a levantar**se** a las ocho.
Ellos **se** están lavando las manos.	Ellos están lavándo**se** las manos.

The reflexive pronoun is always attached to the end of an affirmative command, but it always precedes the negative command.

¡Despiérta**te** temprano!

¡No **te** levantes tarde!

◆ **Actividad 1**

Supply the correct form of the reflexive verb in parentheses.

Modelo: El señor Báez (despertarse) _____ a las seis.
El señor Báez se despierta a las seis.

1. La señora de Báez (levantarse) _____ a las seis y cuarto.

2. Rolando y Samuel (despertarse) _____ a las siete.

3. El señor Báez (afeitarse) _____ .

4. Yo (levantarse) _____ a las siete y cuarto.

5. Tú (bañarse) _____ y después (secarse) _____ .

6. La señora de Báez (lavarse) _____ la cara.

7. Rolando y yo (cepillarse) _____ los dientes a las siete y media.

8. Maritza (peinarse) _____ .

9. Los señores Báez y sus hijos (sentarse) _____ a la mesa.

10. Yo (lavarse) _____ las manos.

◆ **Actividad 2**

Ask the following questions to a fellow classmate.

Modelo: ¿A qué hora te despiertas?
Me despierto a las seis y media.

1. ¿A qué hora te levantas los sábados?

2. ¿Te secas el pelo con una toalla o con un secador de pelo?

3. ¿Te peinas antes del desayuno o después?

4. ¿Te bañas por la noche o por la mañana?

5. ¿A qué hora te acuestas los viernes?

6. ¿Te levantas en seguida (*right away*) cuando suena la alarma?

7. ¿Cuántas veces al día te cepillas los dientes?

◆ **Actividad 3**

First determine if the reflexive form of each verb in parentheses is necessary. Then supply the correct form of each verb.

1. Mis hermanos (cepillar) _____ los dientes después de comer.

2. Ramonita siempre (peinar) _____ a su hermanita antes de ir a la escuela.

3. Carlos (lavar) _____ el auto de su padre los sábados.

4. Cuando hace calor, yo (bañar) _____ dos veces al día.

5. Yo nunca (dormir) _____ en la clase de español.

El reflexivo: los verbos de movimiento

Certain verbs of movement are used in the reflexive form.

darse prisa *(to hurry)*	Debo **darme prisa** porque es tarde.
irse (a) *(to leave [for])*	**Se va** al trabajo a las ocho.
marcharse *(to leave)*	Son las once; voy a **marcharme.**
quedarse *(to stay)*	**Me quedo** en casa cuando estoy enfermo.
reunirse (con) *to meet with*	Marcos **se reúne** con sus amigos después del almuerzo.

◆ **Actividad 4**

Supply the appropriate form of each verb in parentheses.

1. Las amigas (reunirse) _____ en la casa de María.

2. No tienen que (darse) _____ prisa porque van a dormir en su casa.

3. Los hermanos de María no van a (quedarse) _____ en la casa esta noche.

4. Ellos (marcharse) _____ de la fiesta a las ocho.

5. Rosana y Carmencita (lavarse) _____ el pelo.

6. Rosita y yo tenemos que (peinarse) _____ .

7. Todas las muchachas (acostarse) _____ , pero no tienen sueño.

8. Después de la medianoche, las muchachas (dormirse) _____ .

9. La madre de María las (despertar) _____ por la mañana.

10. Las muchachas (levantarse) _____ y (darse) _____ prisa para llegar a tiempo a la escuela.

◆ **Actividad 5**

Write a paragraph of at least eight sentences telling what you do in the morning to get ready for school. Use as many of the reflexive verbs as possible.

Más verbos reflexivos

When used in the reflexive form, the following verbs usually mean "to get" or "to become."

aburrirse	*to get bored*
acostumbrarse (a)	*to get used to*
alegrarse (de)	*to get / be happy (because of)*
calmarse	*to get / become calm*
divertirse (e→ie)	*to have fun*
enfermarse	*to get sick*
enojarse (con)	*to get angry at*
hacerse	*to become*
mejorarse	*to get better*
ocuparse (de)	*to occupy oneself (in)*
ponerse	*to get / become*
preocuparse (por)	*to get worried / be concerned*
sentirse (e→ie) (triste)	*to feel (sad)*
enamorarse (de)	*to fall in love (with)*
comprometerse (con)	*to become engaged (to)*
casarse (con)	*to get married (to)*

◆ **Actividad 6**

Complete each sentence using an appropriate reflexive construction from the list above.

Modelo: Cuando saco una *A* en español . . .
  Cuando saco una A en español, me alegro.

1. Cuando el/la profesor(a) no llega a la clase . . .

2. Cuando escucho música . . .

3. Cuando como demasiado . . .

4. Cuando voy al zoológico . . .

5. Cuando saco malas notas . . .

6. Después que uno se compromete . . .

7. Cuando mi mejor amigo está enfermo . . .

◆ **Actividad 7**

Conteste las preguntas.

1. ¿Quién se preocupa por tu futuro?

2. ¿Quién se enoja frecuentemente contigo?

3. ¿Con quién te diviertes más?

4. ¿Quién se enferma más frecuentemente?

5. ¿Quién se siente orgulloso cuando sacas buenas notas?

Hacerse means "to become" and may be combined with a noun or an adjective.

El agua en el congelador se hace hielo.
The water in the freezer becomes ice.

Héctor quiere hacerse rico y famoso.
Hector wants to become rich and famous.

Ponerse means "to get" or "to become" suddenly or involuntarily and usually combines with adjectives referring to a physical, mental, or emotional state.

Si no come, **se pone** enfermo . . . delgado . . . triste.
If he doesn't eat, he gets sick . . . thin . . . sad.

◆ **Actividad 8**

Describe your reaction to the following circumstances. The following adjectives may help you: *contento, triste, furioso, nervioso, rojo.*

Modelo: Tu hermana usa tu perfume.
Me pongo furiosa.

1. Tu mejor amiga te llama por teléfono.

2. No tienes la tarea para la clase de español.

3. Alguien se burla (*makes fun*) de ti.

4. Un(a) chico(a) te sonríe.

5. Es tarde y tus padres te esperan en casa.

Vocabulario adicional ▲▲▲▲▲▲▲▲▲▲▲▲▲▲▲▲▲▲▲▲▲▲▲▲▲▲▲▲▲▲

The nouns in the column on the right are related to verbs you already know.

Verbo	Sustantivo
bañarse	la bañera (el baño)
peinarse	el peine (el peinado)
despertarse	el despertador
cepillarse	el cepillo
secarse	el secador
divertirse	la diversión
preocuparse	la preocupación

¡Aló!

De más estima es el buen
nombre que las muchas riquezas,
y la buena fama más que la plata
y el oro.   **Proverbios 22:1**

4-1 UNA LLAMADA TELEFÓNICA

Diálogo ▲▲▲

El Sr. Martín Vázquez descuelga el teléfono, escucha el tono, marca el número y espera. Al momento oye una voz.

Operadora: Habla la operadora Alicia Núñez. ¿En qué puedo servirle?

collect

Sr. Vázquez: Quiero hacer una llamada *a cobro revertido* a Managua, Nicaragua.

Operadora: ¿Cuál es el número en Managua?

Sr. Vázquez: 68452.

Operadora: ¿La llamada es de persona a persona o de estación a estación?

Sr. Vázquez: Es de estación a estación.

Operadora: Muy bien. Su nombre, por favor.

Sr. Vázquez: Martín Vázquez.

Operadora: Un momento.

El teléfono suena.

Miguel: ¡Bueno!

Operadora: Tengo una llamada a cobro revertido de parte del Sr. Martín Vázquez. ¿Acepta la llamada?

Miguel: Sí, señorita.

Sr. Vázquez: Hola, ¿qué tal? ¿Con quién tengo el gusto de hablar?

Miguel: Habla Miguel. ¿De dónde llama, don Martín?

delayed

Sr. Vázquez: Estoy todavía en San Salvador. Mi vuelo está *atrasado*.

Miguel: Lo siento. Lo estamos esperando.

Sr. Vázquez: Voy a tomar el avión que sale el sábado. ¿Está tu padre?

Miguel: No, está en su oficina. ¿Quiere dejarle *un recado*?　　a message

Sr. Vázquez: Sí, por favor. Dile que estoy listo para la reunión del lunes. Espero llegar mañana por la tarde. Lo voy a llamar desde el aeropuerto.

Miguel: Muy bien.

Sr. Vázquez: Saludos a todos. ¡Nos vemos pronto!

Miguel: ¡Adiós!

◆ **Conversación**

1. ¿Cuáles son las cuatro cosas que el Sr. Martín Vázquez hace antes de oír la voz de la operadora?

2. ¿Qué clase de llamada hace? (Dé dos características.)

3. ¿Qué le pregunta la operadora a Miguel?

4. ¿Qué problema tiene el Sr. Vázquez en San Salvador?

5. ¿Cuál es el recado que deja?

Vocabulario ▲▲▲▲▲▲▲▲▲▲▲▲▲▲▲▲▲▲▲▲▲▲▲▲▲▲▲▲▲▲▲▲▲▲

El teléfono

colgar (o→ue) el teléfono (*to hang up the phone*)
descolgar (o→ue) el teléfono (*to pick up the phone*)
el tono; la señal (*the dial tone*)
la línea ocupada (*a busy signal*)
marcar el número equivocado (*to dial the wrong number*)

Los tipos de llamadas

a cobro revertido / por cobrar (*collect*)
de estación a estación
de persona a persona
de larga distancia
internacional
local

Frases para la comunicación

- **To answer the telephone:**
  ¡aló!
  ¡bueno!
  ¡dígame!
- **To announce yourself:**
  Habla Juan.
- **To request speaking to somebody:**
  ¿Podría hablar con Miguel, por favor?
- **To ask who is calling:**
  ¿De parte de quién?
- **To ask if someone would like to leave a message:**
  ¿Le gustaría dejar un recado (un mensaje)?

◆ **Actividad 1**

Complete los diálogos.

1. Tú descuelgas el teléfono y escuchas _____ . Marcas el número
   "_____" para llamar a la operadora.

   operadora: _____ la operadora Alicia Núñez. ¿En qué puedo
   servirle?

   tú: Quiero hacer una llamada de _____ distancia,
   estación a _____ , a los Estados Unidos.

   operadora: Su nombre, por favor.

   tú: _____ .

   operadora: ¿A qué número desea llamar?

   tú: _____ .

   operadora: Un momento.

2. El teléfono _____ y María lo contesta.

   María: ¡Aló!

   tú: ¡Aló! ¿ _____ con Marcos, por favor?

   María: ¿ _____ quién?

   tú: De _____ .

   María: Lo siento, Marcos no está en casa. ¿Quiere dejarle un
   _____ ?

   tú: No, gracias. ¡ _____ !

Gramática ▲▲▲

Los días de la semana

Voy a tomar el primer avión que sale **el sábado.**

- The definite article usually precedes the days of the week.

    El lunes es mi día favorito.   Yo te llamo **el martes.**

- When the day of the week is listed on the calendar or is used with a noun or adverb referring to time (hoy, mañana, etc.), the article is not used.

    Hoy es **miércoles.**   Voy a llegar mañana **jueves.**

- Only *sábado* and *domingo* add an *s* to form the plural. The other days of the week use the same form for both the singular and the plural.

    Mi amigo me llama **los viernes**   *My friend calls me on Fridays*
      y **los sábados.**   *and Saturdays.*
    Yo lo llamo **los domingos.**   *I call him on Sundays.*

(For a complete listing of the days of the week and the months of the year, see Reference Tables, pp. 339-340.)

Adverbios de tiempo

ayer	*yesterday*	ahora	*now*
anoche	*last night*	a veces	*sometimes*
hoy	*today*	luego / más tarde	*later*
esta noche	*tonight*	nunca	*never*
mañana	*tomorrow*	pronto	*soon, at once*
pasado mañana	*the day after tomorrow*	siempre	*always*
el fin de semana	*(on) the weekend*		

ᴬ◆ Actividad 2

Conteste las preguntas.

1. ¿Qué día es hoy?
2. ¿Cuántos días hay en una semana?
3. ¿Cuál es tu día favorito?
4. ¿Qué haces los fines de semana?
5. ¿Qué día es mañana?
6. ¿Qué día es pasado mañana?
7. ¿Qué planes tienes para esta noche?
8. ¿Qué actividad haces ahora?
9. ¿Estudias siempre en tu dormitorio?
10. ¿Cuántas veces al día hablas por teléfono?

Los números ordinales

El español es la **primera** lengua extranjera (*foreign*) que estudio.
Roberto está en el **sexto** grado, pero su hermana está en el **quinto.**
Marzo es el **tercer** mes del año.
Los dos **primeros** meses del año son enero y febrero.

Ordinal numbers must agree with the noun they modify in number and gender. They usually precede the noun they modify.

primero, primera	1º	1ª	sexto, sexta	6º	6ª
segundo, segunda	2º	2ª	séptimo, séptima	7º	7ª
tercero, tercera	3º	3ª	octavo, octava	8º	8ª
cuarto, cuarta	4º	4ª	noveno, novena	9º	9ª
quinto, quinta	5º	5ª	décimo, décima	10º	10ª

- Before masculine singular nouns, the shortened forms **primer** and **tercer** are used. The abbreviated forms are 1ᵉʳ and 3ᵉʳ.

  Yo no estoy en el **tercer** grado.

- When both cardinal and ordinal numbers are used, the cardinal number precedes the ordinal number: las **dos primeras** lecciones. (In English we would say, "the first two lessons.")
- Beyond *décimo,* most people prefer to use cardinal numbers instead.

  Alfonso XIII (trece)   Luis XVI (dieciséis)

✎ ◆ Actividad 3

Conteste las preguntas.

1. Si el lunes es el primer día de la semana, ¿qué día es el viernes?
2. ¿Qué mes del año es julio?
3. ¿Cuál es el décimo mes?
4. ¿En qué fila (*row*) te sientas en la clase de español?
5. ¿Qué letra del alfabeto es la letra *e*?
6. ¿Qué mes del año es marzo?
7. ¿En qué grado estás?
8. ¿En qué grado está tu hermano(a) menor?
9. ¿En qué grado estudian Uds. álgebra?
10. ¿En qué grados estudian Uds. la historia de los Estados Unidos?

Palabras indefinidas

Palabras indefinidas			
algo	*something*	nada	*nothing*
alguien	*someone*	nadie	*no one, nobody*
alguno, alguna algunos, algunas	[adj.] *some, any* [pron.] *someone, something, one*	ninguno, ninguna ningunos, ningunas	*none, not any*
tambien	*also*	tampoco	*neither*
o . . . o	*either . . . or*	ni . . . ni	*neither . . . nor*

- If negative words such as *nada* and *nadie* follow the verb in the sentence, *no* or another negative word must precede the verb.

> ¿Tienes algo en la mano? —No, **no** tengo **nada.**
> ¿Hay alguien en casa a estas —No, **no** hay **nadie.**
>   horas?

- When used as indefinite pronouns, the forms of *alguno* and *ninguno* may refer to either things or people.

> **Alguno** de mis libros tiene esa   *One of my books has that information.*
>   información.
> **Ninguna** de las chicas está   *None of the girls is sick.*
>   enferma.

- When *alguno* and *ninguno* are used as adjectives (that is, before a noun), the following forms are used: *algún, alguna, algunos, algunas; ningún, ninguna, ningunos, ningunas.*

Hay **algún** señor a la puerta.	*There is **some** man at the door.*
Ofrecieron **algunas** ideas interesantes.	*They offered **some** interesting ideas.*
No hay **ningún** dinero en mi cartera.	*There is **not any** money in my wallet.*
Ninguna clase tiene más de 25 alumnos.	*No class has more than 25 students.*

• *Tampoco* expresses agreement with negative statements.

Yo voy a llamar a mi amiga por teléfono.	—Yo **también.**
Yo **no** hago llamadas de larga distancia.	—Yo **tampoco.**

◆ **Actividad 4**

The members of the committee in charge of planning the next youth fellowship are in a very negative frame of mind. Pretend you are one of them and answer the following questions in the negative.

Modelo: Roberto, ¿tienes alguna idea para la fiesta?
   Roberto: No, no tengo ninguna idea.

1. Carmen, ¿tenemos dinero para la fiesta?

2. Carlos, ¿alguien va a preparar la música especial?

3. Rafael no quiere cantar. Y tú, Miguel, ¿quieres cantar?

4. ¿Tienes algo que decir?

5. Sara, ¿algún chico va a preparar las invitaciones?

6. Pepe, ¿crees que Tomás o Lucinda van a poder venir?

7. Jóvenes, ¿alguien quiere tener una fiesta?

Refrán ▲▲▲

This proverb discourages the procrastination so prevalent among students of all nationalities.

   No dejes para mañana lo que puedes hacer hoy.

¡Debo darme prisa si quiero hacer esto hoy!

INTERNATIONAL DATE LINE

EL SALVADOR

- **AREA:** *8,100 sq. mi.*
  (approximately the size of Massachusetts)

- **POPULATION:** *5.7 million*

- **GOVERNMENT:** *Republic*

- **CAPITAL:** *San Salvador*

E l Salvador, the smallest of the Central American republics, is the most densely populated and the only one with no Carribean coastline. On September 15, 1821, El Salvador, Honduras, Guatemala, Nicaragua, and Costa Rica declared their independence from Spain and joined the Mexican empire. They broke with Mexico in 1823 and organized the United Provinces of Central America. This league began making definite improvements in the lives of Central Americans but lasted only about fifteen years. As each country became completely independent, it faced serious political and economic difficulties.

Independence for El Salvador initiated a succession of violent power struggles. The first half of the twentieth century brought relative stability and economic development. Several events, however, severely set back the cause of progress: a border war with Honduras in 1969, an earthquake in San Salvador in 1986, and a civil war throughout the 1980s that claimed some 75,000 lives.

Among El Salvador's resources is the fertile soil produced by lava and ash from erupted volcanoes. This soil is ideal for growing coffee, El Salvador's chief crop.

4-2 Una Cuenta de Ahorros

Diálogo ▲▲▲

salary

Yolanda acaba de recibir su primer *salario*. Ella va al banco y abre una cuenta de ahorros.

Banquero: Buenos días, señorita. ¿En qué puedo servirle?

I would like

Yolanda: *Quisiera* abrir una cuenta.

Banquero: ¿Una cuenta corriente o una de ahorros?

Yolanda: De ahorros, por favor.

application

to sign

Banquero: Tenga la bondad de completar este *formulario*. Debe escribir su nombre, dirección, fecha de nacimiento, y número de identificación. Después debe *firmar* en esta línea . . .

Yolanda: Aquí tiene el formulario. Es mi primera cuenta de ahorros.

Banquero: ¿Sí? La felicito. ¿Cuánto quiere depositar hoy?

Yolanda: Ciento diecisiete dólares. El cheque es por $130. Me puede dar $13 en efectivo.

Banquero: Muy bien. ¿Puede endosar el cheque, por favor?

Yolanda: Sí, como no.

booklet

Banquero: Todo está listo. Ya tiene $117 en su cuenta y aquí tiene $13 en efectivo. Ésta es su *libreta* de ahorros. Favor de traer su libreta cada vez que deposite dinero.

Yolanda: Sí, señor. Muchas gracias.

◆ **Conversación**

1. ¿Por qué va Yolanda al banco?
2. ¿Tiene Yolanda ya una cuenta en el banco?
3. ¿Qué clase de cuenta quiere abrir?
4. ¿Por cuánto es el cheque?
5. ¿Cuánto dinero quiere depositar en la cuenta?
6. Antes de darle el cheque al banquero, ¿qué tiene que hacer Yolanda?
7. ¿Qué piensas que va a hacer Yolanda con los trece dólares?

Vocabulario ▲▲▲▲▲▲▲▲▲▲▲▲▲▲▲▲▲▲▲▲▲▲▲▲▲▲▲▲▲▲▲▲▲▲▲▲

El dinero y el banco (*money and banking*)

- **Transacciones bancarias**
  abrir una cuenta corriente
     (*to open a checking account*)
  abrir una cuenta de ahorros
     (*to open a savings account*)
  hablar con el/la cajero(a) (*the teller*)
  cambiar dinero (*to exchange money*)
  cobrar un cheque (*to cash a check*)
  endosar (*to endorse*) un cheque
  depositar dinero
  pedir un préstamo
     (*to apply for a loan*)
  retirar (*to withdraw*) dinero

- **Otras palabras financieras**
  la bolsa; el mercado de valores
     (*the stock market*)
  la bancarrota (*bankruptcy*)
  el diezmo (*the tithe*)
  dinero en efectivo (*cash money*)
  la economía (*the economy*)
  los intereses (*the interest*)
  el mercado común
     (*the common market*)

el billete

el cheque

la tarjeta de crédito

el cheque de viajero

las monedas

Gramática ▲▲

Traer

Notice the verb *traer* (to bring) in the following sentences.

Siempre **traigo** visitas a la iglesia.   Roberto **trae** visitas también.

The verb *traer* is irregular in the first-person singular form of the present tense but is regular in the other forms of the present tense. The present participle is *trayendo*.

Traer			
yo	traigo	nosotros(as)	traemos
tú	traes	vosotros(as)	traéis
Ud., él, ella	trae	Uds., ellos(as)	traen
Present Participle:	trayendo		

◆ **Actividad 1**

Los jóvenes traen regalos para los misioneros. Complete las oraciones con la forma correcta del verbo *traer.*

Modelo: Samuel _____ artículos personales.
    Samuel trae artículos personales.

1. Carmen y su hermana _____ dinero en efectivo.

2. Rebeca y yo _____ nuestros ahorros de moneda.

3. Felipe y Andrés _____ herramientas (*tools*).

4. Tú _____ cheques de viajero.

5. Yo _____ artículos para el hogar.

6. Ramón _____ una computadora.

7. Yolanda _____ libros.

8. Todos nosotros _____ ofrendas.

Escoger (g→j)

The verb *escoger* (to choose) has a spelling change in the first-person singular form of the present tense but is regular in the other forms of the present tense.

Escoger			
yo	escojo	nosotros(as)	escogemos
tú	escoges	vosotros(as)	escogéis
Ud., él, ella	escoge	Uds., ellos(as)	escogen

Other verbs like *escoger:*

coger	*to grasp, take hold of*
dirigir	*to direct*
proteger	*to protect*
recoger	*to gather, to pick up*

◆ **Actividad 2**

Conteste las preguntas.

1. ¿Quién dirige tu escuela?

2. ¿Diriges tú alguna organización en tu escuela?

3. ¿Recoges los papeles del piso (*floor*)?

4. ¿Escoges tu propia (*your own*) ropa, o la escogen tus padres?

5. ¿Te proteges del sol en el verano?

Expresiones de cortesía

The following phrases are commonly used to ask someone a favor in a public setting.

Por favor	Cierre la puerta, por favor.
¿Me puede hacer el favor de + infinitive?	¿Me puede hacer el favor de completar este formulario?
Haga el favor de + infinitive	Haga el favor de firmar este documento.
Favor de + infinitive	Favor de no fumar.
Tenga la bondad de + infinitive	Tenga la bondad de tomar asiento.

◆ **Actividad 3**

Write a dialogue between a bank officer and a client. Incorporate at least three different expressions of courtesy. You may also include the following vocabulary items:

tomar asiento

abrir una cuenta corriente / de ahorros

completar el formulario

firmar el formulario / el cheque

traer / presentar la libreta

depositar el dinero

cambiar cheques de viajero

Los números del cero al cien

Review the numbers up to one hundred.

0	cero	10	diez	20	veinte	30	treinta
1	uno	11	once	21	veintiuno	31	treinta y uno
2	dos	12	doce	22	veintidós	32	treinta y dos
3	tres	13	trece	23	veintitrés	40	cuarenta
4	cuatro	14	catorce	24	veinticuatro	50	cincuenta
5	cinco	15	quince	25	veinticinco	60	sesenta
6	seis	16	dieciséis	26	veintiséis	70	setenta
7	siete	17	diecisiete	27	veintisiete	80	ochenta
8	ocho	18	dieciocho	28	veintiocho	90	noventa
9	nueve	19	diecinueve	29	veintinueve	100	cien

Note:
- *Dieciséis* (16), *veintidós* (22), *veintitrés* (23), and *veintiséis* (26) contain accent marks.
- The twenties are written as one word, but the thirties through the nineties are written as three words.
- Numbers that end in *uno* (1, 21, 31, etc.) change to *un* before masculine nouns and to *una* before feminine nouns.
    Andrés tiene **veintiún** años.
    Hay **treinta y ún** chicos en la clase.
    Hay **cuarenta y una** alumnas en la escuela.

Los números del 101 al millón

101	ciento uno	199	ciento noventa y nueve	800	ochocientos
102	ciento dos	200	doscientos	900	novecientos
103	ciento tres	201	doscientos uno	1.000	mil
114	ciento catorce	300	trescientos	2.000	dos mil
120	ciento veinte	400	cuatrocientos	3.500	tres mil quinientos
121	ciento veintiuno	500	quinientos	10.000	diez mil
131	ciento treinta y uno	600	seiscientos	100.000	cien mil
145	ciento cuarenta y cinco	700	setecientos	1.000.000	un millón

Note:

- Between 101 and 199, *ciento* is used.

    ciento veinte niñas

    ciento noventa y nueve ovejas

- The two hundreds through the nine hundreds must agree in gender and number with the noun they modify.

    trescientas mujeres

    doscientos hombres

- Most Spanish-speaking countries employ the use of a period (instead of a comma) to indicate the thousands place and the place values beyond. A comma is used instead of a decimal point.

    3.100 = tres mil cien (*three thousand one hundred*)

    3,1 = tres coma uno (*three and one tenth*)

♦ **Actividad 4**

Escriba los números siguientes.

1. 95 años
2. 21 años
3. 126 libros
4. 142 mujeres
5. 200 camisas
6. 588 soldados
7. 731 hombres
8. 2.000 niños
9. 1492
10. 1997
11. 2002
12. 1.893.564

La fecha

When giving a date in Spanish, say the day first, then the month, and finally the year. When referring to the first day of the month, Spanish-speakers usually say *el primero*.

Mañana es **el primero de noviembre.**
Mi cumpleaños es **el diez de marzo.**
Hoy es **el 25 de octubre de 1994.**

• The months of the year are not capitalized unless they are the beginning word of a sentence.
• The year in a date is read as follows:

1821   mil ochocientos veintiuno
1962   mil novecientos sesenta y dos
1995   mil novecientos noventa y cinco

♦ **Actividad 5**

Give the dates that are associated with the following events.

1. la independencia de los Estados Unidos 1776 July 4
2. Cristobal Colón y el descubrimiento de América 1492
3. la fecha de hoy 2002 Jun 8
4. tu fecha de nacimiento 1987 April 8
5. las próximas elecciones presidenciales en los Estados Unidos Nov 8
6. la Navidad Dec 24
7. el día de Acción de Gracias (*Thanksgiving*) Nov 24

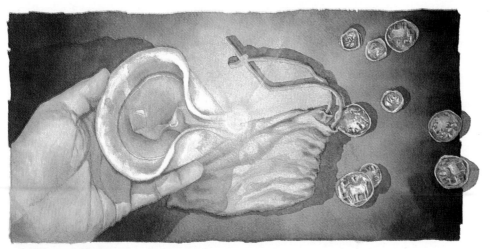

Lectura bíblica ▲▲▲▲▲▲▲▲▲▲▲▲▲▲▲▲▲▲▲▲▲▲▲▲▲▲▲▲▲▲▲▲▲

Lucas 15:8-10

¿O qué mujer que tiene diez *dracmas*, si pierde una dracma, no enciende la **monedas** lámpara, y barre la casa, y busca con diligencia hasta encontrarla? Y cuando la encuentra, reúne a sus amigas y vecinas, diciendo: Gozaos conmigo, porque he encontrado la dracma que había perdido. Así os digo que hay gozo delante de los ángeles de Dios por un pecador que se arrepiente.

El volcán más famoso de Nicaragua, el Momotombo, situado en el Lago Managua, aún humea y tira cenizas sobre la ciudad.

NICARAGUA

- **AREA:** *50,200 sq. mi.*
  (slightly larger than
  New York State)

- **POPULATION:** *4 million*

- **GOVERNMENT:** *Republic*

- **CAPITAL:** *Managua*

In terms of land area, Nicaragua is the largest Central American country. Its name comes from Nicarao, an Indian chief whose tribe lived in the country when the Spaniards began settling there in the 1500s. One of Nicaragua's most notable sites is Lake Nicaragua, the largest lake in Central America (96 miles long) and the world's only freshwater lake with saltwater animal life, such as sharks and swordfish. The lake also contains over 400 small islands.

Nicaragua suffered much turmoil in the 1980s. A revolutionary group called the Sandinistas overthrew the powerful Somoza regime and established a government based on Marxist ideology. A civil war ensued between the Sandinistas and the Contras (counterrevolutionaries), who received financial aid from the United States. Finally, in the 1990 elections, the moderate socialist Violeta Chamorro defeated the incumbent Sandinista president Daniel Ortega, and Nicaragua began a challenging return to stability.

4-3 EL HOTEL

Diálogo ▲▲

La familia Casillas llega al hotel donde va a pasar una semana de vacaciones.
El señor Casillas habla con la recepcionista.

Sr. Casillas:	Perdone, ¿tiene una habitación a nombre de Rafael Casillas?
Recepcionista:	Vamos a ver. Sí, Sr. Casillas, tengo una habitación doble para Ud. y su familia. Bienvenidos al Hotel Intercontinental.
Sr. Casillas:	Gracias.
Recepcionista:	Hágame el favor de llenar este formulario y firmar en este espacio.
Sr. Casillas:	Como no.
Recepcionista:	Su habitación es la 308. Les va a gustar porque tiene vista a la *piscina*. Aquí tiene las llaves. ¿Necesita ayuda con el *equipaje*?
Sr. Casillas:	Sí, por favor.
Recepcionista:	¡Botones! Lleve las maletas a la habitación 308. (Volviéndose al Sr. Casillas) El comedor está en el segundo piso. Está abierto desde las seis de la mañana hasta las diez de la noche.
Sr. Casillas:	¡Qué bien! Hace cinco horas que no comemos.

swimming pool
luggage

La familia Casillas toma el ascensor al tercer piso. Encuentran su habitación
y entran.

Sra. Casillas:	Es una habitación *cómoda* y limpia.
Marcos:	El baño es grande.
Yolanda:	Pero, mamá—hay solamente dos toallas y somos cuatro personas.
Sra. Casillas:	Pues, llama a la recepcionista y pide más toallas.

comfortable

Yolanda llama a la recepcionista por teléfono. Unos minutos más tarde alguien toca a la puerta. Es la camarera.

Camarera: Aquí tienen más toallas y jabón.

Sra. Casillas: Gracias, señorita.

Camarera: De nada. Estoy para servirles. ¿Necesitan algo más?

Sra. Casillas: No, creo que eso es todo. Aquí tiene su propina.

◆ **Conversación**

1. ¿Cuántas personas hay en la familia Casillas?
2. ¿Qué clase de habitación tienen reservada?
3. ¿Qué tiene que hacer el señor Casillas para registrarse?
4. ¿Qué vista tiene la habitación?
5. ¿En qué piso está la habitación de la familia Casillas?
6. Describe la habitación. ¿Cómo es?
7. ¿Qué problema encuentran en su habitación?
8. ¿Dónde está el comedor y cuándo está abierto?
9. ¿Adónde va de vacaciones tu familia?

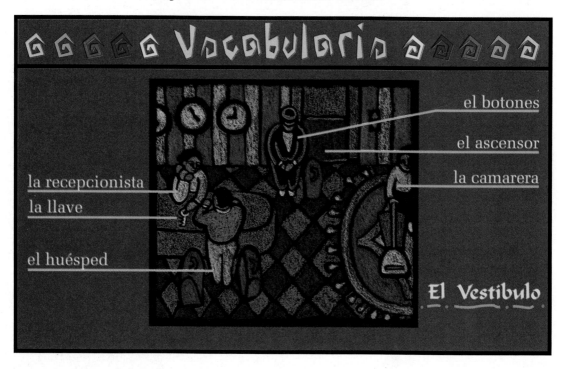

Vocabulario

la recepcionista
la llave
el huésped

el botones
el ascensor
la camarera

El Vestíbulo

La Habitación

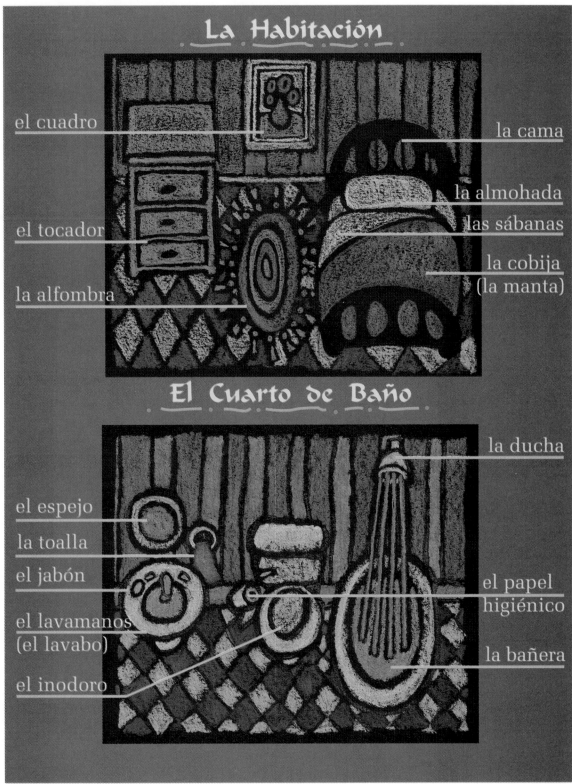

el cuadro

la cama

el tocador

la almohada

las sábanas

la cobija
(la manta)

la alfombra

El Cuarto de Baño

la ducha

el espejo

la toalla

el jabón

el papel
higiénico

el lavamanos
(el lavabo)

el inodoro

la bañera

La Sala

la cortina

el sofá

la lámpara

el sillón

el florero

la alfombra

Gramática ▲▲▲▲▲▲▲▲▲▲▲▲▲▲▲▲▲▲▲▲▲▲▲▲▲▲▲▲▲▲▲▲▲▲▲▲▲▲▲

Las preposiciones

en	*in, on, at*
encima de / arriba de	*on top of*
debajo de	*under*
sobre	*over*
al lado de	*beside, next to*
junto a	*next to*
entre	*between / among*
en medio de	*in the middle of*
delante de / en frente de	*in front of*
detrás de	*behind*
a la derecha de	*to the right of*
a la izquierda de	*to the left of*
adentro (de)	*inside*
afuera (de)	*outside*

◆ **Actividad 1**

Choose the appropriate preposition for each sentence by referring to the illustrations in the vocabulary section.

1. El botones está parado (detrás / en frente) del ascensor.

2. El huésped está (adentro / afuera) del vestíbulo.

3. La camarera puso la almohada (encima / debajo) de la cama.

4. Hay un cuadro (en / arriba de) la pared.

5. El cuadro está (a la izquierda / a la derecha) del tocador.

6. Hay una alfombra (sobre / entre) el tocador y la cama.

7. La ducha está (debajo de / sobre) la bañera.

8. El inodoro está (entre / afuera de) la bañera y el lavamanos.

9. En la sala, el sillón está (al lado del / en medio del) sofá.

10. También hay una alfombra (encima / debajo) de la mesa.

Los pronombres después de las preposiciones

The personal pronouns used after prepositions are the same as the subject pronouns except for *mí* and *ti*. The following chart contains the pronouns used as objects of the preposition.

mí	*nosotros/nosotras*
ti	*vosotros/vosotras*
él, ella, Ud.	*ellos/ellas, Uds.*

Voy a preparar un postre **para ti.**   ¿Es verdad que es **para mí**?
El señor va a tomar fotos **de ellos.**   ¿Puedo estudiar **con Ud.**?

- Notice that **mí** has an accent mark to distinguish it from the possessive adjective **mi.**
- The special endings -*migo* and -*tigo* occur with the preposition con: **conmigo** (*with me*) / **contigo** (*with you*).

◆ **Actividad 2**

Los jóvenes acaban de decidir con quién van a ir al juego de baloncesto. ¿Con quién va a ir cada uno? Use los pronombres en sus respuestas.

Modelo: Pedro / tú
    Pedro va a ir contigo.

1. Mario / yo

2. Rafael y Rosa / Susana

3. Enrique / tú

4. Manuel / María y Rosana

5. Pepe / Luis

6. nosotros / Carolina

◆ **Actividad 3**

Replace the words in italics with an appropriate object pronoun.

Modelo: David y Paco piensan que el árbitro está enojado con *David y Paco.*
David y Paco piensan que el árbitro está enojado con **ellos.**

1. David y Paco buscan al árbitro para hablar con *el árbitro.*

2. El árbitro está hablando con *Rosa.*

3. David y Paco recuerdan que Pepita y Lucía son hijas del árbitro y que Rosa es amiga de *Pepita y Lucía.*

4. Rosa, Pepita y Lucía van con *David y Paco* para hablar con el árbitro.

5. El árbitro les dice a David y Paco: «¡No estoy enojado con *David y Paco*!»

Verbo + preposición + infinitivo

When one verb directly follows another verb, the second verb is usually in the infinitive.

Margarita **quiere escribir** un libro.
Ella **espera comenzar** el libro en el verano.

Some verbs must be followed by a preposition before the infinitive is added. Look at these sentences.

Este verano Marcos **aprende a manejar.**
En junio **comienza a tomar** clases.
Todas las semanas él **trata de ahorrar** dinero.
El examen **consiste en contestar** 25 preguntas.
El **sueña con manejar** un auto deportivo.

The list below contains some of the most common verbs that follow the pattern *verb + preposition + infinitive.*

• The following verbs are usually followed by the preposition *a.*

acostumbrarse a (*to get used to*)	**Me acostumbro a** llegar temprano.
aprender a	Los chicos **aprenden a** hablar español.
ayudar a (*to help*)	Los maestros les **ayudan a** pronunciar las palabras.
comenzar a	¿Cuándo **comienzan a** leer libros en español?
empezar a	**Empiezan a** escribir el primer día.
enseñar a	El señor Ruiz nos **enseña a** hacer piñatas.
invitar a	Marcos me **invita a** comer.
ir a	Mañana **vamos a** cenar en un restaurante.
venir a	Marcos **viene a** buscarme a las siete.

- The following verbs are usually followed by the preposition *de*.

alegrarse de *(to rejoice)*	**Me alegro de** verle a Ud. aquí.
cansarse de *(to tire of)*	Los niños no **se cansan de** jugar.
dejar de *(to cease doing)*	Si **dejo de** comer, me enfermo.
terminar de / acabar de *(to finish)*	A las once **termino de** trabajar.
tratar de *(to try to)*	Hoy **tratamos de** aprender los verbos.

- The following verbs are usually followed by the preposition *en*.

consistir en	La tarea **consiste en** escribir frases.
insistir en	**Insisto en** comprarlo esta noche.
tardar en *(to delay)*	Pablo no **tarda en** llegar.

- The following verb is usually followed by the preposition *con*.

soñar con *(to dream about)*	**Sueño con** viajar a Europa.

◆ **Actividad 4**

Help Alicia narrate her story by supplying the missing prepositions.

Sueño _____ viajar a España algún día. Tengo una amiga que vive ahí. Ella me invita _____ visitarla. Voy _____ tratar _____ ahorrar suficiente dinero para hacer el viaje. Voy _____ trabajar en un restaurante. El trabajo consiste _____ servir las mesas y limpiar. Aunque trabajo, no dejo _____ estudiar. Para mí, es importante ganar suficiente dinero para hacer el viaje. Voy _____ cansarme _____ trabajar tanto, pero no importa. No puedo tardar _____ ir porque mi amiga viene _____ visitarme aquí en dos años.

Hacer + tiempo + que + verbo en el presente

To express the lapse of time from the beginning of an action that began in the past and is still in progress, Spanish speakers use the following construction: *hacer* **+ a period of time +** *que* **+ present tense verb.**

Hace tres años que vivo en San Juan.
Hace dos semanas que Raquel está en México.

Notice the construction for the interrogative form:

¿Cuánto tiempo hace que + present tense verb?

¿Cuánto tiempo hace que estudias español?

♦ **Actividad 5**

Do you know your classmates? Use the clues below to obtain information about a classmate. After interviewing each other, report the most interesting findings to the rest of the class.

¿Cuánto tiempo hace que . . . ?

1. estudiar / español?

2. ser / cristiano(a)

3. asistir / a esta escuela

4. asistir / a la misma iglesia

5. no comer

6. saber / leer

7. vivir / en esta ciudad

♦ **Actividad 6**

Supply a question for each of the following statements.

Modelo: Hace un mes que no tomo café.
¿Cuánto tiempo hace que no tomas café?

1. Hace dos años que no voy al dentista.

2. Hace seis meses que no salimos de esta ciudad.

3. Hace cuatro años que estudio piano.

4. Hace tres años que Carlos escucha buena música.

5. Hace dos días que están enfermos.

La posición de los adjetivos

The meaning of the adjectives *grande, nuevo,* and *pobre* may vary if the adjective precedes the noun it modifies.

Su abuelo viene de una **gran** ciudad.	*His grandfather comes from a great city.*
Ahora vive en una ciudad **grande.**	*Now he lives in a big city.*
Necesito un **nuevo** auto.	*I need a new (different) car.*
Quiero un auto **nuevo.**	*I want a brand new car.*
El **pobre** muchacho nunca llega a tiempo.	*The unfortunate boy never arrives on time.*
Carlos es un muchacho **pobre.**	*Carlos is a poor boy (does not have any money).*

◆ **Actividad 7**

How many sentences can you make in five minutes using the following nouns, verbs, and adjectives? You may make affirmative or negative sentences. Be sure to place the adjectives correctly in order to convey the intended meaning.

Nouns	Verbs	Adjectives	Nouns
el hombre	necesitar	bueno	amigo
la profesora	querer	malo	auto
los jóvenes	tener	grande	idea
nosotros		nuevo	libro
tú		pobre	zapatos

Nota cultural ▲▲▲▲▲▲▲▲▲▲▲▲▲▲▲▲▲▲▲▲▲▲▲▲▲▲▲▲▲▲▲▲▲▲▲▲▲▲▲

Hoteles y hostales

Es costumbre en algunos hoteles *del extranjero* tener que dejar el pasaporte en la oficina del hotel cuando uno se registra. Al pagar la cuenta antes de salir, el *huésped* recibe su pasaporte *de vuelta.* En muchos hoteles el huésped sólo tiene que dejar su número de pasaporte. **abroad** / **guest** / **again**

En España, el viajero más *cuidadoso* de su dinero tiene la opción de *hospedarse* en un **hostal.** Los hostales son casas o edificios antiguos que se han remodelado para *alojar* a varias personas cómodamente. Normalmente, son más económicos que los hoteles, pero a veces no tienen baños privados. Muchos viajeros, sin embargo, prefieren hospedarse en los hostales para conocer la cultura y *disfrutar* de la comida *casera.* **careful** / **to lodge** / **to lodge** / **to enjoy** / **homemade**

Poesía ▲▲

Nicaragua's most well-known poet and writer is Rubén Darío (1867-1916). He is one of the great Spanish-American poets of modern times.

Lo Fatal
(a René Pérez)

Dichoso el árbol que es *apenas* sensitivo,
y más la *piedra* dura, porque ésta ya no siente,
pues no hay *dolor* más grande que el dolor de ser vivo,
ni mayor *pesadumbre* que la vida consciente.
Ser, y no saber nada, y ser sin *rumbo* cierto,
y el *temor* de haber sido y un futuro terror . . .
Y el *espanto* seguro de estar mañana muerto,
y sufrir por la vida y por la sombra y por
lo que no conocemos y apenas *sospechamos,*
y la carne que tienta con sus frescos *racimos,*
y la *tumba* que *aguarda* con sus fúnebres ramos,
¡Y no saber adónde vamos,
ni de dónde venimos . . . !

Glossary (margin):
- fortunate / scarcely
- stone
- pain
- grief; affliction
- direction; course
- fear
- dread
- *sospechar* = to suspect
- bunches
- tomb / *aguardar* = to await

◆ **Cuestionario**

1. Why does the poet seem to admire *el árbol* and *la piedra?*

2. How does Darío view human existence?

3. What does he seem to fear the most?

4. Does it reflect any of your own fears or those of someone you know?

5. How does Darío's poem contrast to a Christian view of life?

6. Many people think that it is impossible to find one's true purpose in life or to know one's own eternal destiny. What does God's Word say about these things?

Jesús le dijo: Yo soy el camino, y la verdad, y la vida; nadie viene al Padre, sino por mí.   **Juan 14:6**

5-1 PROBLEMAS AUTOMOVILÍSTICOS

Diálogo ▲▲▲▲▲▲▲▲▲▲▲▲▲▲▲▲▲▲▲▲▲▲▲▲▲▲▲▲▲▲▲▲▲▲▲▲▲▲

Son las diez de la noche y Carlos está al lado de la carretera. Tiene problemas y decide llamar a casa desde un teléfono público.

Carlos: Hola, papá. Habla Carlos.

Padre: Carlos, ¿qué pasó? Hace media hora que te estamos esperando.

Carlos: Lo siento, papá; es que tuve problemas con el auto.

Padre: ¿Tuviste un accidente?

Carlos: No precisamente, pero—

Padre: ¿Se gastó *la batería*?

Carlos: No, papá, es que—

Padre: Se te acabó la gasolina, ¿verdad?

Carlos: No, papá.

Padre: ¿Qué pasó entonces?

Carlos: Una de las llantas traseras se reventó.

Padre: ¿Y la rueda de repuesto?

Carlos: Está desinflada.

Padre: ¿Desinflada? ¡El mecánico acaba de revisar el automóvil esta semana!

Carlos: Pues no sé que pasó. ¿Qué puedo hacer?

Padre: ¿Hay una gasolinera cerca?

Carlos: No creo. Paré el auto cerca de la salida 24. Estoy llamando desde el Hotel Punta Arenas.

Padre: Voy para allá *en seguida.* Usa las luces de emergencia.   at once

Carlos: ¡Papá! No se te olvide traer una buena rueda de repuesto.

◆ **Conversación**

1. ¿Por qué llama Carlos a casa?
2. ¿De dónde llama?
3. ¿Qué pasó con el auto?
4. ¿Por qué no puede usar la rueda de repuesto?
5. ¿Piensas que el padre de Carlos está enojado con el mecánico?
6. ¿Qué harías tú (*would you do*) en la situación de Carlos?

Vocabulario

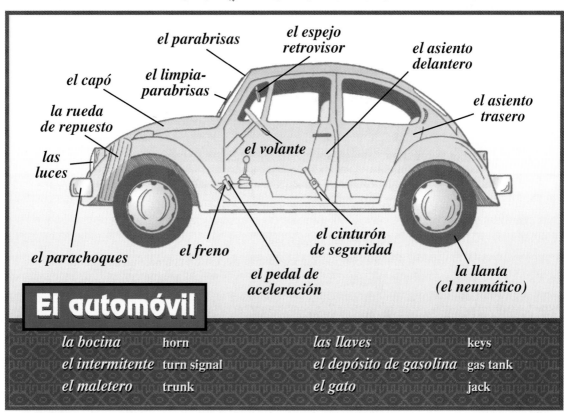

El automóvil

- el parabrisas
- el espejo retrovisor
- el asiento delantero
- el capó
- el limpia-parabrisas
- el asiento trasero
- la rueda de repuesto
- las luces
- el volante
- el parachoques
- el freno
- el cinturón de seguridad
- el pedal de aceleración
- la llanta (el neumático)

la bocina	horn	*las llaves*	keys
el intermitente	turn signal	*el depósito de gasolina*	gas tank
el maletero	trunk	*el gato*	jack

¿Qué pasó?

Fallaron los frenos.

Se recalentó el motor.

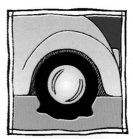

Se reventó la llanta.

Tuvieron un accidente.

Usaron el gato.

Se gastó la batería.

Antes de hacer un viaje, tienes que—

- llenar el depósito de gasolina.

- cambiar el aceite.

- revisar el agua.

- revisar la presión del aire en las llantas.

◆ **Actividad 1**

Choose the letter of the statement that best completes the sentence.

1. Antes de conducir es muy importante _____ .

    a. abrochar el cinturón de seguridad

    b. revisar el maletero

2. Para conducir de noche se necesita encender _____ .

    a. el radiador

    b. las luces

3. Para poner el automóvil en marcha necesitas usar _____ .

    a. los frenos

    b. el pedal de aceleración

4. Para parar el automóvil debes usar _____ .

    a. los frenos

    b. el volante

5. Si las luces no funcionan, debes recargar _____ .

    a. la batería

    b. el depósito de gasolina

6. Cuando está lloviendo, debes usar _____ .

    a. los limpiaparabrisas

    b. el espejo retrovisor

7. Si una de las llantas está desinflada, _____ .

    a. usa la rueda de repuesto

    b. abre el capó

Gramática ▲▲

Acabar de

El mecánico **acaba de** revisar el automóvil.
Rafael y Fernando **acaban de** salir.
Nosotros **acabamos de** cambiar el aceite.

In the examples above, the person or persons in each sentence have just finished doing something. To express recent past actions, the construction **acabar de + infinitivo** is commonly used.

◆ Actividad 2

Tell what the following people have just finished doing.

Modelo: Rosa / lavar el auto
    Rosa acaba de lavar el auto.

1. yo / cambiar el aceite

2. tú / llenar el depósito de agua

3. Carlos / revisar los frenos delanteros

4. Maribel y Noemí / limpiar el interior del auto

5. Maricela y yo / comprar un mapa

El pretérito: los verbos regulares *-ar*

The preterite tense is used to describe actions that took place in the past. Most *-ar* verbs form the preterite like the verb *hablar.*

Hablar			
yo	hablé	*nosotros(as)*	hablamos
tú	hablaste	*vosotros(as)*	hablasteis
Ud., él, ella	habló	*Uds., ellos(as)*	hablaron

The *-ar* verbs that have an *e→ie* or an *o→ue* stem change in the present tense do not have this change in the preterite tense.

Present Tense	**Preterite Tense**
Yo **pienso** cambiar la llanta.	Yo **pensé** cambiar la llanta.
Los frenos **cuestan** doscientos pesos.	Los frenos **costaron** doscientos pesos.
¿No **recuerdas** tu número de licencia?	¿No **recordaste** tu número de licencia?

◆ **Actividad 3**

Cambie cada oración al pretérito.

Modelo: Ricardo y Mario llegan tarde.
   *Ricardo y Mario **llegaron** tarde.*

1. Carlos habla con su padre por teléfono.

2. Yo pienso revisar el agua.

3. Mis hermanos llevan el automóvil al mecánico.

4. Yo oro antes de salir a la carretera.

5. Papá revisa la presión en los neumáticos.

6. Mamá llena el depósito de gasolina.

7. Yo me lavo las manos antes de conducir.

8. Tomás y Felipe compran refrescos en la gasolinera.

9. La señorita Vázquez les enseña los nuevos modelos de automóviles.

10. Las clases de conducir terminan el martes.

El pretérito: los verbos *-car, -gar, -zar*

Verbs that end in *-car, -gar,* and *-zar* have a spelling change in the *yo* form of the preterite in order to preserve the consonant sound before the **e.**

sacar	c → qu	**Saqué** fotos de mi nuevo automóvil.
entregar	g → gu	Le **entregué** el automóvil al mecánico.
empezar	z → c	El lunes **empecé** a trabajar en el taller de autos.

Other verbs of this kind are *buscar, comenzar, jugar, llegar, pagar*, and *practicar*.

◆ **Actividad 4**

The following students are talking about things they are going to do. Tell them that you did each activity yesterday.

Modelo: Roberta: Voy a jugar al tenis hoy.
      Yo jugué al tenis ayer.

1. Marta: Voy a practicar el piano dos horas esta noche.

2. Ana: Voy a sacar fotos de mi familia mañana.

3. Rosa: Voy a pagar la cuenta esta tarde.

4. Élida: Voy a entregar mi tarea al profesor.

5. Carolina: Yo empiezo a trabajar en el banco el lunes.

6. Sonia: Yo juego al baloncesto por la mañana.

7. Belinda: Comienzo mi nuevo libro esta noche.

8. Raquel: Voy a llegar temprano a la escuela mañana.

9. Tomasina: Voy a buscar un taxi.

El pretérito: los verbos *ir* y *ser*

The verbs *ir* and *ser* share the same forms in the preterite. The context determines which verb is being used.

Ir / ser			
yo	fui	*nosotros(as)*	fuimos
tú	fuiste	*vosotros(as)*	fuisteis
Ud., él, ella	fue	*Uds., ellos(as)*	fueron

◆ **Actividad 5**

Supply the correct preterite form of *ir* or *ser.* Indicate which verb is being used.

1. Nosotros _____ a Costa Rica en autobús.

2. Margarita _____ la primera en llegar.

3. Ellos _____ de vacaciones con sus padres.

4. Sus padres _____ amables conmigo.

5. Yo _____ al volcán Irazú.

6. El viaje _____ largo.

7. Maritza _____ a las montañas también.

8. ¿Adónde _____ tú de vacaciones?

9. Carlos y yo _____ a San José también.

10. Las vacas _____ sorprendidas (*surprised*) en el camino por el auto de Maritza.

◆ **Actividad 6**

Supply the correct preterite form of each verb in parentheses.

Mi viaje a Irazú

Una mañana (yo/levantarse) _____ muy temprano y
(yo/prepararse) _____ para hacer un viaje con mi familia al
volcán Irazú. Todos (nosotros/ir) _____ en automóvil.

Cuando (nosotros/comenzar) _____ el viaje aquel día, mis
hermanos y yo (sentarse) _____ en el asiento trasero. Pero más
tarde, mamá y yo (cambiar) _____ , y yo (sentarse) _____
adelante con papá.

Al salir de San José, (nosotros/empezar) _____ a ver las
bellas montañas. (Yo/sacar) _____ muchas fotos de las flores.
Pronto (nosotros/llegar) _____ a un valle y (nosotros/mirar)
_____ los campos sembrados de papas y otros vegetales. También (nosotros/pasar) _____ por pequeños pueblos y la ciudad
de Cartago, la antigua capital de Costa Rica.

Después, (nosotros/comenzar) _____ a subir la montaña.
A la distancia pudimos ver el volcán. ¡Por fin (llegar) _____ !
Otras personas (llegar) _____ para ver el volcán también. Un
turista simpático (sacar) _____ fotos de nuestra familia al lado
del gran cráter. ¡(Ser) _____ una experiencia inolvidable!

Lectura bíblica ▲▲▲▲▲▲▲▲▲▲▲▲▲▲▲▲▲▲▲▲▲▲▲▲▲▲▲▲▲▲▲▲▲▲▲▲▲▲

Isaías 53:3-6

Despreciado y desechado entre los hombres, varón de dolores, experimen-
tado en quebranto; y como que escondimos de él el rostro, fue menospreciado,
y no lo estimamos.

Ciertamente llevó él nuestras enfermedades, y sufrió nuestros dolores; y
nosotros le tuvimos por azotado, por herido de Dios y abatido.

Mas él herido fue por nuestras rebeliones, molido por nuestros pecados; el
castigo de nuestra paz fue sobre él, y por su llaga fuimos nosotros curados.

Todos nosotros nos descarriamos como ovejas, cada cual se apartó por su
camino; mas Jehová cargó en él el pecado de todos nosotros.

COSTA RICA

- **AREA:** 19,600 sq. mi.
  (slightly smaller
  than West Virginia)

- **POPULATION:** 3.3 million

- **GOVERNMENT:** Democratic
  republic

- **CAPITAL:** San José

COSTA RICA

osta Rica is the most stable Central American country. Its government is democratic, and no need exists for a standing army. Costa Ricans pride themselves in their excellent educational system which has produced a 93 percent literacy rate.

Costa Rica's eastern shore consists largely of thick tropical rain forests which abound with wild vegetation, especially orchids. A mountain range runs through the center of the country and includes the Meseta Central (Central Plateau), home to 75 percent of the population and the base of the country's agriculture. The Pacific coastal strip, however, produces much of the banana crop.

Volcanoes constitute a significant part of Costa Rica's landscape. Among the most famous are the Poás, containing the world's largest crater (one mile in diameter), and the Irazú, which erupted in the 1960's.

Because of the peaceful atmosphere, beautiful scenery, excellent climate, friendly people, and low taxes, many U.S. citizens have chosen Costa Rica as their place of retirement.

5-2 EN LA ESTACIÓN DE FERROCARRIL

Diálogo ▲▲▲▲▲▲▲▲▲▲▲▲▲▲▲▲▲▲▲▲▲▲▲▲▲▲▲▲▲▲▲▲▲▲▲▲▲▲

Ana y su madre están en la estación de ferrocarril de Chamartín en Madrid.
Están esperando a Marta, la hija mayor, que viene de Bilbao.

Voz: El tren procedente de Bilbao está entrando por la vía 11.

Ana: Mamá, ¿escuchaste el anuncio? Estamos en el andén
equivocado; ésta es la vía 7.   **wrong**

Madre: Ana, nosotras miramos el horario en la pantalla, ¿recuerdas? Yo ví "Bilbao, vía 7."

Ana: Pues acaban de decir que está en la vía 11. Miremos
otra vez . . .

Voz: Señores viajeros con destino a Bilbao, diríjanse a la vía
número 7.

Madre: *¡Qué despistada estoy!* El tren con destino a Bilbao está   **I'm really out of it!**
en la vía 7, y el tren procedente de Bilbao está en la vía
11.

Ana: Pues, vamos; hace dos minutos que llegó el tren.

Cuando llegan, Marta está esperando.

Marta: ¡Mamá! ¡Ana! Aquí estoy. ¿Por qué llegaron tarde?

Ana: Leímos mal la pantalla y fuimos al andén equivocado.

Marta: Bueno, no importa; me alegro mucho de verlas.

Madre: ¿Cómo lo pasaste en Bilbao, Marta?

Marta: Muy bien. Hizo mucho frío, pero fue muy divertido.
Esquié y jugué en la nieve.

Madre: ¿Cómo están los abuelos? Nos sorprendió cuando la
abuela llamó y dijo que no venías hasta hoy.

Marta: Sí, cancelaron las salidas de los trenes a causa de la nieve, pero todo está bien ahora.

Ana: ¿Tuviste que hacer trasbordo?

Marta: No, pero el tren hizo escala en Burgos y Segovia.

Madre: Bueno, llegaste bien y eso es lo importante.

◆ **Conversación**

1. ¿Por cuál vía entra el tren procedente de Bilbao?
2. ¿De dónde viene Marta? ¿Qué hizo allí?
3. ¿Qué estación del año piensas que es?
4. ¿Por qué cancelaron las salidas de los trenes?
5. ¿Fue un viaje directo?
6. ¿Cuál fue el itinerario de Marta?

Vocabulario ▲▲▲▲▲▲▲▲▲▲▲▲▲▲▲▲▲▲▲▲▲▲▲▲▲▲▲▲▲▲▲▲▲▲▲▲▲▲▲

La estación de ferrocarril

el tren / el ferrocarril
el andén (*station platform*)
la vía (*train tracks*)
la llegada (*arrival*)
la salida (*departure*)
la cabina (*compartment*)
el pasajero (*passenger*)

el pasaje de ida y vuelta
  (*round-trip ticket*)
primera clase (*first-class*)
segunda clase (*economy class*)
el cobrador (*conductor*)

el conductor (*engineer*)
procedente de (*originating from*)
con destino a (*with a destination of*)
hacer escala (*to make a stop*)
hacer trasbordo (*to change trains*)

parar (*to stop*): El tren paró en la estación.

subir (a) (*to board*): Los pasajeros subieron al tren.

bajar (de) (*to get off*): Marta bajó del tren.

◆ **Actividad 1**

Choose the correct vocabulary word(s) for each sentence.

1. Los pasajeros miran (el horario / la cabina) en la pantalla.

2. El billete de (primera clase / segunda clase) cuesta más.

3. Los pasajeros hacen (escala / trasbordo) en Chamartín porque tienen que cambiar de tren.

4. El tren procedente de Bilbao hizo (escala / trasbordo) en Burgos y Segovia.

5. Los pasajeros esperan en (la vía / el andén) número 5.

6. El tren entra por (la vía / el andén) número 4.

7. El (cobrador / conductor) cobra los billetes de los pasajeros.

Gramática ▲▲

El pretérito: los verbos regulares *-er / -ir*

Most of the *-er* and *-ir* verbs form the preterite tense like *comer* and *salir.* Notice that the endings are the same.

	comer	salir
yo	comí	salí
tú	comiste	saliste
Ud., él, ella	comió	salió
nosotros(as)	comimos	salimos
vosotros(as)	comisteis	salisteis
Uds., ellos(as)	comieron	salieron

The *-er* verbs that have an *e→ie* or an *o→ue* stem change in the present tense do not have the change in the preterite tense.

Los pasajeros no **entienden** el anuncio.

¿**Vuelve** este tren a la estación?

Los pasajeros no **entendieron** el anuncio.

¿**Volvió** este tren a la estación?

EN LA ESTACIÓN DE FERROCARRIL

143

◆ **Actividad 2**

Conteste las preguntas con la ayuda de las palabras en paréntesis.

Modelo: ¿Perdiste el pasaje? (No, yo . . .)
No, no perdí el pasaje.

1. ¿Corrió Manuel hasta el andén? (Sí, . . .)

2. ¿Comiste en el comedor del tren? (Sí, . . .)

3. ¿Bebió Ud. un refresco? (No, . . . agua)

4. ¿Perdió Lucía el tren? (No, . . . las maletas)

5. ¿Devolvieron Uds. el pasaje? (Sí, . . .)

6. ¿Conociste al conductor? (No, . . .)

7. ¿Volvió Ud. el mismo día? (Sí, . . .)

◆ **Actividad 3**

Use the cues provided to state what each person did yesterday. Supply any missing articles or prepositions.

Modelo: Juan / salir de / ciudad
Juan salió de la ciudad.

1. Samuel / perder / tren

2. Rosa / escribir / carta / a / su tío

3. Pablo y Marcos / repartir / tratados / estación

4. Ana María y su hermana / aprender / versículos de la Biblia

5. Rafaela / practicar / guitarra / en / tren

6. cuatro jóvenes / viajar / juntos

7. Julián y Teresa / recibir / cartas / Panamá

8. Pepe / preparar / sermón / para los jóvenes

9. mi familia / comer / restaurante español

El pretérito: los verbos *dar* y *ver*

The verbs *dar* and *ver* take the regular -*er* / -*ir* endings in the preterite. The accent marks are not used in the *yo* and *él* forms, however, since these forms are one-syllable words.

	dar	ver
yo	di	vi
tú	diste	viste
Ud., él, ella	dio	vio
nosotros(as)	dimos	vimos
vosotros(as)	disteis	visteis
Uds., ellos(as)	dieron	vieron

◆ **Actividad 4**

Answer the following questions using the cues given in parentheses.

Modelo: ¿A qué hora viste el tren llegar a la estación? (9:15)
Vi el tren llegar a la estación a las nueve y cuarto.

1. ¿Quién te dio el dinero para comprar los billetes? (mi padre)
2. ¿Quién vio el horario del tren? (nosotros)
3. ¿Vieron Uds. la cabina de primera clase? (sí)
4. ¿Quién le dio los billetes al cobrador? (mi amigo)
5. ¿Cuándo vio tu amigo la estación correcta? (demasiado tarde)
6. ¿Dieron Uds. una vuelta por esta ciudad? (sí)
7. ¿Quién te dio la información necesaria? (los otros pasajeros)
8. ¿Vieron Uds. la importancia de poner atención a los detalles? (¡sí!)

El pretérito: los verbos *caer, creer, leer, oír*

The **i** in the stem of the following verbs changes to **y** in both the third-person singular and plural forms. Note also that the **í** is accented in all the other forms.

	caer	creer	leer	oír
yo	caí	creí	leí	oí
tú	caíste	creíste	leíste	oíste
Ud., él, ella	cayó	creyó	leyó	oyó
nosotros(as)	caímos	creímos	leímos	oímos
vosotros(as)	caísteis	creísteis	leísteis	oísteis
Uds., ellos(as)	cayeron	creyeron	leyeron	oyeron

PANAMÁ

- **AREA:** *29,200 sq. mi.*
  (slightly larger
  than West Virginia)

- **POPULATION:** *2.6 million*

- **GOVERNMENT:** *Constitutional
  democracy*

- **CAPITAL:** *Panamá*

Panamá is an S-shaped neck of land that connects Central America to the South American continent. In 1513 when Balboa discovered that this narrow strip of land was all that separated the Atlantic and Pacific Oceans, Panamá took on new significance for Spain. The Spaniards began transporting gold and silver from South America up the Pacific coast, across the isthmus, and on to Spain. This route became known as *el camino real*.

Centuries later, in 1903, the United States decided to resume the work of a French company and build a canal through the isthmus. President Teddy Roosevelt sought to negotiate a treaty with Colombia, which had jurisdiction over the area at that time. When Colombia refused, the Panamanians revolted and declared their independence. They then signed a treaty with the United States for the construction of the canal. The project was completed in 1904.

Today some 15,000 vessels traverse the canal annually. The Panama Canal Commission of the U.S. government currently operates the canal, but Panamá will exercise full control of it by the turn of the century.

5-3 Un Viaje En Avión

Diálogo ▲▲

Rosa y Carmen son dos muchachas que viven en Miami. Ellas van a pasar unas semanas de vacaciones en Panamá con la tía de Rosa. El avión va a *aterrizar* to land en unos minutos.

Asistente:	Señores pasajeros, nos estamos aproximando al aeropuerto. Vamos a aterrizar en unos minutos. Rogamos que ajusten sus cinturones de seguridad. Gracias.
Rosa:	El avión despegó a las cuatro y son las ocho. Llegamos pronto.
Carmen:	Sí, el piloto dijo que el viento nos ayudó y por eso llegamos temprano.
Rosa:	Tenemos que pasar por inmigración y aduana.
Carmen:	Y después, ¡la playa!

En el aeropuerto, las chicas reclaman su equipaje y van hacia inmigración.

Agente:	Buenos días, ¿puedo ver sus papeles?
Rosa:	Sí, aquí tiene mi pasaporte y mi visa de turista.
Agente:	¿Dónde nació usted, señorita?
Rosa:	En Bogotá, Colombia.
Agente:	Este avión vino de los Estados Unidos. ¿Vive usted allí?
Rosa:	Sí, señor, soy residente de los Estados Unidos. Vengo a Panamá como turista.
Agente:	Muy bien, ya puede ir a la aduana.
Carmen:	Buenos días. Aquí tiene mis papeles. Yo viajo con ella.

citizen

Agente: ¿Es Ud. *ciudadana* americana?

Carmen: Sí, señor.

Agente: Bueno, pase a la aduana también.

En la aduana . . .

Aduanero: Buenos días, ¿tiene algo que declarar?

Rosa: No.

Aduanero: Gracias, puede seguir.

Carmen: Buenos días. Aquí tiene mi tarjeta de aduana.

Aduanero: ¿Tiene algo que declarar?

Carmen: Traigo esta cámara de video personal.

Aduanero: ¿Es para uso propio?

Carmen: Sí.

Have a good stay

Aduanero: Adelante. *Que tenga una buena estancia* en Panamá.

◆ **Conversación**

1. ¿Adónde van Rosa y Carmen?
2. ¿Cuál es el propósito del viaje?
3. ¿De dónde son ellas?
4. Normalmente, ¿qué papeles se necesitan para viajar a otro país?
5. ¿Adónde te gustaría ir para practicar el español?
6. Cuenta (*tell*) a la clase de un viaje que hiciste.

Vocabulario

Un viaje en avión

la aduana	customs	*carro de equipaje*	luggage cart
el equipaje	luggage	*reclamación de equipaje*	baggage claim
la maleta	suitcase	*facturar / registrar*	register (luggage)
el pasaporte	passport	*el inspector (de aduana)*	customs official

Capítulo 5-3

el aterrizaje	landing	*el asistente de vuelo*	flight attendant
el despegue	take off	*la azafata (aeromoza)*	stewardess
el destino	destination	*la demora / el retraso*	delay
la inmigración	immigration	*embarcar / desembarcar*	to board / exit the plane
la pista	landing strip	*la puerta de embarque*	boarding gate
revisar	to inspect	*la puerta de salida*	gate of departure
la salida	exit	*la tarjeta de embarque*	boarding pass
la sala de espera	waiting room	*viajar al extranjero*	to travel abroad
la terminal	terminal	*¿Tiene algo que declarar?*	Do you have anything to declare?
la visa (el visado)	visa		

◆ **Actividad 1**

Choose the vocabulary expressions that best fit the story.

Carmen acaba de regresar a Panamá después de pasar un mes en Nueva York en la casa de unos amigos. Le está contando a su hermana Diana cómo le fue el viaje en avión.

Diana: ¿Te gustó el viaje (en avión / en tren)?

Carmen: Sí, me gustó mucho. Al llegar a Nueva York (el aterrizaje / el despegue) estuvo un poco brusco, pero no tuve miedo.

Diana: ¿Qué hiciste en el aeropuerto?

Carmen: En el avión conocí a (una azafata / una inspectora) de la línea aérea que fue muy amable. Ella me ayudó en el aeropuerto. Primero tuvimos que presentar el pasaporte en (la aduana / la sala de espera). Después fuimos a recoger (el equipaje / el visado) a la reclamación de equipaje. Entonces un inspector de aduana revisó (mis maletas / el destino).

Diana: ¿No tuviste que (declarar / revisar) nada?

Carmen: No, no fue necesario. Después, (un mozo / un asistente de vuelo) llevó las maletas a la salida de (la terminal / la pista). En eso, vi a la Sra. Mendoza y viajamos (en metro / en avión) a su casa.

Gramática ▲▲▲

El pretérito: más verbos irregulares

The irregular verbs presented in this section use the following preterite endings.

-e	-imos
-iste	-isteis
-o	-ieron

These verbs have irregular stems. Notice the two groups of irregular stems below.

"u" group

andar	anduv-	Ellos **anduvieron** por toda la terminal.
estar	estuv-	**Estuve** en Aguascalientes dos semanas.
poder	pud-	No **pudimos** comprar billetes.
poner	pus-	El **puso** el equipaje en el coche.
saber	sup-	No **supimos** a donde fue.
tener	tuv-	¿**Tuviste** suficiente dinero para viajar?

"i" group

hacer	hic-	Anoche **hice** planes para el viaje.
querer	quis-	Mi hermano no **quiso** venir.
venir	vin-	No **vinimos** a la puerta de embarque a tiempo.

In order to preserve the sound of the stem, the *él* form of *hacer* has a spelling change from **c** to **z**: *El avión hizo escala en Guadalajara.*

The irregular verbs in the preterite also have a difference in pronunciation. The *yo* and *él* forms do not have an accent mark in the ending; thus the last syllable is not stressed. Notice the difference between the regular verb *comer* and the irregular verb *hacer.*

comer	**hacer**
comí	hice
comió	hizo

◆ **Actividad 2**

Use the following information to ask questions in the preterite to a classmate.

1. estar enfermo(a) el mes pasado

2. andar a la escuela algún día

3. hacer un viaje la Navidad pasada

4. poder viajar solo(a) a los 13 años

5. poner el nombre en el libro de español

6. venir a la última excursión

7. querer viajar al extranjero el verano pasado

8. tener un examen la semana pasada

◆ **Actividad 3**

David just arrived home from a trip to Barcelona, Spain. He is telling his brother about his experiences in the New York airport. Supply the correct preterite form of each verb in parentheses.

1. El avión (llegar) _____ tarde a Nueva York.

2. Cuando (yo / bajar) _____ del avión, (ir) _____ a la inmigración.

3. El inspector (ver) _____ mi pasaporte, (poner) _____ un sello y (yo / salir) _____ .

4. Después (yo / ir) _____ a buscar mis maletas.

5. Al principio no (poder) _____ encontrarlas.

6. Por fin el mozo (ver) _____ una y después yo (ver) _____ la otra.

7. El mozo las (recoger) _____ y las (llevar) _____ a la aduana.

8. El inspector de aduana (revisar) _____ las maletas.

9. Nosotros (tener) _____ que caminar mucho para llegar al automóvil.

10. Papá (poner) _____ las maletas en el automóvil y (nosotros / ir) _____ a casa.

El pretérito: los verbos como *decir*

Decir			
yo	dije	nosotros(as)	dijimos
tú	dijiste	vosotros(as)	dijisteis
Ud., él, ella	dijo	Uds., ellos(as)	dijeron

Verbs whose preterite stem ends in **j** conjugate like *decir.*

Infinitive	**Pret. Stem**	
conducir	conduj-	¿**Condujiste** el auto de tu padre al aeropuerto?
decir	dij-	No me **dijeron** la hora de llegada.
traducir	traduj-	Me **tradujo** la información del billete.
traer	traj-	¿Qué nos **trajeron** del Perú?
reducir	reduj-	Las aerolíneas **redujeron** los precios de vuelo.
bendecir	bendij-	Dios **bendijo** al pueblo de Israel.

◆ **Actividad 4**

Use the elements given to form complete sentences in the preterite.

Modelo: Elena / decir que / hay que facturar (*check*) el equipaje.
Elena dijo que hay que facturar el equipaje.

1. los directores de Lacsa / reducir / los precios

2. Mi madre / bendecirme / antes de salir de viaje

3. las primas / decir que / quieren ir a Sudamérica

4. tú / traer / los billetes de avión al aeropuerto

5. yo / traducir / el formulario de aduana

6. Mi padre / conducir / al aeropuerto

7. la azafata / traducir / las instrucciones al español

◆ **Actividad 5**

The following people have missed their flights. They want to get tickets for the next one. Give an excuse for each passenger.

Modelo: Tomás: no poder encontrar su billete
Señor, Tomás no pudo encontrar su billete.

1. Ricardo: no saber el número del vuelo

2. Marisa: no poder encontrar la puerta de salida

3. Miguel y Edgar: conocer a unas muchachas simpáticas

4. Santiago y Ana: no hacer planes a tiempo

5. Rebeca y Diana: tener problemas con sus maletas

El pretérito: los cambios de sentido

A few verbs have special meanings when they are used in the preterite. Look at the following sentences.

No **conozco** a muchas personas famosas. *(acquainted with)*
Anoche **conocí** a Octavio Paz, un escritor famoso. *(met for the first time)*

Rosa María **quiere** viajar a Europa en el verano. *(wants to)*
Ella **quiso** viajar el año pasado. *(wanted to but couldn't)*

Carmen **no quiere** acompañarme a Europa. *(doesn't want to)*
Le invité a venir conmigo, pero **no quiso.** *(refused)*

Sabemos el horario de los aviones a Miami. *(know)*
Ayer **supe** que Rafael llega a las diez esta mañana. *(found out)*

◆ **Actividad 6**

Supply the correct preterite form of the appropriate verb: *conocer, querer, no querer, saber.*

1. Nosotros _____ viajar el año pasado pero no pudimos.

2. Martín _____ a María ayer.

3. Los estudiantes _____ del examen ayer.

4. El pasajero _____ cambiar de avión.

5. Ellas no _____ el número de vuelo a tiempo.

Lectura bíblica ▲▲▲▲▲▲▲▲▲▲▲▲▲▲▲▲▲▲▲▲▲▲▲▲▲▲▲▲▲▲▲▲▲

El credo cristiano

Creo que la Biblia es la Palabra de Dios.

Creo que "en el principio" Dios creó (hizo) el mundo.

Creo que Dios creó al hombre.

Creo que Adán, el primer hombre, pecó y así el pecado pasó a todos los hombres. Por eso todos merecemos la condenación eterna.

Creo que Dios ama al hombre y por eso envió a su hijo, el Señor Jesucristo, al mundo para morir por nosotros y para darnos vida eterna.

Creo que Jesús nació de una virgen.

Creo que Jesús vivió una vida perfecta.

Creo que Jesús murió en la cruz, y al tercer día, resucitó de la tumba.

Creo que Jesús ascendió al cielo y ahora está en el cielo intercediendo por nosotros.

Creo que Jesús me salvó y me perdonó cuando confesé mis pecados y creí en Él y le recibí como mi Salvador.

Creo que ahora tengo vida eterna y que algún día iré al cielo.

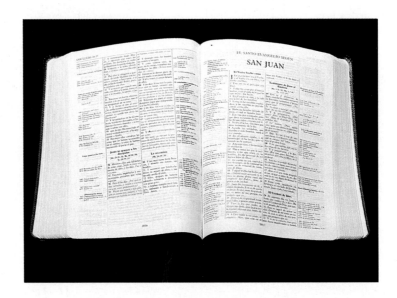

Vestíos de toda la armadura de
Dios, para que podáis estar firmes
contra las asechanzas del diablo.
Efesios 6:11

CAPÍTULO SEIS

6-1 INDEPENDENCIA PARA LATINOAMÉRICA

Lectura ▲▲

A principios del siglo XIX (diecinueve), España todavía dominaba gran parte del Nuevo Mundo al sur de los Estados Unidos. Una de sus colonias más prósperas era el territorio de la Nueva Granada, que *incluía* lo que hoy son los países de Colombia, Venezuela y Ecuador.

Los Estados Unidos ganó su independencia de Inglaterra *a fines del* siglo XVIII (dieciocho). El *éxito* de la revolución norteamericana *animó* a otros países que también querían liberarse de monarquías absolutistas.

Un evento que *impulsó* el movimiento de independencia en las colonias de Latinoamérica fue la invasión francesa de España en 1808, dirigida por Napoleón. Esta ocupación militar *provocó* en *España misma* una rebelión popular *contra* los franceses. Los latinoamericanos *compartían* ese sentimiento, y sus gobiernos coloniales *se negaron a someterse* al gobierno napoleónico. *Una tras otra,* las colonias declararon su independencia.

Cuando el *rey* español Fernando VII (séptimo) regresó a su *trono* en 1814, el movimiento de independencia dominaba las antiguas colonias. La *próxima década* trajo una serie de guerras revolucionarias en las cuales Fernando no fue lo suficientemente agresivo. Para el año 1825, España se encontraba *casi* sin *imperio.*

Glosario (margen):
- included
- toward the end of
- success / encouraged
- prompted
- incited / Spain itself
- against / shared
- refused to submit
- One after another
- king / throne
- next
- decade
- almost
- empire

◆ Conversación

1. ¿Qué países actuales formaban parte del territorio de la Nueva Granada?

2. ¿Piensas que la revolución norteamericana fue de ejemplo a las colonias de Latinoamérica?

3. ¿Qué evento impulsó el movimiento de independencia en las colonias latinoamericanas?

Simón Bolívar, el Gran Libertador

Simón Bolívar fue una de las figuras más importantes en la *lucha* por la **struggle**
independencia. Nació en Caracas a una familia aristócrata el 24 de julio de

1783. Como joven recibió su educación en Europa,
donde aceptó las filosofías políticas de los gran-
des *intelectuales* del día. *Tras la muerte* de su **intellectuals / after the**
esposa en 1807, Bolívar *se unió a* la causa **death / joined**
revolucionaria en Venezuela, un año antes
de la invasión napoleónica de España.

Por muchos años los ejércitos de
Bolívar y del gran revolucionario ar-
gentino José de San Martín lucharon por
la independencia de Sudamérica. Las fuerzas españolas sufrieron su derrota final en
el año 1824. *Sin embargo,* las varias guerras **However**
civiles que *estallaron* a consecuencia de la **broke out**
independización *frustraron* el sueño más grande **frustrated**
de Bolívar—el de ver unificadas *bajo* un gobierno **under**
central a todas las repúblicas de la América del Sur. El
nombre del país de Bolivia *conmemora* la labor del gran libertador. **commemorates**

◆ **Conversación**

1. ¿Dónde y en qué año nació Bolívar?

2. ¿Dónde recibió Bolívar su educación?

3. ¿Qué gran revolucionario le ayudó a Bolívar en su lucha por la inde-pendencia de Sudamérica?

4. ¿Cuál era el sueño más grande de Bolívar para la América del Sur?

5. ¿Se pudo cumplir el sueño de Bolívar?

6. ¿Crees que Bolívar merece (*de-serves*) ser llamado el Gran Liber-tador?

Vocabulario

Las armas de guerra

el cañón
la espada (sword)
la granada (grenade)
la metralleta (machine gun)
el revólver
el rifle

Las acciones de guerra

avanzar (to advance)
la batalla
combatir (to combat)
la conquista (conquest)
la derrota

derrotar (to defeat)
pelear (to fight)
rescatar (to rescue)
la victoria
la paz

El personal militar

el soldado (soldier)
la guardia (guard)
el ejército (army)
los guerrilleros

el general
el coronel
el capitán
el sargento

Gramática ▲▲▲

Hacer + que con el pretérito

— ¿Cuánto tiempo **hace que saliste** de Venezuela?

— **Hace** cuatro años **que salí.**

— ¿Cuánto tiempo **hace que** los venezolanos **ganaron** su independencia?

— **Hace** más de ciento setenta años **que ganaron** su independencia.

— ¿Cuántos minutos **hace que** las chicas **se fueron**?

— **Se fueron hace** diez minutos.

— Llegué a casa **hace** una hora.

— Llamé a Rubén **hace** cinco minutos.

Spanish speakers use *hace (que)* with a preterite verb to show how much time has elapsed since an event took place and the present time. This construction has the corresponding English meaning of *ago*.

Note that if the verb comes before *hace*, the *que* is dropped.

◆ Actividad 1

Conteste las preguntas según el tiempo indicado en paréntesis. Siga el modelo.

Modelo: ¿Cuánto tiempo hace que llegaste? (diez minutos)
   Hace diez minutos que llegué.

1. ¿Cuánto tiempo hace que Juan salió? (una hora)

2. ¿Cuánto tiempo hace que estudiaste español? (dos años)

3. ¿Cuántos años hace que Colón descubrió América? (más de 500 años)

4. ¿Cuántos meses hace que entramos en el colegio? (tres meses)

5. ¿Cuánto tiempo hace que recibiste a Cristo como tu Salvador? (un año)

6. ¿Cuánto tiempo hace que José y María fueron a Belén? (casi dos mil años)

7. ¿Cuántos días hace que tuvimos un examen? (dos días)

8. ¿Cuánto tiempo hace que fuiste a México? (seis meses)

El imperfecto: los verbos regulares *-ar*

> A principios del siglo diecinueve, España todavía **dominaba** gran parte
> del Nuevo Mundo al sur de los Estados Unidos.
> (*At the beginning of the nineteenth century, Spain still dominated a
> great portion of the New World to the south of the United States.*)

The verb tense used in Spanish to describe situations in the past is the imperfect
tense (*el imperfecto*). The imperfect is formed by adding a set of endings to
the stem. The endings for the *-ar* verbs are highlighted in the table below.

Hablar			
yo	hablaba	nosotros(as)	hablábamos
tú	hablabas	vosotros(as)	hablabais
Ud., él, ella	hablaba	Uds., ellos(as)	hablaban

All *-ar* verbs are regular in the imperfect tense, even those that are irregular in
the present or preterite. Also, note that the first- and third-person singular forms
are the same.

> Yo no **hablaba** en la clase, pero Juan **hablaba** mucho.

◆ **Actividad 2**

Everyone in the Hernández household always has to work. Yesterday
David went to their home. Describe what each family member was doing
when he arrived.

Modelo: La señora Hernández (cocinar) _____ .
    La señora Hernández cocinaba.

1. El señor Hernández (trabajar) _____ en el patio.
2. Eliseo y Maritza (ayudar) _____ a su papá.
3. Los tíos (limpiar) _____ la sala.
4. Roberto (cortar) _____ el césped (*to mow the lawn*).
5. Tú (lavar) _____ el carro.
6. Sara (cuidar) _____ a su hermanita.
7. Nosotros (lavar) _____ la ropa.
8. Todos (limpiar) _____ la casa.

◆ **Actividad 3**

Write about Simón Bolívar according to the information given. Use the imperfect tense.

Modelo: querer un gobierno central
Bolívar quería un gobierno central.

1. ayudar a Venezuela

2. luchar para Colombia

3. no estar contento con España

4. desear sacar a América del poder de España

5. ayudar a San Martín en el Perú

6. tener que resolver los problemas entre Colombia y el Perú

7. desear la felicidad para su patria

◆ **Actividad 4**

Veteran soldiers are reminiscing about "the good ol' days." Supply the questions asked them by the recruits according to the answers given.

Modelo: ¿ _____ ? —¡Sí, señor! Siempre lavábamos nuestros uniformes.
¿Siempre lavaban Uds. sus uniformes?

1. ¿ _____ ? —¡Claro que sí! Yo siempre jugaba al fútbol en el tiempo libre.

2. ¿ _____ ? —Sí, a veces paseábamos por las plazas con nuestros amigos.

3. ¿ _____ ? —¡Sí! El capitán cantaba durante las batallas. ¡Qué inspiración!

4. ¿ _____ ? —¡Sí, señor! Limpiábamos los cuartos todos los días.

5. ¿ _____ ? —Sí, de vez en cuando mi unidad de combate nadaba en el océano.

6. ¿ _____ ? —¡Oh sí! Viajábamos por barco a varias islas.

7. ¿ _____ ? —Sí, hombre, luchabamos contra el enemigo.

El imperfecto: los verbos regulares *-er / -ir*

In the imperfect, the *-er* and the *-ir* verbs have the same endings.

	comer	vivir
yo	comía	vivía
tú	comías	vivías
Ud., él, ella	comía	vivía
nosotros(as)	comíamos	vivíamos
vosotros(as)	comíais	vivíais
Uds., ellos(as)	comían	vivían

Notice that all the forms are accented and that the *yo* and *él* forms are the same.

Note: The imperfect of the verb form **hay** is **había**.

El año pasado **había** tres estudiantes de Venezuela en mi clase; ahora **hay** seis.

◆ **Actividad 5**

You do not do the same things now that you did when you were ten years old. Tell what each young person used to do and what he does now.

Modelo: Roberto: leer las historietas (*comics*) / biografías
Antes Roberto leía las historietas, pero ahora lee biografías.

1. Fernando: escribir cartas a Papá Noel / a su novia

2. Tomás: querer ser deportista / doctor

3. Felipe: beber leche / café

4. Raquel y Rosalina: dormir a las ocho / a las diez y media

5. nosotros: asistir a la escuela primaria / la escuela superior

6. Pedro: repartir periódicos / vender hamburguesas

7. yo: aprender inglés / español

8. tú: decir mentiras / la verdad

9. Samuel: comer poco / mucho

10. Manuel: no escribir mucho / buenas redacciones (*compositions*)

◆ **Actividad 6**

Write about the independence period and Simón Bolívar by completing the information provided below. Use the reading for this lesson as a guide. The verbs should be in the imperfect tense.

1. España: *dominar* mucho de Latinoamérica

2. La Nueva Granada: *incluir* los países modernos de . . .

3. Como los Estados Unidos, otros países: *querer* liberarse de . . .

4. Todos los hispanoamericanos: *oponerse* a la ocupación . . .

5. Algunos hispanoamericanos: *querer* vivir independientes de . . .

6. Simón Bolívar: *desear* la independencia para Latinoamérica

7. Bolívar: *querer* para toda Latinoamérica un gobierno . . .

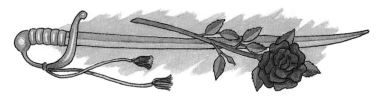

Poesía ▲▲

The following poem about Simón Bolívar is by Luis Lloréns Torres (puertorriqueño, 1878-1944).

Bolívar

Político, militar, héroe, orador y poeta.
Y un todo grande. Como las tierras libertadas por él.
Por él, que no nació hijo de patria alguna,
sino que muchas patrias nacieron de él.

Tenía la *valentía* del que lleva una espada.　　　　　　　bravery
Tenía la cortesía del que lleva una flor.
Y entrando en los salones *arrojaba* la espada;　　　　　would throw (down)
y entrando en los combates arrojaba la flor.

Los *picos* del Ande no eran más, a sus ojos,　　　　　　peaks
que *signos admirativos de sus arrojos.*　　　　　　　　exclamation points
Fue un soldado poeta. Un poeta soldado.　　　　　　　for his boldness
Y cada pueblo libertado
era una *hazaña* del poeta　　　　　　　　　　　　　deed; feat
y era un poema del soldado.
Y fue crucificado . . .

- **AREA:** 44,200 sq. mi.
  (approximately the size
  of Pennsylvania)

- **POPULATION:** 11 million

- **GOVERNMENT:** Communist state

- **CAPITAL:** La Habana

uba is an island 750 miles long ranging in width from 25 to 125 miles. It is the largest of the Greater Antilles, a group of islands in the Caribbean Sea, just south of Florida. The semitropical climate and fertile soil favor the growing of sugar cane, Cuba's chief product.

Cuba served as a key commercial port in the Spanish empire and was the last major colony to gain its independence. Patriot and author José Martí led the uprising that finally ended in the Spanish-American War and the signing of the Treaty of Paris on December 10, 1898. Under this treaty Spain relinquished control of Cuba to the United States, and the island obtained complete independence in 1903. Cuba granted the United States a permanent lease on Guantánamo Bay, where American forces built a large naval base which still remains in operation.

In 1959, the dictator Fulgencio Batista was forced to flee Cuba as Fidel Castro assumed power and established a communist government. As a result, some 700,000 Cubans fled the island. In 1962 the United States imposed a trade embargo, and Cuba became dependent upon the Soviet Union for trade and economic aid. With the collapse of the Soviet Union in 1991, Cuba found herself in serious economic straits.

6-2 José Martí, Patriota Cubano

Lectura ▲▲▲

Cuando nació José Martí en 1853, Cuba había estado bajo el dominio de España por más de trescientos años. En 1868 los cubanos comenzaron una lucha intensa para obtener la independencia.

Aunque José Martí tenía sólo quince años al comienzo de la guerra, un día le comentó a su madre que después de las muchas generaciones de esclavos en su país, *tendría que haber* una generación de mártires. No sabía que él mismo *moriría* como un mártir más tarde.

there would have to be

would die

Martí era escritor. Escribió prosa y *poesía* para *promover* la causa de la independencia de su patria. A los dieciocho años comenzó a sufrir por sus *obras,* siendo *exiliado* a España en dos ocasiones.

poetry / to promote

works / exiled

Después de diez años de guerra y destrucción, España *convino mejorar* las condiciones en Cuba, pero no *otorgó* la autonomía *tan deseada.* En 1879 Martí fue a vivir a Nueva York donde organizó un movimiento revolucionario. Su deseo era ver a Cuba libre del dominio español.

agreed to improve

granted / much desired

Martí y dos amigos militares regresaron a Cuba en 1895, determinados a ganar la independencia. Martí no era militar, pero decidió acompañar a los soldados a las batallas. Seis semanas más tarde, murió de un *balazo.*

gunshot

Aunque Martí no vivió para ver la liberación de su patria, sus obras literarias influenciaron a los cubanos a continuar la lucha por la independencia. Por fin *obtuvieron* la victoria *como resultado* de la guerra hispano-americana en 1898.

obtained / as a result

◆ **Conversación**

1. ¿En qué año comenzó la guerra de la independencia en Cuba?
2. ¿Cuántos años tenía José Martí cuando comenzó la guerra de la independencia?
3. ¿Cuál era la profesión de Martí?
4. ¿Por qué fue exiliado?
5. ¿Qué hizo Martí en Nueva York?
6. ¿Cuál era el sueño de Martí?
7. ¿Con qué propósito regresó Martí a Cuba?
8. ¿Con quiénes regresó?
9. ¿Cómo murió Martí?
10. ¿Vio Martí a su patria libre de España antes de morir?

Vocabulario ▲▲▲▲▲▲▲▲▲▲▲▲▲▲▲▲▲▲▲▲▲▲▲▲▲▲▲▲▲▲▲▲▲▲▲▲▲▲▲

Una colonia española

la cárcel (*jail*)

la catedral (*cathedral*)

el cementerio (*cemetery*)

la fortaleza (*fort*)

la plaza

la bandera (*flag*)

el mar (*sea*)

la playa (*beach*)

el colono (*colonist*)

el mártir (*martyr*)

el sacerdote (*priest*)

el soldado

Causas y motivos

la esclavitud (*slavery*)

los impuestos (*taxes*)

la independencia

la libertad (*freedom*)

el patriotismo

la revolución

Gramática ▲▲▲

El imperfecto de *ser, ir* y *ver*

There are only three irregular verbs in the imperfect tense: *ser, ir,* and *ver.*

	ser	ir	ver
yo	era	iba	veía
tú	eras	ibas	veías
Ud., él, ella	era	iba	veía
nosotros(as)	éramos	íbamos	veíamos
vosotros(as)	erais	ibais	veíais
Uds., ellos(as)	eran	iban	veían

Only the *nosotros* form of *ser* and *ir* has an accent mark. All the forms of *ver* have an accent mark.

◆ **Actividad 1**

Use the information given to form questions about life in the Americas before the various countries received their independence.

Modelo: tener su propio rey
> *¿Tenían su propio rey? —No, no tenían su propio rey.*

1. tener cada país una bandera propia
2. pagar impuestos a España
3. ser colonias españolas
4. ver muchos problemas con la forma de gobierno
5. los jóvenes ir a España para estudiar

◆ **Actividad 2**

Choose one of the adjectives given to describe how the following people used to be when they were kids.

Modelo: tu padre / alto, bajo
> *Mi padre era alto cuando era niño.*

1. tú / tímido, hablador
2. Abraham Lincoln / pobre, rico
3. yo / estudioso, vago
4. tus hermanos / guapos, feos
5. tu hermana / bonita, fea

Usos del imperfecto: acciones continuas

The imperfect tense is used to describe repeated or habitual actions in the past.

Todos los veranos **íbamos** a la playa por una semana.
Every summer we went (would go) to the beach for a week.

Carlitos **caminaba** a la escuela todos los días.
Carlitos walked (would walk) to school every day.

Mi abuelo siempre **hablaba** de España.
My grandfather always used to talk about Spain.

In these sentences the imperfect tense conveys the idea of the English expression *used to*.

Ana siempre **hacía** sus tareas a tiempo.

A veces **íbamos** a la playa para las vacaciones.

Su tía **viajaba** a Costa Rica todos los años.

The following adverbs convey the idea of continual or habitual action: *siempre, a veces, a menudo* (often), *todos los días (años)*.

◆ **Actividad 3**

You and your classmates are recalling your summers at youth camp and all the things you would do each summer. Form sentences with the elements provided to tell what people used to do at camp.

Modelo: Nosotros: lavar nuestros trajes de baño
Siempre lavábamos nuestros trajes de baño.

1. yo: jugar al fútbol por las tardes

2. David y Miguel: pasear por el campo en el tiempo libre

3. nosotros: cantar junto a la fogata (*campfire*) todas las noches

4. las chicas: nadar (*to swim*) en el río todos los días

5. los chicos: viajar en autobús a la playa cada tarde

6. todos: limpiar nuestras cabañas cada mañana

◆ **Actividad 4**

Ana attended her first Bible camp. She kept a diary of the things she used to do every day. Pretend you are Ana and tell what you used to do.

Modelo: 7:00 levantarse

Todas las mañanas me levantaba a las siete.

1. 7:15 cepillarse los dientes
2. 7:20 vestirse
3. 7:50 tender la cama
4. 8:00 desayunar
5. 8:30 tener devociones
6. 8:45 limpiar el dormitorio
7. 9:00 estudiar la Biblia
8. 10:00 nadar en la piscina
9. 11:00 jugar al baloncesto
10. 12:00 almorzar
11. 1:00 tomar una siesta
12. 2:00 hacer trabajos manuales (crafts)
13. 3:00 hacer deportes
14. 5:00 bañarse
15. 5:45 cenar
16. 6:30 escuchar la predicación
17. 7:45 dar testimonio
18. 10:00 acostarse

◆ **Actividad 5**

A girl from Venezuela was sixteen years old when Bolívar declared her country's independence. She wrote about the changes that took place. Complete the story with the correct tense of the verb in parentheses.

Cuando (tener) _____ 16 años, (vivir) _____ en Venezuela. Mi padre (tener) _____ una hacienda y toda mi familia (trabajar) _____ allí. Mi padre (decir) _____ que como nosotros (ser) _____ independientes, ya no (tener) _____ que pagar impuestos a España. Ahora (tener) _____ que pagarle a nuestro gobierno. La bandera de España ya no (hondear) _____ en el cielo. Ahora (haber) _____ una nueva bandera. (Ser) _____ amarilla, azul, y roja. No (ser) _____ fácil acostumbrarse al cambio, pero nosotros (estar) _____ felices de tener nuestro propio país.

El uso del imperfecto: acción en progreso

Another use of the imperfect tense is to describe actions that were in progress over a period of time in the past. (For actions that took place at a specific time in the past, however, the preterite tense is used.) Contrast the following sentences.

Ricardo **leía** muchos libros cuando era niño.

Ricardo **escribió** un poema anoche.

El señor Gómez **trabajaba** en una oficina.

El **renunció** (*resigned*) ayer.

Marcos **asistía** a una escuela cristiana.

Mi amigo **asistió** a la iglesia el domingo conmigo.

When the imperfect tense is used to describe past actions in progress, it often sets the scene for some further action.

Cuando Juan **viajaba** por la carretera 12, un policía lo paró.

When Juan was traveling on Hwy. 12, a policeman stopped him.

Cuando Luisa **tenía** 16 años, Venezuela se independizó.

When Luisa was 16, Venezuela became independent.

Los Fernández **vivían** en Colombia cuando Bolívar murió.

The Fernández family was living in Colombia when Bolívar died.

◆ **Actividad 6**

These students were engaged in many different activities during their summer vacations. Using the imperfect tense, tell what each one did.

Modelo: Susana: estudiar francés
　　　　Susana estudiaba francés durante las vacaciones.

1. Carmen: visitar a sus abuelos

2. Pedro y Ramón: trabajar en un restaurante

3. Diego y yo: jugar al ténis

4. Ana y Lucía: nadar en la piscina

5. Rafael: tomar muchas fotos

6. yo: ir a las montañas

7. Felipe: practicar la trompeta

8. tú: tocar el trombón

◆ **Actividad 7**

Marcos does not like interruptions, so he is having an especially hard day! For each sentence below, use the imperfect tense for the action that was in progress and the preterite for the specific interruption.

Modelo: Marcos (desayunar) _____ cuando (sonar) _____ el teléfono.
        Marcos desayunaba cuando sonó el teléfono.

1. Mientras (dormir) _____ profundamente, su mamá le (llamar) _____ .

2. Cuando (pensar) _____ lavar el carro, (llegar) _____ dos amigos.

3. Le (escribir) _____ una carta a su amiga, cuando (entrar) _____ su hermana.

4. El día que no (saber) _____ la respuesta, la maestra le (hacer) _____ una pregunta.

5. (Leer) _____ la revista, cuando su perro le (saltar) _____ encima.

6. (Querer) _____ ir a la piscina, cuando (empezar) _____ a llover.

◆ **Actividad 8**

Complete the sentences with the correct form of each verb (preterite or imperfect).

Modelo: El señor Ortiz (trabajar) _____ en México cuando yo le conocí.
        El señor Ortiz trabajaba en México cuando yo le conocí.
        La familia Ortiz (comprar) _____ una casa nueva ayer.
        La familia Ortiz compró una casa nueva ayer.

1. Margarita (cantar) _____ en la iglesia el domingo.

2. Cuando Rafael vivía en Miami, (cantar) _____ en el coro de su iglesia.

3. La semana pasada Rafael (venir) _____ a mi casa.

4. Durante las vacaciones, él (ir) _____ a la playa todos los sábados.

5. El sábado pasado, él (ir) _____ otra vez.

6. Anoche yo (decidir) _____ acostarme temprano.

7. A las nueve y media, Rafael me (llamar) _____ .

8. Por fin (dormirse) _____ a las once.

El imperfecto progresivo

We learned that the present progressive tense is used to express that something is happening right now and is formed by using the present of *estar* + **present participle.**

> Juan **está tomando** un examen de inglés ahora.

The past progressive tense expresses that some event was taking place at a definite time in the past. It is formed by using an imperfect form of *estar* + **present participle.**

> A las once de la noche, Pedro **estaba hablando** por teléfono.

> María **estaba estudiando** cuando Pedro la llamó.

> ¿Qué **estaban haciendo** los estudiantes cuando entró la profesora?

◆ Actividad 9

Francisco's friends are always busy. He is telling his cousin what his friends were doing when he called them. Play the role of Francisco.

Modelo: Rolando: cantar en el coro
   Rolando estaba cantando en el coro cuando lo llamé.

1. Pedro y Alfonso: estudiar para un examen
2. Rosa María: cuidar a su hermanito
3. Tomás: hacer ejercicio
4. Sergio: levantar pesas (*weights*)
5. Orlando y Marcos: jugar al baloncesto
6. Ana: comer pizza

◆ Actividad 10

Ask your friends in class what they were doing last night at 9 o'clock. Share the answers given with the rest of the class.

Refrán ▲▲▲

It is good to dream, but learn to be realistic and count only on what you actually have. *Más vale pájaro en mano que cien volando.*

6-3 La Hacienda En México

Diálogo ▲▲

Santiago está de vacaciones en México. Conoce a un señor americano en una *hacienda* y comienzan a conversar.   large ranch

Santiago: ¿Cuánto tiempo hace que llegó a México?

Don Pepe: Nací aquí. ¿Quieres oír la historia de esta hacienda?

Santiago: *¡Por supuesto!* Debe ser interesante.   Of course!

Don Pepe: Hace más de cien años, un señor americano de Ohio compró este *terreno* para dárselo *de herencia* a su hijo.   land / as an inheritance

Santiago: ¿Cuánto terreno compró?

Don Pepe: Bueno, él tenía mucho dinero; compró 2.220 hectáreas, que es más o menos 5.600 acres. El padre y el hijo trabajaron juntos durante un tiempo, pero el hijo no tenía interés en seguir viviendo en México y *regresó* a Ohio. Su padre trató de vender la hacienda pero no pudo.   returned

Santiago: Y entonces, ¿qué hizo el padre?

Don Pepe: En 1901, el señor viajó a Texas, y allí conoció a mi abuelo. Le contó que tenía una hacienda en México que tenía casa, animales y buen terreno. Mi abuelo decidió comprar la hacienda. Mi abuelo vendió su casa y toda su propiedad en Texas *para reunir suficiente* dinero para pagarle al señor. Llevó a su esposa y sus nueve hijos a vivir a México.   to gather enough

Santiago: ¡Qué interesante vivir en una hacienda en México!

Don Pepe: No fue fácil. Hubo una guerra en 1910 que duró siete años. Todas las mujeres tuvieron que salir. Los hombres *se quedaron* para trabajar y *proteger* la propiedad.

stayed / to protect

Santiago: ¿Se quedó también su padre?

Don Pepe: Sí. Él ayudaba a mi abuelo. En 1921 se casó con mi madre, y luego mi abuelo le entregó la hacienda a mi padre.

Santiago: ¿Él tenía que hacer todo el trabajo?

Don Pepe: No. Había más de dos mil personas que vivían en la hacienda y trabajaban para mi padre. Todos tenían sus propias casas. La hacienda era como un pequeño *pueblo*. Había una tienda y una escuela para los niños de los obreros. Yo asistí a la escuela con los niños mexicanos, pero también mi madre me daba clases de inglés.

village

Santiago: Ahora no hay tantos hombres en la hacienda, ¿verdad?

Don Pepe: No. La hacienda no es tan grande ahora. Hace muchos años el gobierno mexicano *repartió* el noventa por ciento de la hacienda en lo que llamaron la *reforma agraria*. Pero mi padre *siguió criando ganado* y cultivando *caña de azúcar* hasta 1959, cuando me entregó la propiedad a mí. Yo tenía treinta y cinco años en ese entonces.

distributed
agrarian reform
kept raising cattle
sugar cane

Santiago: ¿Todavía tiene ganado?

Don Pepe: No. Hace más de treinta años que vendí los animales. Ahora que me estoy poniendo viejo, no puedo trabajar en el campo. ¿Ves las casas ahí? Las *alquilo* a turistas. A muchos americanos les gusta pasar aquí unos meses al año.

alquilar = to rent

◆ **Conversación**

1. ¿Quién compró la hacienda de los mexicanos?

2. ¿Por qué quería venderla?

3. ¿Cuándo la compró el abuelo de don Pepe?

4. ¿Qué pasó en México desde 1910 hasta 1917?

5. ¿Cuándo recibió la hacienda el padre de don Pepe?

6. Describa la hacienda cuando don Pepe era niño.

7. ¿Por qué es más pequeña la hacienda ahora?

Vocabulario ▲▲▲▲▲▲▲▲▲▲▲▲▲▲▲▲▲▲▲▲▲▲▲▲▲▲▲▲▲▲▲▲▲▲▲▲▲▲

La política

Tipos de gobierno
el comunismo
la democracia
la dictadura (*dictatorship*)
la monarquía
la oligarquía
la república
el socialismo
la teocracia

Partidos políticos
conservador
democrático
independiente
liberal
popular
republicano
revolucionario
socialista

Divisiones de gobierno
la cámara de diputados
   (*house of representatives*)
la cámara de senadores
   (*senate*)
el congreso
las cortes (*courts*)
el parlamento
la presidencia

Otras palabras políticas
el candidato
las elecciones
la huelga (*strike*)
las manifestaciones
las protestas
las reformas
votar

Fidel Castro comenzó su dictadura de Cuba en el año 1959.

Gramática ▲▲

El uso del imperfecto: descripción en el pasado

Había una vez una niña.	*Once upon a time there was a girl.*
La niña **era** bonita.	*The girl was pretty.* (physical appearance)
Tenía diez años.	*She was ten years old.* (age)
Era domingo.	*It was Sunday.* (day of the week)
Era el 6 de junio.	*It was the sixth of June.* (date)
Hacía calor.	*It was hot.* (weather)
La niña **estaba** asustada.	*The girl was afraid.* (emotional state)
No **quería** ir al infierno.	*She did not want to go to hell.* (attitude)
Aquel día **escuchó** el evangelio y **recibió** a Cristo.	*That day she heard the gospel and received Christ.*

The imperfect tense is used to describe circumstances and conditions in the past: physical appearance, age, hour, day of the week, date, weather, emotional state, and attitudes. It is used to describe *what was going on.*

The preterite tense, however, is used to tell *what events happened* in the past. Thus, the sentence *escuchó el evangelio y recibió a Cristo* is in the preterite tense.

◆ Actividad 1

¿Conoces la historia de David y Goliat? Lisa quiere contarles la historia a los niños de su clase pero tiene problemas con los verbos. ¿Puedes ayudarla?

Modelo: David (ser) _____ un joven que (tener) _____ más o menos veinte años.
      *David **era** un joven que **tenía** más o menos veinte años.*

1. Goliat (ser) _____ un gigante que (tener) _____ más de nueve pies de altura. Cada mañana Goliat (salir) _____ delante del ejército de Israel y (pedir) _____ que algún hombre peleara contra él.

2. David (vivir) _____ en Belén con su padre, que (llamarse) _____ Isaí. Su padre (ser) _____ anciano. El (tener) _____ ocho hijos y David (ser) _____ el menor. Los tres hermanos mayores (estar) _____ en el ejército peleando contra Goliat. Un día Isaí (llamar) _____ a David y le (enviar) _____ a llevar comida a sus hermanos.

3. (Ser) _____ un día bonito. David (tener) _____ deseos de ver la batalla. Cuando (llegar) _____ , (ver) _____ a Goliat. David (saber) _____ que él (poder) _____ pelear contra Goliat, porque Dios (estar) _____ con él.

4. David (buscar) _____ cinco piedras y las (poner) _____ en su bolsillo. (Tomar) _____ una y la (tirar) _____ con su honda (*slingshot*). Goliat (caer) _____ muerto. David (confiar) _____ en Dios y Dios le (dar) _____ la victoria.

Jacopo Vignali, *The Triumph of David,* Bob Jones University Art Gallery

El uso del imperfecto: estado mental o emocional en el pasado

Look at the imperfect verbs in the following sentences.

Yo **pensaba** que el español era fácil.	*I thought that Spanish was easy.*
Raúl **creía** que Margarita lo **amaba.**	*Raúl believed that Margarita loved him.*
Siempre **quería** comer golosinas.	*I always wanted to eat candy.*

To describe how a person continually thought or felt in the past, the imperfect tense is used. Verbs like *amar, creer, entender, pensar,* and *querer* describe one's mental or emotional state.

Notice the use of the preterite in the following sentences.

Por mucho tiempo tenía dudas, pero un día **creí** lo que Dios dice en la Biblia.	*I had doubts for a long time, but one day I believed what God says in the Bible.*
Miguel siempre me invitaba a su iglesia, y el domingo **decidí** ir con él.	*Miguel always invited me to his church and Sunday I decided to go with him.*

The preterite is used to describe the beginning of one's mental or emotional state.

♦ **Actividad 2**

Mario está pensando en su niñez. Ayúdelo a expresar sus pensamientos.

Modelo: Cuando era niño, (amar) a Dios.
   Cuando era niño, amaba a Dios.

1. . . . (querer) ser médico

2. . . . (no entender) la Biblia

3. . . . (gustarse) ir a la casa de mi abuela

4. . . . (amar) a todo el mundo

5. . . . (no querer) dormir temprano

6. . . . (creer) que no (haber) nada que papá no (poder) hacer

♦ **Actividad 3**

Rafael quiere dar su testimonio en la iglesia. Está escribiéndolo en un papel. ¿Qué dice?

Modelo: Cuando yo (tener) diez años, (comprender) que era pecador.
   Cuando yo tenía diez años, comprendí que era pecador.

1. No (gustarse) _____ ir a la iglesia, pero un día (ir) _____ con un amigo.

2. (Escuchar) _____ la música, y (gustarse) _____ .

3. (Tener) _____ dudas de que Dios me amara, pero ese día (comprender) _____ que Dios es amor.

4. Mi amigo me (hablar) _____ de Cristo, y me (decir) _____ que Cristo me (amar) _____ .

5. Por fin (reconocer) _____ que (ser) _____ pecador e (invitar) _____ a Cristo a entrar en mi corazón.

6. Aquel día Dios me (salvar) _____ .

Ir + *a* + infinitivo

Compare the following sentences.

   Los Moyano **iban a viajar** a Barcelona el año pasado.

   *(The Moyanos **were going to** travel to Barcelona last year.)*

   Los Moyano **fueron a vivir** en Barcelona el año pasado.

   *(The Moyanos **went to** live in Barcelona last year.)*

In the first sentence, the imperfect form ***iban a* + infinitive** shows intention. The Moyanos had the intention of traveling to Barcelona last year, but something must have happened. (They were going to . . .)

   In the second sentence, the preterite form *fueron a* + **infinitive** tells us that they did go to live in Barcelona last year. (They went to . . .)

◆ **Actividad 4**

Los jóvenes tenían muchos planes para el fin de semana, pero no hicieron lo que pensaban hacer. Diga lo que pasó.

Modelo: Ramón: ir al centro / ir al partido de fútbol

Ramón iba a ir al centro, pero fue al partido de fútbol.

1. Marcos: ir a la biblioteca / ir a la casa de su amigo

2. Roberto y Rosa María: ir al parque / ir al campo

3. Sergio y yo: ir a la tienda de departamentos / ir a K-Mart

4. Norma: viajar a Miami / viajar a Orlando

5. Carlos: ir al museo / ir a la casa de sus abuelos

6. Tú: visitar al circo / ir al hospital

Resumen de los usos del pretérito y el imperfecto

1. The preterite is used to refer to—

    a. the beginning of an action or event in the past.

    Tenía doce años cuando la guerra **comenzó.**

    b. completed actions or events in the past.

    Colón **descubrió** América en 1492.

    c. actions or events that began and were completed in the past.

    Reagan **fue** presidente durante ocho años.

2. The imperfect is used to describe—

    a. actions that were in progress in the past; that is, they were ongoing, or continuous.

    En esos años, más de dos mil personas **vivían** en la hacienda.

    b. habitual or repeated actions in the past.

    Todos los años **visitaban** la hacienda.

    c. conditions and circumstances that surrounded an action or event in the past.

    Había vacas en la hacienda.
    Era un día de sol.

    d. a physical, emotional, or mental state in the past.

    Ricardo **era** un hombre alto y fuerte.
    Era una casa grande.
    Estaba contento.
    Sabía inglés y español.

    e. intention or potential in the past: imperfect of **ir + a + infinitive.**

    Carlos me dijo que **iba a ser** presidente.

◆ **Actividad 5**

Termine las frases usando su imaginación.

Modelo: Cuando mi padre era niño, . . .
    vivía con su tío.

1. Cuando Kennedy era presidente, . . .

2. Cuando Rusia era comunista, . . .

3. Cuando los Estados Unidos tenía trece colonias, . . .

4. Cuando yo tenía diez años, . . .

5. Todos los años, mi familia . . .

◆ **Actividad 6**

Escriba acerca de su niñez. Describa su familia, su iglesia, sus actividades, dónde vivía, a qué escuela asistía, y eventos importantes de su vida. Debe usar verbos en el imperfecto y en el pretérito.

◆ **Actividad 7**

Give the appropriate preterite or imperfect form of the verb in parentheses.

(Haber) _____ una vez un soldado que (llamarse) _____ Gedeón. Gedeón era un hombre muy valiente que (vivir) _____ durante los días cuando los israelitas (hacer) _____ lo malo ante los ojos de Dios. Por eso, Jehová les puso en la mano de los madianitas. Los israelitas (llorar) _____ y (rogar) _____ al Señor que los librara de los madianitas. Un ángel del Señor vino y le habló a Gedeón diciendo: Jehová te ha escogido para luchar contra los madianitas. Gedeón (orar) _____ mucho y (pedir) _____ tres señales. Dios (contestar) _____ sus oraciones.

(Haber) _____ muchos hombres que (querer) _____ luchar, pero Dios (querer) _____ tener menos para mostrar su poder. Trescientos soldados fueron escogidos. Gedeón (tocar) _____ la trompeta y los israelitas (marchar) _____ a la batalla y (matar) _____ a los madianitas. Dios (ayudar) _____ a su siervo Gedeón.

◆ **Actividad 8**

Choose a hero and write a brief composition describing his life. You may wish to include personal characteristics, battles, and victories. (You may write about Cristobal Colón, José Martí, Simón Bolívar, or another hero of your choice.)

Nota Històrica ▲▲▲▲▲▲▲▲▲▲▲▲▲▲▲▲▲▲▲▲▲▲▲▲▲▲▲▲▲▲▲▲▲▲▲▲▲▲▲

La reforma agraria en México

Cuando Porfirio Díaz era presidente de México al comienzo del siglo XX, las tierras estaban en manos de unos pocos propietarios. En 1910, *el pueblo* de **the people** México se rebeló y Díaz tuvo que renunciar el próximo año. La revolución continuó hasta que en 1917 fue aprobada una nueva constitución que incluía reformas sociales.

Al subir a la presidencia en 1920, el general Álvaro Obregón comenzó la reforma agraria y la distribución de las grandes haciendas entre los *campesi-* **farmers; peasants** *nos.* Desde entonces, la mitad del territorio nacional *ha llegado a ser* parte de **has become** la reforma agraria.

Vocabulario adicional ▲▲▲▲▲▲▲▲▲▲▲▲▲▲▲▲▲▲▲▲▲▲▲▲▲▲▲▲▲▲▲▲

El prefijo *des-* en español es equivalente al prefijo *un-* o *dis-* en inglés.

aparecer (*to appear*)	desaparecer (*to disappear*)
conocido (*known*)	desconocido (*unknown*)
esperar (*to wait; to hope*)	desesperar (*to despair*)
hacer (*to do*)	deshacer (*to undo*)
ocupar (*to occupy*)	desocupar (*to vacate*)
ordenar (*to arrange in order*)	desordenar (*to throw into disarray*)

Llene el espacio.

cansar (*to tire*)	_____ (*to rest*)
cargar (*to carry, to load*)	_____ (*to discharge, to unload*)
colgar (*to hang*)	_____ (*to take down, to unhook*)
consolar (*to comfort*)	_____ (*to grieve, to sadden*)

Para formar los siguientes sustantivos, reemplaza la terminación *-ar* o *-ir* del verbo con la terminación *-ador(a)* o *-idor(a)*.

Verbos	**Sustantivos**
colonizar	colonizador(a)
comentar	comentador(a)
conquistar	conquistador(a)
descubrir	descubridor(a)
explorar	explorador(a)

¿Puedes dar otros ejemplos?

Todos nosotros nos descarriamos
como ovejas, cada cual se apartó
por su camino; mas Jehová cargó
en él el pecado de todos nosotros.
Isaías 53:6

CAPÍTULO SIETE

7-1 LOS MÚSICOS DE BREMEN

Lectura ▲▲▲

master
demanding / to flee

· Había una vez un burro que estaba cansado de trabajar. Su *amo* era muy *exigente*, y el pobre burro quería *huir*. Un día el burro salió de su casa y fue hacia la ciudad de Bremen para ser músico en la banda municipal.

hunting dog
no longer

Iba el burro camino a Bremen cuando encontró a un viejo *perro de caza*. El pobre perro *ya no* podía ayudar a su amo a cazar, y por eso había huído en busca de libertad. El burro le dijo al perro:

—Perro viejo, ven conmigo a la ciudad de Bremen; podemos ser músicos en la banda municipal.

Y el perro contestó:

—Es mejor ir contigo que morir en la casa de mi amo.

Así que los dos fueron camino a Bremen.

Iban los dos caminando cuando vieron a un gato en el camino. El burro dijo:

—¿Qué te pasa, pobre gato? —Y el gato respondió:

—Soy muy viejo y no puedo cazar ratones; mi ama quiere matarme.

—Ven con nosotros —dijo el burro. —Vamos a ser músicos.

all of a sudden

Los tres animales siguieron su camino. *De repente* oyeron el cantar de un gallo y fueron para ver lo que pasaba.

—¡Mi ama va a cocinarme para la fiesta de mañana! ¡Tengo mucho miedo! ¡Quiquiriquí! —*gritó* el gallo.

***gritar* = to scream**

—Ven con nosotros —dijo el burro. —Vamos a ser músicos, y tú cantas muy bien.

And so

De modo que el gallo fue con el burro, el perro y el gato hacia la ciudad de Bremen.

to grow dark / the forest
nearby / there
bandits

Empezaba a *anochecer* y los animales no querían dormir en *el bosque*. Vieron luz en una casa *cercana* y decidieron pasar *allí* la noche. Cuando llegaron a la casa, vieron que había unos *bandidos* comiendo.

—Vamos a *asustarlos* —dijo el burro.

Los cuatro animales hicieron tanto *ruido* que los bandidos salieron asustados. El burro, el perro, el gato y el gallo entraron en la casa, comieron mucho, y luego fueron a dormir.

Los bandidos estaban en el bosque y querían volver a la casa; así que mandaron a uno de ellos para investigar. La casa estaba tranquila y *a oscuras;* y el bandido entró a la cocina para encender *el fuego.* Cuando encendió *una cerilla*, el gato se asustó, saltó sobre él y lo *arañó.* El bandido salió corriendo por *la puerta trasera* pero el perro estaba allí y lo *mordió.* El burro le dió una *coz,* y el gallo gritó con todas sus fuerzas —¡Quiquiriquí!

El bandido fue corriendo a sus compañeros y dijo:

—En la casa hay una *bruja* horrible. Me arañó, me mordió, me *golpeó*, y me gritó. Tuve que salir corriendo.

Los bandidos estaban tan asustados que *nunca jamás* volvieron a la casa, y los animales decidieron quedarse allí *para siempre.*

to scare them
noise

dark
the fire / a match
scratched
the back door / bit
kick

a witch / *golpear* = to beat

never ever
forever

Vocabulario ▲▲▲▲▲▲▲▲▲▲▲▲▲▲▲▲▲▲▲▲▲▲▲▲▲▲▲▲▲▲▲▲▲▲▲▲▲▲

Los animales de la finca

el buey (*ox*)	el cerdo (*pig*)	el pavo (*turkey*)
el burro (*donkey*)	la gallina (*hen*)	el pollo (*chicken*)
el caballo (*horse*)	el gallo (*rooster*)	el ratón (*mouse*)
la cabra (*goat*)	la oveja (*lamb*)	la vaca (*cow*)

Los animales domésticos

el canario (*canary*)	el gato (*cat*)	el perro (*dog*)
el conejo (*rabbit*)	el loro (*parrot*)	el pez de color (*goldfish*)

◆ **Actividad 2**

Fill in each blank with the appropriate past participle form of the verb in parentheses. Watch for agreement.

1. La profesora mira a los estudiantes con los libros _____ . (cerrar)

2. Las estudiantes estaban _____ porque no había suficientes sillas. (parar)

3. Los niños estaban _____ al ver tantos gatos. (sorprender)

4. Yo ví a María _____ en la clase. (dormir)

5. Mis padres estaban _____ porque llegué tarde a casa. (preocupar)

6. Todos estamos _____ para el examen. (preparar)

7. Rebeca y Amelia están _____ con Marcos. (enojar)

8. Fernando estaba muy _____ ayer. (ocupar)

9. Noelia siempre está _____ durante sus vacaciones. (aburrir)

10. El relampago dejó el perro _____ . (asustar)

◆ **Actividad 3**

Read the following paragraph and then choose the correct picture.

La familia Lozano está en la sala. Felipe está parado junto a la puerta. El padre está acostado en el sofá, pero aunque está muy cansado no está dormido. Rosa y Pablo están reclinados en el sillón de la madre. En la pared está colgada una foto antigua de los bisabuelos.

◆ **Actividad 4**

Conteste las preguntas con oraciones completas.

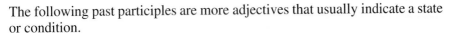

1. ¿Estás cansado(a) ahora?

2. ¿Estás interesado(a) en aprender español?

3. ¿Estás preocupado(a) por algo (*about something*)?

4. ¿Quién está sentado(a) a tu derecha?

5. ¿Está cerrada la puerta de tu cuarto?

The following past participles are more adjectives that usually indicate a state or condition.

encendido (*turned on*)	La lámpara estaba **encendida.**
apagado (*turned off*)	Ahora la lámpara está **apagada.**
quebrado (*broken*)	El espejo está **quebrado.**
quemado (*burnt*)	¿Qué vamos a comer? La carne está **quemada.**
escondido (*hidden*)	Los animales estaban **escondidos** en la casa.
perdido (*lost*)	El dinero de la señora está **perdido.**

◆ **Actividad 5**

Complete the sentences in a logical way by adding past participles (for state or condition).

Modelo: No veo bien. Las luces . . . *están apagadas.*

1. Hace calor en la casa. El aire acondicionado . . .

2. No puedo comer la tostada. La tostada . . .

3. Al niño le duele el brazo. El brazo . . .

4. No puedo ver las noticias. El televisor . . .

5. La señora busca a la cabra debajo de la mesa. La cabra está . . .

6. Había mucha luz en la casa. Todas las lámparas . . .

7. No encontré mi libro. El libro . . .

Lectura bíblica ▲▲▲▲▲▲▲▲▲▲▲▲▲▲▲▲▲▲▲▲▲▲▲▲▲▲▲▲▲▲▲▲▲▲▲▲▲

Lucas 18:35-42

Aconteció que acercándose Jesús a Jericó, un ciego estaba sentado junto al camino mendigando; y al oír a la multitud que pasaba, preguntó qué era aquello. Y le dijeron que pasaba Jesús nazareno. Entonces dio voces, diciendo: ¡Jesús, Hijo de David, ten misericordia de mí! . . . Jesús . . . le preguntó, diciendo: ¿Qué quieres que te haga? Y él dijo: Señor, que reciba la vista. Jesús le dijo: Recíbela, tu fe te ha salvado.

MADRID

The city of Madrid, with its elaborate National Palace, serves as the center of all government activities in Spain. Madrid is also the hub of Spanish commerce, communications, and culture. Among the city's cultural institutions is the Royal Spanish Academy. The Academy seeks to preserve the Spanish language by publishing a dictionary which serves as the standard for Spanish speakers worldwide.

Madrid is also home to numerous touristic attractions, such as the world-renowned art museum El Prado and several historic plazas. The Puerta del Sol plaza marks the center of the city; the Plaza Mayor witnessed the burning of Christians during the Inquisition; and the Plaza de España contains a brass monument of Cervantes and his famous character Don Quixote.

7-2 PLATERO

Lectura ▲▲▲

Juan Ramón Jiménez (1881-1958), a Spanish poet and the 1956 winner of the Nobel Prize for Literature, wrote one of his most famous works, *Platero y yo*, (published in 1914) in prose. Platero, a little burro, is the writer's companion during many adventures. Chapter one of the book introduces Platero. For your comprehension, review the following words before reading the story.

peludo	*furry*
blando	*soft*
por fuera	*on the outside*
duro	*hard*
dejar suelto	*to let loose*
el prado	*meadow*
tierno	*tender*
seco	*dry*
por dentro	*on the inside*
acero	*steel*

Capítulo uno: Platero

Platero es pequeño, peludo, suave; tan blando por fuera, *que se diría* todo de algodón, que no lleva *huesos.* Sólo los *espejos de azabache* de sus ojos son duros *cual dos escarabajos* de cristal negro.

that one might say / bones / jet-black mirrors / like two beetles

Lo dejo suelto, y se va al prado, y *acaricia* tibiamente con su *hocico, rozándolas apenas,* las florecillas rosas, celestes y *gualdas* . . . Lo llamo dulcemente: «¿Platero?» y viene a mí con un *trotecillo* alegre que parece que se ríe en no sé qué *cascabeleo* ideal . . .

caresses / snout / barely brushing against / yellow flower / little trot / jingle bell

Come cuanto le doy. Le gustan las naranjas, mandarinas, las *uvas moscateles,* todas de *ámbar,* los *higos* morados, con su cristalina *gotita de miel* . . .

a delicate type of grape / amber / figs / little drop of honey

Es tierno y *mimoso* igual que un niño, que una niña . . .; pero fuerte y seco por dentro, como de *piedra.* Cuando paseo sobre él, los domingos, por las últimas *callejas* del pueblo, los hombres del campo *vestidos de limpio* y despaciosos se quedan mirándolo:

spoiled; pampered / stone / alley streets / dressed up

—Tiene acero . . .

Tiene acero. Acero y *plata de luna,* al mismo tiempo.

moon silver

◆ **Conversación**

Answer in English.

1. Describe Platero.

2. Name some contrasting words that the author uses to describe Platero.

3. Where does Platero go when the writer lets him loose?

4. When the writer calls him, what does Platero do?

5. What does Platero like to eat?

6. Where do the writer and Platero go on Sundays?

7. Why do the men from the fields say that Platero is made of steel and moon silver at the same time?

8. Do you think that *Platero* is a good name for this burro? Why?

Vocabulario ▲▲▲

Los animales del bosque

el águila (*eagle*)   el mapache (*raccoon*)   el sapo (*toad*)

el búho (*owl*)   el oso (*bear*)   el venado (*deer*)

el lobo (*wolf*)   el pájaro (*bird*)   el zorro (*fox*)

Los animales de la selva

la cebra (*zebra*)   el hipopótamo   el leopardo

la culebra (*snake*)   la jirafa (*giraffe*)   el mono (*monkey*)

el elefante   el león   el tigre

Los animales del mar

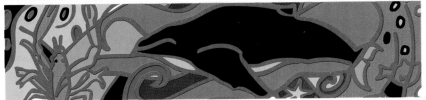

la ballena (*whale*)   el delfín (*dolphin*)   el pez (*fish*)

el calamar (*squid*)   la foca (*seal*)   el pulpo (*octopus*)

el cangrejo (*crab*)   el pescado (*fish as a food*)   el tiburón (*shark*)

Gramática ▲▲▲▲▲▲▲▲▲▲▲▲▲▲▲▲▲▲▲▲▲▲▲▲▲▲▲▲▲▲▲▲▲▲▲▲▲▲▲

El pronombre impersonal *se*

In sentences with reflexive verbs, the pronoun *se* refers to the person doing the action.

María **se baña.**   *María bathes herself.*
Pedro y Marta **se sientan**   *Pedro and Marta sit (themselves)*
   a la mesa.   *down at the table.*

The reflexive pronoun *se,* however, may also be used in an impersonal construction as shown in the following sentences.

Se come bien en mi casa.   ***One*** *eats well at my house.*
Se habla castellano en Madrid.   ***They*** *speak Castillian in Madrid.*
¿Cómo **se** dice . . .?   *How does* ***one*** *(do you) say . . .?*
¿Cómo **se** escribe . . .?   *How does* ***one*** *(do you) write . . .?*
Se sabe que . . .   ***People*** *know that . . .*

In each of the Spanish sentences above, no specific person is named. The pronoun *se* refers to people in general. In English we might say *one, they, you, we,* or *people;* but in Spanish, the impersonal subject is not expressed.

◆ Actividad 1

Write an equivalent sentence using the impersonal pronoun *se*.

Modelo: En Cuba la gente habla español.
      En Cuba se habla español.

1. Ellos venden buena comida aquí.

2. Las personas comen bien en Puerto Rico.

3. Ellos venden carne en el mercado.

4. Todos compran helados en la heladería.

5. La gente dice que las mandarinas son buenas para la salud.

◆ Actividad 2

Conteste las preguntas.

Modelo: ¿Dónde se come buena comida china?
      Se come buena comida china en el restaurante el Vesuvio.

1. ¿Dónde se habla el mejor inglés? ¿en el norte o en el sur de los Estados Unidos?

2. ¿Dónde se come bien en tu ciudad?

3. ¿Dónde se compra ropa a buen precio?

4. ¿Cómo se dice «bear» en español?

5. ¿Cómo se escribe el nombre del burrito en la historia de Juan Ramón Jiménez?

Expressions using the impersonal *se* are often found in signs or advertisements.

Aquí **se** habla español.	*Spanish is spoken here.*
Se prohibe fumar.	*Smoking is prohibited. (No smoking!)*
Se vende una casa.	*House for sale.*
Se alquilan autos.	*Cars for rent.*

In the sentences above the construction is **se + verb + noun.** Notice that each verb agrees with the noun which follows it.

◆ Actividad 3

The following people want to place an ad in the newspaper. Write an ad for each of them by using the impersonal pronoun *se*.

Modelo: María Torres quiere vender un Taurus del 88.
      Se vende un Taurus del 88.

1. El señor Cordero quiere vender un perro pastor alemán.

2. La señora Pérez quiere comprar una casa para perro.

3. La hacienda Santiago quiere comprar caballos de carrera.

4. Los jóvenes quieren vender cinco conejitos blancos.

5. El Hotel Miramar necesita una recepcionista.

6. Los niños necesitan una jaula para pájaros.

7. Una compañía solicita mecánicos.

8. El restaurante Jinotepe solicita dos cocineros.

El diminutivo

Tengo una **hermanita**.	*I have a little sister.*
Se llama **Rosita.**	*Her name is Rosie (little Rose).*
Tiene un **gatito.**	*She has a kitten.*
Platero juega con las **florecillas** del campo.	*Platero plays with the little field flowers.*
Yo amo a mi **noviecita.**	*I love my dear girlfriend.*

In Spanish, diminutive endings are attached to words to convey the idea of smallness or endearment. The most common diminutive endings are **-ito(a)**, **-cito(a)** and **-cillo(a).**

As a general rule, use *-ito(a)* with words ending in *a, o,* and *l: mamá→mamita, papá→papito, ángel→angelito.* Use *-cito(a)* and *-cillo(a)* with other words: *mujer→mujercita, león→leoncito, trotes→trotecillos.*

When a word ends in a vowel, drop the vowel before adding a diminutive that begins with a vowel.

◆ **Actividad 4**

Supply the diminutive form of each word in parentheses. Use the diminutives **-ito(a)** or **-cito(a).**

1. Su (burro) se llama Platero.

2. Le gusta comer las (flores) del prado.

3. No tengo un (burro) pero tengo un (gato) en mi casa.

4. A mi (hermana) le gusta jugar con sus (animales).

5. ¡Los (dedos) de los niños son tan pequeños!

6. Mi (abuela) vive en una (casa) amarilla cerca de la iglesia.

7. Mamá se llama Carmen, pero papá le dice (Carmen).

8. Yo quiero mucho a mis (perros).

Los adjetivos posesivos enfáticos

In Spanish there are two forms of possessive adjectives. The **simple** possessive adjectives *mi, tu, su, nuestro,* and *vuestro* go before the noun they modify.

Carmen tiene **mi** libro de literatura.

The **stressed** possessive adjectives go after the word they modify.

Rolando tiene unos **libros míos.**   *Rolando has some **books of mine.***
Una **amiga nuestra** vive en Toledo.   *A **friend of ours** lives in Toledo.*

All the forms of the stressed possessive adjectives and their English equivalents are listed below.

Possessive adjectives			
mío, mía míos, mías	*mine*	nuestro, nuestra nuestros, nuestras	*ours*
tuyo, tuya tuyos, tuyas	*yours*	vuestro, vuestra vuestros, vuestras	*yours (familiar plural)*
suyo, suya suyos, suyas	*his, hers, yours (formal)*	suyo, suya suyos, suyas	*theirs, yours (plural)*

The stressed possessive adjective must agree in number and gender with the thing possessed (the noun that follows): *libros míos, amiga nuestra.*

Note that the stressed possessive adjective is usually the equivalent of the English expression *of mine, of yours, of his,* and so on.

In Spanish, the indefinite article may be left out when the noun modified by the stressed possessive adjective follows the verb **ser.**

Mariana es **prima mía.**   *Mariana is **a cousin of mine.***

Mateo es **amigo nuestro.**   *Mateo is **a friend of ours.***

¿Es **pariente tuyo** Miguel?   *Is Miguel **a relative of yours?***

◆ **Actividad 5**

Sergio is showing pictures of his recent mission trip to a classmate who in turn is asking Sergio if the following people are friends of his. Do this activity with a partner.

Modelo: Compañero: ¿Es amiga tuya Margarita Pérez?
       Sergio: Sí, es amiga mía.

1. Oscar y Pablo Alonzo
2. Diego López
3. Isabel Torres
4. Fabio y Cecilia Moreno
5. Rosana y Ester Hernández
6. Viviana Bonilla

◆ **Actividad 6**

The students in the Spanish class are making plans to travel to Uruguay during vacation. They are deciding what each one is going to take.

Modelo: Esteban / los tratados *(tracts)*
  Esteban lleva los tratados.

1. Tomás / la cámara de fotos
2. todos / los zapatos deportivos
3. Benjamín / dos diccionarios
4. nosotras / la cámara de video
5. yo / los lentes de sol *(sunglasses)*
6. ellas / las toallas de playa
7. tú / tres revistas de turismo
8. nosotros / la música para el coro

Los pronombres posesivos

Look at the possessives in the following sentences.

  Paco y yo tenemos automóviles. **El suyo** es rojo y **el mío** es verde.

The expressions in bold print above are possessive pronouns replacing the nouns **mi automóvil** and **su automóvil.**

  The possessive pronouns are formed with **a definite article + a stressed possessive adjective.** Both the definite article and the stressed possessive adjective must agree in gender and number with the noun they replace.

mis libros - **los míos**	nuestras casas - **las nuestras**
tu cámara - **la tuya**	sus primos - **los suyos**

The definite article is generally omitted after the verb *ser.*

Aquella pizza es **tuya** y esta es **mía.**	*That pizza is **yours**, and this one is **mine**.*

◆ **Actividad 7**

Diego siempre sabe dónde están sus cosas, pero su hermano nunca sabe dónde están las suyas. Diego le pregunta a su hermano dónde están ciertos artículos.

Modelo: bicicleta
  Aquí está mi bicicleta, pero ¿dónde está la tuya?

1. calculadora
2. libros
3. camisa
4. zapatos

◆ **Actividad 8**

Conteste cada pregunta usando un pronombre posesivo.

1. Yo leo mi libro de español. ¿Lees tú el tuyo?

2. Nosotros queremos a nuestros padres. ¿Quieren Uds. a los suyos?

3. Mateo baña a su perra. ¿Bañas a la tuya? (No, yo no baño a . . .)

4. Marta acabó su tarea. ¿Acabó Manuel la suya? (Sí, acabó . . .)

5. ¿Te comes mi pizza o la tuya? (Me como . . .)

Nota Informativa▲▲▲▲▲▲▲▲▲▲▲▲▲▲▲▲▲▲▲▲▲▲▲▲▲▲▲▲▲▲▲▲▲▲▲▲▲▲

The government of Spain is a parliamentary monarchy. Approved in 1978, the Spanish constitution retained the king as the symbolic head of state and upheld the *Cortes,* an elected legislature. The leader of the majority party in the *Cortes* serves as the President (or Prime Minister) and, along with his cabinet, is responsible for many of the nation's affairs.

The political divisions of Spain constitute another important feature of the nation's makeup. Spain is divided into seventeen "autonomous communities," large regions possessing a measure of self-government but still answerable to the central government. These communities consist of smaller provinces, fifty in all, which have their own governors and legislators.

TOLEDO

Toledo, one of Spain's oldest cities, rests on a hill surrounded by the Tagus *(Tajo)* River. The city served as the capital for the Visigoths and the Moors and, until 1561, for the Spaniards. Although it represents the heart of Spanish Catholicism, Toledo cherishes a tradition of tolerating Jews and Arabs.

Toledo's numerous historic sites provide, according to one writer, a complete history of Spain. The city is rich in bridges, monuments, churches, and castles which attract tourists. One of the city's most famous sites is the home of the mannerist painter El Greco, who worked in Toledo during the seventeenth century.

7-3 Alegría

Lectura ▲▲

Before reading the following selection of *Platero y yo,* familiarize yourself
with the following terms.

parecerse (a)	*to resemble*	embestir	*to attack*
la luna creciente	*crescent moon*	rodar	*to roll*
gris	*gray*	patas	*animal feet*
saltar	*to jump; leap*	brincar	*to jump; hop*
hacer como que	*to act as if*	hacerse el tonto	*to pretend not to know*

Capítulo tres: Alegría

Platero juega con Diana, la bella perra blanca que se parece a la luna creciente;
con la vieja cabra gris, con los niños . . .

ringing her little bell
straight up
like two horns of the
century plant
pulling with her teeth
the cattails in his load
bumps / forehead
bleats
toy / pranks
lingering / so they do
not fall off

Salta Diana, ágil y elegante, delante del burro, *sonando su leve campanilla,*
y hace como que le muerde los hocicos. Y Platero, poniendo las orejas *en punta,
cual dos cuernos de pita,* la embiste blandamente y la hace rodar sobre la hierba
en flor.

La cabra va al lado de Platero, rozándose a sus patas, *tirando con los dientes*
de la punta de *las espadañas de la carga.* Con una clavellina o con una
margarita en la boca se pone frente a él, le *topa* en el *testuz* y brinca luego, y
bala alegremente, mimosa igual que una mujer . . .

Entre los niños, Platero es de *juguete.* ¡Con qué paciencia sufre sus *locuras!*
¡Cómo va despacio, *deteniéndose,* haciéndose el tonto, *para que ellos no se
caigan!* ¡Cómo los asusta, iniciando, de pronto, un trote falso!

◆ Conversación

1. Who is Diana?

2. What does Diana resemble?

3. What does Diana do to Platero when they play?

4. What kind of flowers does the goat have in her mouth?

5. Name at least three things that the goat does when she plays with
   Platero.

6. How does Platero tease the children?

7. Why is *Alegría* a good title for this chapter?

Vocabulario

La creación

el espacio	space
los planetas	planets
el sistema solar	solar system
la hierba	grass, weeds
las plantas	plants
las aves	birds
los peces	fish
la fauna	animals

el sol
las estrellas
la luna
las nubes
los árboles
la montaña
el cielo
las flores
el mar

Gramática ▲▲

Los pronombres demostrativos neutros

In Lesson 7 you studied the demonstrative pronouns *éste, ése,* and *aquél* and learned that they agree with the nouns they replace in gender and number. Now look at the demonstrative pronouns in the following sentences.

¿Qué es **esto**?
¿Qué es **eso**?
Las computadoras son maravillosas.
Ayer robaron el Banco Central y se
   llevaron millones de pesos.

—Es una fórmula geométrica.
—Es mi nueva computadora.
—**Eso** es verdad.
—¡**Aquello** fue una barbaridad!

The demonstrative pronouns *esto, eso,* and *aquello* refer to objects that are as yet unnamed, or to ideas or situations as a whole; therefore, they are called **neuter demonstratives.** They never change forms and never have a written accent mark.

◆ **Actividad 1**

After reading each sentence, indicate your reaction by choosing a statement from the list below.

¡Eso es horrible!	¡Eso es mentira!
¡Eso es normal!	¡Eso es tremendo!
¡Eso es increíble!	¡Eso es magnífico!

Modelo: El director de la escuela acaba de anunciar que mañana no hay clases.
  ¡Eso es magnífico!

1. Mi tío tiene una mansión grande con piscina y canchas de tenis. Nos invitó a pasar el fin de semana con él.

2. El reportero comentó que hace varios años que aquel país está en guerra y que la gente no tiene nada para comer.

3. Su escritorio está lleno de libros y papeles.

4. El profesor dijo que eres inteligente, cortés, y que te gusta trabajar.

5. La computadora que tienes puede traducir palabras de un idioma a otro.

El uso de *lo que*

Notice the use of *lo que* in the following sentences.

Repita **lo que** dijo Pablo.	*Repeat **what** Pablo said.*
Los niños hacen **lo que** hacen sus padres.	*Children do **that which** their parents do.*
¡Haz **lo que** te dije (yo)!	*Do **what** I told you.*

The Spanish expression **lo que** is comparable to the English expression *what, that which,* or *the thing(s) which.* It does not refer directly to a noun, but rather to an idea. Notice the word order:
  lo que + verb + subject.

◆ **Actividad 2**

Marisol is quizzing a friend on the story of Platero. Write her questions. Then quiz a friend.

Modelo: hacer / Platero en el prado.
  ¿Recuerdas lo que hace Platero en el prado?

1. decir / los hombres del campo acerca de Platero

2. llevar / Diana en el cuello

3. tirar / la cabra con los dientes

4. tener / en la boca la cabra

5. hacer / Platero con los niños

◆ **Actividad 3**

Explain everyday experiences at school by using *lo que* and the correct form of the verbs given. Follow the model.

Modelo: en el examen: contestar / saber
       En el examen contesto lo que sé.
       En el examen no (siempre) contesto
       lo que sé.

1. en la cafetería: comer / servir(se)

2. con tus amigos: jugar / querer

3. en la clase: entender / oír

4. en la biblioteca: comprender / leer

5. en los deportes: hacer / poder

Qué + adjetivo o adverbio

¡Qué hermosa es la rosa!	*How beautiful is the rose!*
¡Qué bueno! / ¡Qué bien!	*How good!*
¡Qué malo! / ¡Qué mal!	*How awful!*

Qué + sustantivo

¡Qué pena!	*What a shame!*
¡Qué lástima!	*What a pity!*
¡Qué lío!	*What a mess (mix-up)!*

Lo + adjetivo

The neuter **lo** before an adjective corresponds to several English expressions.

Lo bueno es que no tengo que pagar.	***The good thing*** *is that I don't have to pay.*
Lo malo es que tengo otra cita.	***The bad part*** *is that I have another date.*
Lo importante es que él me invitó.	***What is important*** *is that he invited me.*
¿Siempre haces **lo fácil** primero?	*Do you always do **the things that are easy** first?*
Lo bonito de la primavera son las mariposas.	***What is beautiful*** *about spring are the butterflies.*

◆ **Actividad 4**

1. ¿Qué es lo bueno de la clase de español?

2. ¿Qué es lo mejor de tu escuela?

3. ¿Qué es lo más necesario para sacar buenas notas?

4. ¿Qué es lo más difícil de aprender español? ¿los verbos?

5. ¿Qué es lo más importante en tu vida?

Refrán ▲▲▲▲▲▲▲▲▲▲▲▲▲▲▲▲▲▲▲▲▲▲▲▲▲▲▲▲▲▲▲▲▲▲▲▲

Has anyone ever told you that you're "a chip off the old block"? This proverb stresses the influence parents have in shaping their children's character.

De tal palo, tal astilla.

Lectura ▲▲▲▲▲▲▲▲▲▲▲▲▲▲▲▲▲▲▲▲▲▲▲▲▲▲▲▲▲▲▲▲▲▲▲▲

Capítulo sesenta y siete: Melancolía

I have gone / grave
male pine tree
quit shouting

Esta tarde *he ido* con los niños a visitar la *sepultura* de Platero, que está en el huerto de la Piña, al pie del *pino paternal.*

. . . Los niños, así que iban llegando, *dejaban de gritar.* Quietos y serios, sus ojos brillantes en mis ojos, me llenaban de preguntas ansiosas.

hairy back
will you, perhaps, have
forgotten me?
as if / light (in weight)
had seen / fluttered /
like a soul

—¡Platero amigo! —le dije yo a la tierra—; si, como pienso, estás ahora en un prado del cielo y llevas sobre tu *lomo peludo* a los ángeles adolescentes, *¿me habrás, quizás, olvidado?* Platero, dime: ¿te acuerdas aún de mí?

Y, *cual* contestando mi pregunta, una *leve* mariposa blanca, que antes no *había visto, revolaba* insistentemente, *igual que un alma,* de lirio en lirio . . .

◆ **Cuestionario**

1. Where does the speaker go with the children?

2. Why did the children stop shouting?

3. According to the speaker, where is Platero now? Whom does Platero carry on his back?

4. What fluttered about from lily to lily? What did it seem to represent to the speaker?

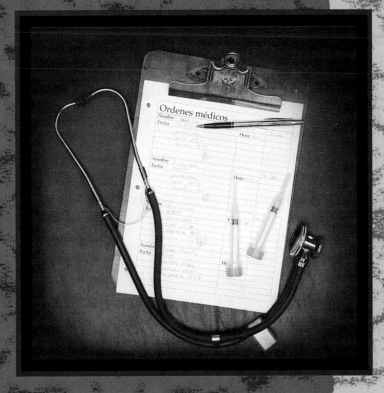

Aun estando nosotros muertos en
pecados, nos dio vida juntamente
con Cristo (por gracia sois salvos).
Efesios 2:5

CAPÍTULO OCHO

8-1 Una visita al médico

Diálogo ▲▲▲

sentirse mal = to feel sick

Luis: Mamá, *me siento mal* esta mañana. No pude dormir nada.

Mamá: ¿Qué te pasa?

since

Luis: He tenido dolor de cabeza y dolor de estómago *desde* anoche.

Mamá: Pues, vamos al médico.

En la oficina del doctor Mendoza . . .

Doctor: Buenos días, Luis. ¿Cómo te sientes?

Mamá: Luis ha tenido dolor de cabeza desde anoche.

Doctor: Perdón, señora. Quiero que Luis me diga lo que le pasa.

Luis: Esta mañana cuando me desperté, tenía dolor de cabeza, doctor.

Mamá: Y tenías dolor de estómago también, ¿no?

Doctor: ¡Señora, por favor!

Luis: También desde anoche he tenido dolor de estómago.

Doctor: Voy a tomarte la temperatura.

thermometer

Le pone el *termómetro* en la boca. Después lo examina.

Doctor: Te he tomado la temperatura y no tienes fiebre. Tu temperatura está normal. Luis, durante las últimas veinticuatro horas, ¿qué has comido?

Mamá: Ayer le preparé . . .

Doctor: Señora, le he preguntado a Luis, por favor.

Luis: Pues, comí . . . lo normal; pero . . . antes de acostarme, me comí dos bocadillos grandes de jamón y chorizo. Nada más.

Doctor: Ahora entiendo por qué has tenido dolor de estómago. No te voy a *recetar* nada. Señora, ¿tiene algún *antiácido* en su casa?   to prescribe / antacid

Mamá: Sí, doctor.

Doctor: Puede darle a Luis dos *cucharadas* de antiácido cada cuatro horas. Él se va a sentir mejor esta noche.   tablespoons

Mamá: Gracias, doctor.

Doctor: Hasta luego, Luis. Y ¡no comas tanto!

◆ **Conversación**

1. ¿Por qué no quiere levantarse Luis?
2. ¿Qué síntomas ha tenido desde anoche?
3. ¿Tiene fiebre?
4. ¿Qué comió Luis durante las últimas veinticuatro horas?
5. ¿Qué remedio le dio el doctor a Luis?

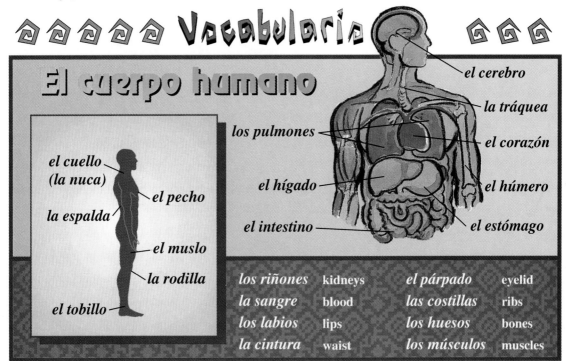

Vocabulario

El cuerpo humano

el cerebro
la tráquea
los pulmones
el corazón
el hígado
el húmero
el intestino
el estómago

el cuello (la nuca)
el pecho
la espalda
el muslo
la rodilla
el tobillo

los riñones	kidneys	el párpado	eyelid
la sangre	blood	las costillas	ribs
los labios	lips	los huesos	bones
la cintura	waist	los músculos	muscles

Los síntomas

el dolor de cabeza (*headache*)
el dolor de espalda (*backache*)
el dolor de estómago (*stomachache*)
la fiebre; la calentura (*fever*)
el malestar (*discomfort*)
la tensión (presión) arterial (*blood pressure*)

desmayarse (*to faint*)
estornudar (*to sneeze*)
toser (*to cough*)

Gramática ▲▲

El presente perfecto

The present perfect tense in Spanish is very similar to its English counterpart (*I have spoken, you have eaten, he has requested*). It is a compound tense made up of a present tense form of the auxiliary verb **haber + the past participle** of the main verb.

In the perfect tenses only the verb *haber* is conjugated. The participle always ends in *-o* when combined with *haber.* This usage sets it apart from that of its role as an adjective. As an adjective when combined with *ser* or *estar,* the participle must agree in gender and number with the noun it modifies.

El presente perfecto			
yo	he hablado	*nosotros(as)*	hemos hablado
tú	has hablado	*vosotros(as)*	habéis hablado
Ud., él, ella	ha hablado	*Uds., ellos(as)*	han hablado

Since the **haber + participle** combination constitutes a unit, the word *no* or any object pronouns must go to the left of *haber.*

¿**Has comido** mucho?	No, **no he comido** mucho.
¿**Ha pedido** la cuenta?	No, él **no** la **ha pedido.**

◆ Actividad 1

Dr. Zeta is examining Daniel by asking him how he has felt recently. Play the part of Dr. Zeta by forming questions with the cues provided.

Modelo: Qué (comer) hoy   *¿Qué has comido hoy, Daniel?*

1. (tener) dolor de cabeza

2. (sentir) dolor de estómago

3. (caminar) en el sol

4. qué (tomar) para el desayuno

5. (estornudar) en estos días

6. (toser) esta semana

◆ **Actividad 2**

Pregunte a un(a) compañero(a) de clase si ha hecho las siguientes cosas.

Modelo: (tener) un examen esta semana

Estudiante 1: ¿Has tenido un examen esta semana?
Estudiante 2: Sí, he tenido un examen en literatura.
(No, no he tenido un examen esta semana.)

1. (hablar) con la directora del colegio hoy
2. (estar) enfermo recientemente
3. (comprar) medicina este mes
4. (ir) al médico este semestre
5. (tener) dolor de cabeza hoy
6. (llamar) a tu mejor amigo(a) esta mañana
7. (servir) de voluntario(a) en un hospital este año
8. (recibir) una carta esta semana

Uso del presente perfecto

The present perfect tense describes an action which has taken place immediately prior to the present and is viewed as continuing to have an impact upon the present. It tells what one has, or has not, done as of the present time.

Jorge **ha tenido** un accidente.	*Jorge **has had** an accident.*
Hemos llegado al hospital.	*We **have arrived** at the hospital.*

◆ **Actividad 3**

Events that have happened in the past may affect one's present physical and emotional state. Use the cues provided to explain why the persons below feel the way they do. Follow the model.

Modelo: Viviana / contento / comprar / un vestido nuevo
*Viviana está contenta **porque** ha comprado un vestido nuevo.*

1. Ana / nervioso / recibir / una invitación a una fiesta importante
2. Ud. / preocupado / perder / un cheque
3. Ramón y Adrián / enfermo / comer / demasiado
4. Ester y yo / contento / nuestros abuelos / llegar hoy
5. Rafael / triste / su equipo / perder / el partido ayer
6. yo / emocionado / mi equipo / ganar / el partido
7. Tabaré / cansado / jugar / tres partidos de fútbol esta semana
8. tú / satisfecho / vender / la bicicleta de Pablo Martín

At the end of a very busy day at the hospital, Dr. Díaz is asking his assistant various questions. You and a partner can play their roles.

Modelo: llegar / el doctor González
   Dr. Díaz: ¿Ha llegado el doctor González?
   Asistente: No, no ha llegado.

1. llamar a los directores del hospital / Ud.

2. toser hoy / el señor Garza

3. tener más dolor de cabeza / Rafael

4. tener fiebre hoy / Anita

5. estornudar esta mañana / el joven Pedro

6. tomarle la temperatura al Sr. Gómez / Ud.

7. tomarle la presión a la señora de Esteban / Ud.

8. comer el almuerzo / Ud.

El participio pasado de verbos como *leer*

When the stems of *-er* and *-ir* verbs end in a strong vowel (a, e, o), the **i** following the strong vowel must have a written accent mark in forming the past participle.

Infinitive	Past participle
leer	leído
caer	caído
creer	creído
oír	oído
reír	reído

◆ Actividad 5

Juan Pablo recalls a recent visit to the doctor. Help him tell his story by supplying the present perfect form of each verb given in parentheses.

Modelo: el doctor (leer) mi historial médico.
   El doctor ha leído mi historial médico.

1. Mis padres (creer) _____ que yo estaba muy enfermo.

2. Yo (leer) _____ las preguntas del cuestionario.

3. Una enfermera bonita me (sonreír) _____ dulcemente.

4. La enfermera (oír) _____ los latidos de mi corazón.

5. Yo me (caer) _____ de la cama de examinación.

6. El doctor no (reírse) _____ mucho.

◆ **Actividad 6**

The new physical education teacher is asking questions about her students'
health backgrounds. Ask the questions she would, using the clues provided.

Modelo: Mario / practicar / deportes antes
Profesora: ¿Ha practicado Mario deportes antes?

1. Tomás / sufrir / del corazón

2. tú / viajar mucho

3. Ana y María / estar / hospitalizadas alguna vez

4. Paco y Patricio / tener / problemas del pulmón

5. Carmen / aumentar / de peso este año

6. Uds. / jugar / al aire libre recientemente

7. Orlando / tomar / alguna medicina hoy

Vocabulario adicional ▲▲▲▲▲▲▲▲▲▲▲▲▲▲▲▲▲▲▲▲▲▲▲▲▲▲▲▲▲▲

¿Puedes adivinar *(guess)* el significado de cada palabra?

Verbo	**Adjetivo**	**Sustantivo**
adorar	adorable	adoración
aparecer	aparente	aparición
explicar	explicable	explicación
imaginar	imaginable	imaginación
recibir	receptivo	recepción
sentir	sensible	sensación
unir	unido	unión

*El Alcázar se encuentra
entre las atracciones
turísticas e históricas
de Segovia.*

SEGOVIA

The city of Segovia, located forty miles north of Madrid, preserves the memory of the Roman domination of Spain. The Romans began occupying Spain in the third century B.C. and initiated a period of peace and development which ended around A.D. 400, with the Visigoths' invasion of the country.

The Romans conquered Segovia in 80 B.C. and realized the need to bring water to the city from a source seven miles away. So they hewed granite blocks from the nearby mountains and built, without mortar, an enormous aqueduct which is 900 yards long, rises as high as 92 feet, and contains 170 arches.

Other notable sites in Segovia include the Alcázar, a fairy-tale castle overlooking the city, and La Granja, a palatial estate modeled after the Versailles in France.

8-2 La farmacia nueva

Diálogo ▲▲▲

Paco: ¿Quieres ir conmigo a la farmacia nueva?

Tito: ¿La han abierto ya?

Paco: Sí, hace dos días. Me han dicho que es grande.

Tito: Voy a ver si tienen la medicina que necesito. El médico me dio la receta hace tres días.

Paco: ¿Para qué es?

Tito: Es que hace una semana *me desmayé*. Me sentí muy *débil* y al fin fui al médico. Me examinó y me tomó la tensión. No encontró nada malo pero me recetó unas pastillas.   I fainted / weak

Paco: ¿Por qué no las has comprado?

Tito: Es que no las he encontrado en ninguna de las farmacias en la ciudad.

Paco: Seguramente aquí las puedes encontrar.

Llegan a la farmacia. Tito va a donde está el farmacéutico y le da la receta.

Tito: ¿Me puede preparar esta receta?

Farmacéutico: Vamos a ver. Ha tenido suerte. Estas pastillas son muy difíciles de encontrar, pero hoy mismo ha llegado una *caja*. En seguida vuelvo . . . Aquí tiene las pastillas. La dosis está en la etiqueta: «una pastilla tres veces al día». Las pastillas pueden causar ciertos *efectos secundarios*. Si tiene problemas, por favor llámenos.   box / side effects

Tito: Gracias, señor.

◆ **Conversación**
1. ¿Cuándo se abrió la farmacia nueva?
2. ¿Qué tiene que comprar Tito?
3. ¿Por qué le dio el médico la receta a Tito?
4. ¿Por qué quería comprar la medicina en la farmacia nueva?
5. ¿A quién le dio la receta?
6. ¿Qué estaba escrito en la etiqueta?
7. ¿Por qué dijo el farmacéutico «Ha tenido suerte»?
8. ¿Lees las etiquetas antes de tomar una medicina?

Vocabulario

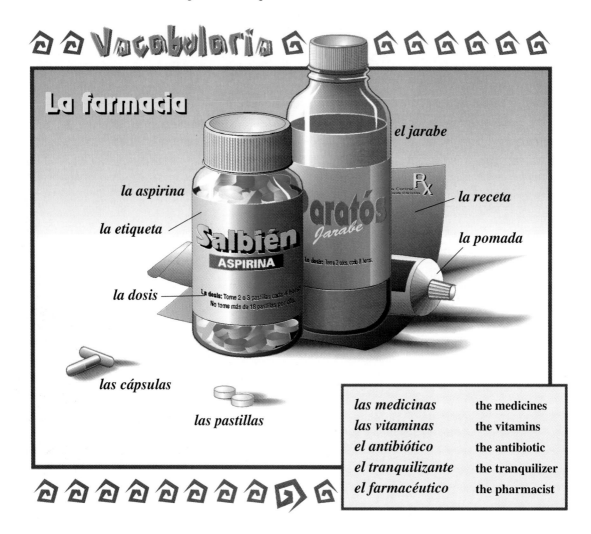

La farmacia

el jarabe

la aspirina

la etiqueta

la receta

la pomada

la dosis

las cápsulas

las pastillas

las medicinas	the medicines
las vitaminas	the vitamins
el antibiótico	the antibiotic
el tranquilizante	the tranquilizer
el farmacéutico	the pharmacist

Gramática ▲▲▲

Los participios pasados irregulares

Some verbs have irregular past participles. The following are some of the most common ones.

abrir	abierto	¿Quién **ha abierto** el frasco de pastillas?
descubrir	descubierto	El doctor **ha descubierto** el problema.
decir	dicho	No me **han dicho** la verdad.
hacer	hecho	**Hemos hecho** una fiesta para los pacientes.
morir	muerto	¡Su perro **ha muerto**!
poner	puesto	Lisa se **ha puesto** pomada en el brazo.
volver	vuelto	Juan no **ha vuelto** del hospital.
escribir	escrito	Nunca **he escrito** una receta.
romper	roto	¿Te **has roto** un brazo alguna vez?
ver	visto	¿**Has visto** la farmacia nueva?

◆ **Actividad 1**

Gustavo has just returned from visiting some friends who have been sick. Tell what happened in each situation. Use the past participle of each verb.

Modelo: Rosamaría: escribir una carta al farmacéutico.
   Rosamaría ha escrito una carta al farmacéutico.

1. Edgardo: ponerse pomada en el pie

2. Omar: decir que no regresa del hospital hasta el jueves

3. la enfermera: hacer la cama del paciente

4. el doctor: escribir una receta para mi amiga Marisa

5. los Moyano: ver la farmacia en la calle Central muchísimo

6. Oscar: romperse un hueso del brazo

7. Ismael: volver a la clínica también

8. el doctor Ruiz: descubrir la solución a la enfermedad de Rolando

◆ **Actividad 2**

Complete each sentence with the correct present perfect form of each verb in parentheses.

Modelo: Mi hermano Miguel (ver) al doctor esta semana.
   Mi hermano Miguel ha visto al doctor esta semana.

1. Nosotros (descubrir) _____ que nuestro amigo está enfermo.

2. Tabaré le (decir) _____ al doctor que tiene dolor de cabeza.

3. Yo (romper) _____ el frasco de medicina.

4. José Manuel le (decir) _____ el problema al farmacéutico.

5. El farmacéutico (escribir) _____ la dosis en la etiqueta.

6. Los directores (ver) _____ los reportajes del departamento.

7. Mi padre se (poner) _____ pomada en la pierna.

8. Pablo (abrir) _____ el frasco de jarabe para la tos.

9. Su madre (volver) _____ a aumentar de peso (*gain weight*).

10. Las dos profesoras (escribir) _____ un artículo para el periódico de farmacología.

Más expresiones de tiempo

Notice how the following expressions of time are used.

ya	*already*	¿Has ido al médico **ya**?
ya no	*no longer*	**Ya no** tengo un resfriado.
		No tengo un resfriado **ya**.
todavía	*still*	¿**Todavía** tienes un resfriado?
todavía . . . no	*not yet*	¿**No** has ido al médico **todavía**?—**Todavía no**.
aún	*still*	¿Tienes un resfriado **aún**?
		El niño está enfermo **aún**.
jamás	*never*	**Jamás** he nadado.
no . . . jamás	*"never ever"*	**No** he nadado **jamás**.

Note: If *jamás* precedes the verb, it is used by itself to mean "never"; however, if *jamás* follows the verb, it has an emphatic connotation and requires a negative word such as *no* preceding the verb.

Todavía and *aún* are interchangeable, and they can occupy more than one place in the sentence.

◆ **Actividad 3**

Ana García asks her students if they have ever done various things. The students answer negatively every time. Play the role of Ana García by asking the questions; then play the students' role by giving the answers.

Modelo: viajar a Canadá

> *Srta. García: ¿Alguna vez has viajado a Canadá?*
> *Estudiante: No, no he viajado a Canadá jamás.*
>> *(No, no he viajado nunca a Canadá.)*

1. escribir una novela

2. decir una mentira

3. ponerse furioso

4. leer un drama de Shakespeare

5. descubrir los secretos de tu hermano(a)

6. volver a la casa después de la medianoche

7. romperse un brazo

8. hacer un viaje en avión

◆ **Actividad 4**

Pretend you are a medical assistant. Answer the questions the doctor is asking you.

Modelo: ¿Has terminado la tarea ya? (afirmativo)

> *Sí, ya la he terminado.*
> ¿Has terminado los informes médicos ya? (negativo)
> *No, no los he terminado todavía.*

1. ¿Ya le has dado el jarabe a Rafael? (afirmativo)

2. ¿Todavía tiene fiebre? (negativo)

3. ¿No le has tomado la temperatura todavía? (afirmativo)

4. ¿Tu padre está enfermo aún? (afirmativo)

5. ¿Aún le duele la cabeza? (negativo)

6. ¿Está abierta la farmacia todavía? (afirmativo)

7. ¿Has visitado otro hospital en esta ciudad? (negativo)

8. ¿Has contestado todas las llamadas ya? (afirmativo)

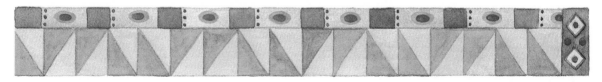

◆ **Actividad 5**

Find a way to express the ideas given using *no . . . todavía, todavía, ya no, ya, aún,* or *jamás.*

1. Has estado enfermo, pero ahora estás bien.

2. Es la primera vez que vas al médico.

3. Es la última vez que vas a jugar al baloncesto.

4. Hacía frío, pero ahora hace calor.

5. Hace cuatro horas que estás estudiando.

6. No has terminado de limpiar y estoy esperando.

7. La semana pasada tenía un resfriado y hoy lo sigo teniendo.

8. ¡No voy a volver a esta farmacia!

◆ **Actividad 6**

Keep a daily journal for a week in which you recount what you have done during each day.

Modelo: *Hoy he escrito una historia para la clase de inglés, y he aprendido diez palabras nuevas en la clase de español.*

◆ **Actividad 7**

Ask three people to tell you about interesting things they have done. You may ask them if they have gone to a foreign country, written a book, played sports, met a famous person, and so on. Then, share the information with your class.

Modelo: *El señor Blanco ha viajado a Australia y ha visto un canguro (kangaroo).*

Refrán ▲▲

According to this proverb, your life will be happier if you deal with problems before they arise.

Más vale prevenir que lamentar.

8-3 ¡Pobre Juan!

Diálogo ▲▲

Paco: ¿Has oído lo que le pasó a Juan?

Tito: No. ¿Qué le pasó?

Paco: Anoche él quería visitar a Amelia. Ya sabes que a él le gusta ir a verla.

Tito: Oh, sí. Todo el mundo sabe eso.

Paco: Antes de salir, Juan llamó por teléfono a la casa de ella. Su hermano Mario contestó; le dijo que Amelia había ido a la farmacia pero que ya regresaba *en cualquier momento.*   at any moment

Tito: Y Juan salió para la casa de Amelia, ¿no?

Paco: Exactamente. Pero nunca llegó.

Tito: ¿Por qué?

Paco: ¿Sabes dónde está el restaurante en la Calle Mayor al lado de la farmacia El Amparo?

Tito: Sí.

Paco: Frente al restaurante Juan tuvo un accidente. Un automóvil que venía en la *dirección opuesta* trató de   opposite direction *adelantar* a otro auto. No lo pudo hacer y chocó con el   to pass auto de Juan.

Tito: ¿Y Juan? ¿Fue mal herido?

Paco: Como él se había abrochado el cinturón de seguridad, no le pasó casi nada. Pero el señor que lo chocó está en el hospital todavía. Su auto destrozó el auto de Juan.

Tito: ¿Lo llevaron a Juan al hospital también?

Paco: Como no. Lo examinaron pero lo dejaron ir a casa. No estuvo ahí ni siquiera una hora.

Tito: ¿Y Amelia?

got tired of

Paco: No la pudo ver. Cuando él la llamó para decirle del accidente, Mario le dijo que ya se había ido con Alfredo porque *se cansó de* esperar a Juan.

Tito: ¡Pobre Juan!

◆ **Conversación**

1. ¿Adónde iba Juan anoche?
2. ¿Qué hizo Juan antes de salir?
3. ¿Quién contestó el teléfono en la casa de Amelia?
4. ¿Dónde estaba ella?
5. ¿Dónde ocurrió el accidente?
6. ¿Cómo sucedió?
7. ¿Quién está aún en el hospital?
8. ¿Por cuánto tiempo estuvo Juan en el hospital?
9. ¿Cómo está el auto de Juan?
10. ¿Cómo piensa Ud. que Juan se sintió cuando supo que Amelia se fue con Alfredo?
11. ¿Por qué no fue herido Juan?
12. ¿Siempre se abrocha Ud. el cinturón de seguridad?

Vocabulario ▲▲▲

El accidente

un choque (*a crash*)
una herida (*a wound*)
peligro (*danger*)
la cruz roja
　(*the red cross*)
la ambulancia
　(*ambulance*)
los primeros auxilios
　(*first aid*)

Gramática ▲▲

El pluscuamperfecto

Amelia se **había ido** cuando
Juan llamó.

*Amelia **had** (already) **left** when
Juan called.*

Juan se **había abrochado** el
cinturón antes del accidente.

*Juan **had buckled** his seatbelt
before the accident.*

The verbs in bold print above are in the pluperfect tense. Like all perfect tenses,
the pluperfect is a compound tense. It is formed as follows:

imperfect form of *haber* + past participle

El pluscuamperfecto			
yo	había llamado	nosotros(as)	habíamos llamado
tú	habías llamado	vosotros(as)	habíais llamado
Ud., él, ella	había llamado	Uds., ellos(as)	habían llamado

The pluperfect tense refers to an action that was completed before a certain
time in the past. It is equivalent to the past perfect tense in English.

◆ **Actividad 1**

Juan had made great plans for a wonderful evening with Amelia. Tell what
he had done before the date was to take place.

Modelo: comprar las entradas
Juan había comprado las entradas.

1. llamar a Amelia

2. pedirle el automóvil a su padre

3. lavar el automóvil

4. ponerse una camisa nueva

5. sacar dinero del banco

6. comprar flores y bonbones de chocolate

◆ Actividad 2

Supply the correct pluperfect form for each verb in parentheses.

Modelo: Martín (pedir) permiso antes de salir con Juana.
      Martín había pedido permiso antes de salir con Juana.

1. Carlos (hacer) las reservaciones antes de llegar al restaurante.
2. Juan (llenar) el tanque de gasolina dos veces antes de llegar.
3. Yo (bañarse) temprano.
4. Martín (afeitarse) y (peinarse) bien antes de salir con Delia.
5. Carmen (lavarse) el pelo.
6. Tú (vestirse).
7. Nosotros (ponerse) nerviosos.
8. Ellos (subir) al automóvil.
9. Ellos (abrocharse) los cinturones.

◆ Actividad 3

Ud. y un amigo iban viajando por la carretera cuando vieron un accidente. Cuando llegó la policía, les preguntó qué habían visto. Complete la historia con la forma correcta de cada verbo en paréntesis.

Mi amigo y yo veníamos por esta carretera cuando vimos que (suceder) _____ un accidente. El auto azul (tratar) _____ de adelantar al auto blanco, pero no vio que venía otro auto en la dirección opuesta. Ya puede ver el resultado. Cuando llegamos nosotros, el que manejaba el auto azul ya (salir) _____ de su auto. Parece que no (abrocharse) _____ el cinturón de seguridad. No sé cómo (poder) _____ salir, porque ahora está inconsciente. Lo bueno es que la unidad de primeros auxilios ya (llegar) _____ . El señor del auto blanco tampoco tenía abrochado el cinturón de seguridad, pero él no está en tan malas condiciones como el otro. Tiene una herida en el brazo y parece que está fracturado. Antes de llegar usted, me dijo que es la segunda vez que le (pasar) _____ un accidente en esta misma carretera. ¡Es un lugar peligroso!

Expresiones afirmativas y negativas

también	*also*	Yo **también** me había puesto el cinturón de seguridad.
tampoco	*not . . . either*	**No** he comprado un radio nuevo **tampoco.**
aun *(without an accent mark)*	*even*	**Aun** Rosa no ha venido esta tarde.
ni siquiera	*not even*	**Ni siquiera** ha venido al hospital a visitarme.
		No ha venido a visitarme en casa **ni siquiera** un día.

Note: *Tampoco* is used in a sentence that agrees with a previous negative statement.

◆ Actividad 4

Margarita's little brother, Manuel, always says he does the same things Margarita does. With another student, play the parts of Margarita and Manuel.

Modelo: escribir para el periódico
  Margarita: Yo escribo para el periódico.
  Manuel: Yo también.

  no escribir para la revista
  Margarita: No escribo para la revista.
  Manuel: Yo tampoco.

1. tocar el piano
2. no conducir el auto de mi padre
3. no cantar muy bien
4. hablar inglés
5. no hablar francés
6. decir siempre la verdad
7. ayudar a mi madre
8. no repetir lo que los otros dicen

Lectura bíblica ▲▲▲▲▲▲▲▲▲▲▲▲▲▲▲▲▲▲▲▲▲▲▲▲▲▲▲▲▲▲▲▲▲▲▲▲▲

Juan 6:15-21

Jesús . . . volvió a retirarse al monte él solo. Al anochecer, descendieron sus discípulos al mar, y entrando en una barca, iban cruzando el mar hacia Capernaum. Estaba ya oscuro, y Jesús no había venido a ellos. Y se levantaba el mar con un gran viento que soplaba. Cuando habían remado como veinticinco o treinta estadios, vieron a Jesús que andaba sobre el mar y se acercaba a la barca; y tuvieron miedo. Mas él les dijo: Yo soy; no temáis. Ellos entonces con gusto le recibieron en la barca, la cual llegó en seguida a la tierra adonde iban.

Escribe las cosas que has visto,
y las que son, y las que han de ser
después de estas.
Apocalipsis 1:19

9-1 Sueños

Diálogo ▲▲

Diana: ¿En qué piensas, Pedro?

some day   **Pedro:** En lo que haré *algún día.*

Diana: ¿De veras? ¿Qué quieres hacer?

Pedro: Quiero ser piloto de un 747—

not even / yet   **Diana:** ¡Piloto! *Ni siquiera* has viajado en avión *todavía.*

Pedro: Viajaré por todo el mundo. Conoceré las grandes ciudades; comeré en los mejores restaurantes de Paris, de Londres, de Atenas y de Tokio—

to pilot   **Diana:** Pero primero tienes que estudiar y aprender a *pilotar* un avión.

Pedro: Visitaré las ruinas de los aztecas en México y de los incas en el Perú; veré las pirámides en Egipto y el Taj Mahal en la India—

dreaming   **Diana:** Pedro, tú no estás pensando, estás *soñando.* Se necesitan más de diez años para llegar a ser piloto de un avión comercial.

Pedro: Iré a Hong Kong y a Australia; a Madrid y a Berlín—

Diana: Pedro, creo que tú nunca llegarás a ser piloto. Lo que tú quieres ser es turista.

◆ Conversación

1. ¿En qué está pensando Pedro?
2. ¿Por qué quiere ser piloto?
3. ¿Tiene experiencia en aviación?
4. ¿Adónde viajará?
5. Según Diana, ¿cuántos años se necesitan para llegar a ser piloto de un avión comercial?
6. ¿Por qué dice Diana que Pedro está soñando?
7. ¿Y tú? ¿Tienes planes para el futuro?

Vocabulario

Las profesiones

el/la abogado(a)	lawyer
el/la administrador(a)	administrator
el/la aeromozo(a) (la azafata)	steward/stewardess
la ama de casa	housekeeper
el/la arquitecto(a)	architect
el/la artista	artist
el/la asistente de vuelo	flight assistant
el/la biólogo(a)	biologist
el/la científico(a)	scientist
el/la contador(a)	accountant
el/la chofer	chauffeur
el/la dentista	dentist
el/la escritor(a)	writer
el/la empresario(a)	entrepreneur
el/la enfermero(a)	nurse
el/la gerente	manager
el/la ingeniero(a)	engineer
el/la juez	judge
el mecánico	mechanic
el/la médico	medical doctor
el/la obrero(a)	worker
el/la oficinista	office worker
el/la pintor(a)	painter
el plomero (el fontanero)	plumber
el/la policía	police officer
el/la secretario(a)	secretary
el/la vendedor(a)	salesman/seller

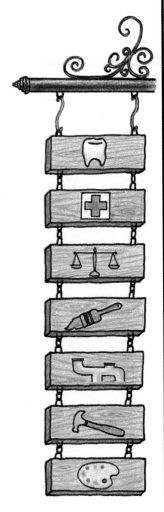

Gramática ▲▲▲

El futuro: las formas regulares

Roberto and Miguel talk about what they will do after they graduate. Notice the verbs in the future tense.

Miguel: ¿Dónde **estudiarás** cuando te gradúes, Roberto?

Roberto: **Estudiaré** en la Universidad de Salamanca.

Miguel: ¿**Viajarás** a Salamanca en tren o en avión?

Roberto: Creo que **iré** en tren.

The future tense in Spanish is a simple tense. As in all simple tenses, a set of endings is added to a stem. In the case of the regular future tense, however, the stem is the complete infinitive. The future endings, given below, are the same for all three verb conjugations.

El futuro		
yo	-é	Estudiaré enfermería en la universidad.
tú	-ás	Estudiarás ingeniería en la universidad.
Ud., él, ella	-á	Aprenderá computación en la universidad.
nosotros(as)	-emos	Aprenderemos muchas cosas en la universidad.
vosotros(as)	-éis	Viviréis en un apartamento en la universidad.
Uds., ellos(as)	-án	Vivirán en los dormitorios de la universidad.

Notice that all the future endings, except for the *nosotros* form, have an accent mark. The endings are the same for -*ar, -er,* and -*ir* verbs.

future tense = infinitive + future endings

When the future action is closely tied to the present, Spanish speakers usually use the expression *ir + a + infinitivo* rather than the future tense. Sometimes even the present tense is used.

Vamos a salir para España mañana.

Salimos para España mañana.

◆ **Actividad 1**

Pedro dice lo que él y sus amigos harán en el verano.

Modelo: Gilberto (estudiar) _____ en España.
   Gilberto estudiará en España.

 1. Tomás (trabajar) _____ en la oficina de su tío.

 2. Patricia (cuidar) _____ a los niños de una vecina.

 3. Yo (visitar) _____ a mis abuelos en Canadá.

 4. Mi familia y yo (ir) _____ en automóvil.

 5. Pedro (tomar) _____ clases de aviación.

 6. Marcos y Ricardo (jugar) _____ al tenis todo el verano.

 7. Tú (tomar) _____ un avión para viajar a España.

 8. Cristina (cumplir) _____ dieciséis años el 2 de julio.

◆ **Actividad 2**

Have you ever thought about how life may be in the future? Use the cues given to make predictions about the future.

Modelo: hombres / viajar / a la luna los fines de semana.
   Los hombres viajarán a la luna los fines de semana.

 1. automóviles / no usar / gasolina

 2. el mundo / estar / en guerra

 3. estudiantes / ir / a la escuela once meses al año

 4. aviones / cruzar / el Atlántico en tres horas

 5. casas / ser / de cristal

 6. todos los automóviles / costar / más de cuarenta mil dólares

 7. todos los jóvenes / ir / a la universidad

 8. jóvenes / hablar / español

◆ **Actividad 3**

Jorge and his family are moving from the country to the city, and Jorge is wondering about their future. What is Jorge saying?

Modelo: ¿Dónde (vivir) _____ nosotros?
  ¿Dónde viviremos nosotros?

1. ¿Dónde (encontrar) _____ trabajo mi padre?

2. ¿Cuánto dinero (ganar) _____ él?

3. ¿Dónde (ir) _____ a la escuela nosotros?

4. ¿A qué iglesia (asistir) _____ nosotros?

5. ¿Cómo (ser) _____ nuestros vecinos?

6. ¿(Conocer) _____ yo a alguien?

7. ¿Me (gustar) _____ los vecinos?

8. ¿Me (llamar) _____ por teléfono mis amigos?

◆ **Actividad 4**

Go back to *Actividad 3* and invent answers to Jorge's questions.

Modelo: ¿Dónde viviremos nosotros? *Vivirán en Buenos Aires.*

El futuro: las formas irregulares

A few verbs have irregular stems in the future, but their endings are regular.

1. The first group forms the irregular future stem by omitting the vowel of the infinitive ending:

haber → habr-	No hay clases hoy, pero **habrá** clases mañana.
poder → podr-	Si practicas mucho, **podrás** jugar mejor.
querer → querr-	No sé si papá **querrá** pagar tanto.
saber → sabr-	Después de leer la próxima página, **sabrás** la respuesta.

2. The second group forms the irregular future stem by replacing the vowel of the infinitive ending with **d:**

poner → pondr-	¿Dónde **pondré** estas flores?
salir → saldr-	¿A qué hora **saldremos** para Nueva York?
tener → tendr-	**Tendrán** que trabajar mucho en el verano.
venir → vendr-	Me dicen que **vendrán** temprano el lunes.

3. The third group of verbs has completely irregular future stems.

decir → dir-	¿Te **dirán** la verdad?
hacer → har-	¿Quién **hará** el mejor modelo de auto en el siglo XXI?

◆ **Actividad 5 ¿Qué pasará?**

Use the correct future form of each verb in parentheses.

1. Si no pongo atención en la clase de español, no _____ cuando es el examen. (saber)

2. Si no sé cuando es el examen, no _____ estudiar para el examen. (poder)

3. Si no estudio para el examen, no _____ el examen. (aprobar)

4. Si no apruebo el examen, _____ una nota baja. (recibir)

5. Si recibo una nota baja, _____ un gran problema en casa. (haber)

◆ **Actividad 6**

¡Preguntas, preguntas, preguntas! No sabemos que pasará de aquí a diez años. Pero podemos imaginar.

Dentro de diez años, ¿dónde estarás? ¿Qué estarás haciendo? ¿Qué profesión tendrás? ¿Estarás casado(a)? Imagina cómo será tu vida. Escribe por lo menos cinco oraciones usando los siguientes verbos: *ser, estar, tener (que), saber, poder, hacer.*

El futuro: para indicar probabilidad

Notice the use of the future tense in these sentences.

¿Qué hora **será?**	*I wonder what time it is.*
Serán las cuatro.	*It's probably four o'clock.*
¿En qué clase **estará** Luis?	*I wonder which class Luis is in.*
Estará en la clase de arte.	*He's probably in art class.*

In Spanish, the future tense has the additional use of expressing probability in the present time. In an interrogative expression, it conveys the idea of *"I wonder"* about a present event.

◆ **Actividad 7**

The Ramos family is expecting a visit from Sara and Viviana, two foreign exchange students. They wonder what these girls will be like.

Modelo: Viviana / tener quince años
   ¿Tendrá Viviana quince años?

1. Sara / ser bonita

2. Viviana y Sara / saber hablar inglés

3. Viviana / tener ojos azules

4. Viviana y Sara / querer ir a nuestra escuela

5. Viviana y Sara / decirnos cómo es su escuela

6. Viviana / saber jugar al fútbol

Por + sustantivo

The preposition *por* followed by a noun is used to express many different ideas. The English equivalent of *por* is not always "for." Note the different ideas expressed by *por.*

- **in exchange for** (*for, in place of*)

    Compré un radio **por** treinta dólares.

    Cambiaré mi bicicleta **por** una motocicleta.

    Cristo murió en la cruz **por** mí.

- **manner or means** (*by*)

    Mandaré el paquete a España **por** correo aéreo.

    Me dieron las noticias **por** teléfono.

- **duration of time** (*for, during, in*)

    Voy a viajar **por** tres semanas.

    Me gusta estudiar **por** la mañana.

- **cause or motive** (*for, because of, on behalf of, for the sake of*)

    ¿Se casó con él **por** amor o **por** dinero?

    ¿A qué hora vienes **por** mí?

    Estoy preocupado **por** ti.

    Rafael hablará al director **por** toda la clase.

    Los padres se sacrifican **por** sus hijos.

- **movement** (*along, through, by, around*)

    El pobre perrito estaba caminando **por** la calle cuando lo vi.

    La carretera Panamericana pasa **por** los países de América Central.

    El cartero pasará **por** nuestra casa a la una.

    Los novios paseaban **por** el parque.

- **other expressions that use** *por:*

    cien **por ciento** (*one hundred percent*)

    sesenta kilómetros **por hora** (*sixty kilometers per hour*)

◆ **Actividad 8**

Use the cues provided in parentheses to answer each question. Use complete sentences.

    Modelo: ¿Por cuánto vende Ud. el diccionario? ($10)
    Lo vendo por diez dólares.

1. ¿Por cuál modo de transporte mandarán Uds. sus cosas a Honduras? (barco)

2. ¿A qué hora del día pasarás tú por tus amigos? (la tarde)

3. ¿Por dónde pasearán Uds.? (el campo)

4. ¿Por quién dio su vida Jesucristo? (todos)

5. ¿Por quién se sacrifica el estudiante? (madre)

6. ¿Por cuánto tiempo estarás de visita en Chile? (tres semanas)

7. ¿Por cuáles países has viajado este año? (España y Francia)

8. ¿Por cuánto compraste los pasajes de avión? ($800)

9. ¿Cómo te mandó los pasajes la agencia de viajes? (correo)

10. ¿Cómo te pusiste en contacto con Carolina? (teléfono)

Poesía ▲▲▲

The following poem by Juan Ramón Jiménez contains eleven verbs in the future tense. List the verbs and then give the infinitive for each.

El viaje definitivo

  . . . Y yo me iré. Y se quedarán los pájaros cantando;
y se quedará mi *huerto,* con su verde árbol,
y con su *pozo* blanco.

  Todas las tardes, el cielo será azul y plácido;
y tocarán, como esta tarde están tocando,
las *campanas* del *campanario.*

  Se morirán aquéllos que me amaron;
y el pueblo se hará nuevo cada año;
y en el *rincón* aquel de mi huerto florido y *encalado,*
mi espíritu *errará,* nostálgico. . .

  Y yo me iré; y estaré solo, sin hogar,
sin árbol verde, sin pozo blanco,
sin cielo azul y plácido. . .
Y se quedarán los pájaros cantando.

orchard or garden
well

bells / bell tower

corner / whitewashed
errar = to roam

Vocabulario adicional ▲▲▲▲▲▲▲▲▲▲▲▲▲▲▲▲▲▲▲▲▲▲▲▲▲▲▲▲▲▲

Dropping the last vowel and adding *-ero* to certain nouns gives the titles of people engaged in activities suggested by those nouns. For example: *carta → cartero* (letter → mailman). Can you determine what each of these people does?

barba	barbero
cocina	cocinero
ganado	ganadero
leche	lechero
marina (*navy*)	marinero
pelota	pelotero
zapato	zapatero

SALAMANCA

Salamanca, a city in the northwestern autonomous community of León, rose to prominence in the thirteenth century when King Alfonso IX founded a university there. The University of Salamanca became one of the leading academic centers in medieval Europe, boasting over 10,000 students. Two of Spain's most prominent poets, Fray Luis de León and San Juan de la Cruz, studied at Salamanca. To this day, the university remains prestigious as an educational institution.

9-2 Una carta al rector

Lectura ▲▲▲

to attend

Pedro escribe una carta a la universidad donde desea *asistir*.

Salamanca, España
1 de junio de 1996

director; registrar

Estimado señor *rector:*
He oído de su programa de aviación y estoy muy interesado. Me
encantaría recibir más información. Quisiera saber cuales son los
requisitos para entrar en la universidad. He estudiado muchas
clases de física y matemáticas a nivel universitario y me interesaría

to take a test / to validate

dar un examen para *convalidar* algunas clases. Agradecería mucho
oír de usted. Sería un placer para mí asistir a su universidad.

Atentamente,

Pedro Rodríguez

Pedro Rodríguez

Vocabulario ▲▲▲

La educación y las materias escolares

a nivel universitario	*on the university level*
la dirección	*principal's office (high school)*
la rectoría	*main office (university)*
especializarse en	*to major in*
matricularse; inscribirse	*to register*
los derechos de matrícula	*fees (registration); tuition*
requisito	*required course*
la beca	*scholarship*

el lenguaje
el español
la gramática
el inglés
el latín
la literatura española

las ciencias
la anatomía
la biología
la física
la química
  (*chemistry*)

los estudios sociales
la ética (*ethics*)
la filosofía (*philosophy*)
la geografía
la historia
la sociología

las matemáticas
el álgebra
la aritmética
el cálculo
la geometría
la lógica matemática
la trigonometría

otras materias
el arte
el drama
la educación física
la psicología
la oratoria (*speech*)

Gramática ▲▲▲▲▲▲▲▲▲▲▲▲▲▲▲▲▲▲▲▲▲▲▲▲▲▲▲▲▲▲▲▲▲▲▲▲▲

El condicional

— ¿Cuándo **enviarías** la carta? ¿hoy o mañana?
— Yo la **enviaría** hoy.
— Ah, sí. ¿Te **gustaría** ir conmigo al correo?

The verbs given above in bold are in the conditional tense. In Spanish, the conditional is a simple tense. It is formed by adding the set of endings below to the future stem.

El condicional			
yo	-ía	*nosotros(as)*	-íamos
tú	-ías	*vosotros(as)*	-íais
Ud., él, ella	-ía	*Uds., ellos(as)*	-ían

Verbs that have an irregular stem in the future tense have the same irregular stem in the conditional.

haber	**habr-**	salir	**saldr-**
poder	**podr-**	tener	**tendr-**
querer	**querr-**	venir	**vendr-**
saber	**sabr-**	decir	**dir-**
poner	**pondr-**		

Note: The conditional of *hay* is *habría*.

In most cases, the Spanish conditional tense is the English equivalent of *would* + verb.

1. It expresses what one would do (or would not do) under certain conditions.

¿Qué **harías** con un caballo en tu casa?	*What would you do with a horse in your house?*

2. It may be used to express probability in the past.

¿Adónde **iría** Marta ayer?	*I wonder where Marta went yesterday.*

3. When used with the verbs *deber* and *poder,* it is used to make polite requests or suggestions.

Deberías ir a la iglesia hoy.	*You should go to church today.*
¿**Podrías** llevar esta carta al correo?	*Could you take this letter to the post office?*

Note:
• If the English *would* means *used to*, Spanish speakers use the imperfect tense.

Él siempre **mandaba** tarjetas de cumpleaños.	*He would (used to) always send birthday cards.*

• If the English *would not* means *refused to,* Spanish speakers usually use the preterite of *querer.*

Marcos **no quiso** venir.	*Marcos would not come. (He did not want to come.)*

◆ **Actividad 1**

Change the following sentences in order to "soften" the following requests or suggestions.

Modelo: Cómprame un refresco, por favor.
   ¿Podrías comprarme un refresco, por favor?

1. Ven conmigo al concierto el viernes.

2. Debes comer afuera.

3. Ayúdame con la tarea en la biblioteca.

4. María debe acompañar a Luis a la iglesia el domingo.

5. Tú debes hacer tu tarea temprano.

6. Ustedes deben obedecer a sus padres.

7. Canta con nosotros el domingo en la noche.

◆ **Actividad 2**

The following students were asked to tell what they would do with one thousand dollars. Report their answers by using the conditional tense.

Modelo: Marta: ir a la Florida.
   Marta iría a la Florida.

1. Roberto: viajar a Los Angeles para visitar a su tío

2. Margarita y Luisa: comprar ropa nueva para ellas y su madre

3. Marcos: dar dinero a todos los misioneros que conoce

4. Carmen : poner el dinero en su cuenta universitaria

5. Pablo y Santiago: juntar su dinero y tomar unas vacaciones

6. Rafael: abrir una cuenta de ahorros en el banco

7. Felipe: comer en el mejor restaurante por un mes entero

8. Y tú, ¿qué harías?

◆ **Actividad 3**

What would be your reaction under the following circumstances?

Alguien te da mil dólares.
1. ¿Qué comprarías?

2. ¿Adónde viajarías?

El equipo de baloncesto de tu escuela gana el campeonato.
3. ¿Qué harían?

4. ¿Qué dirían?

El director de tu colegio anuncia que no hay clases mañana.
5. ¿A qué hora te levantarías?

6. ¿Adónde irías?

El pastor pide las ideas de los jóvenes para las actividades de la iglesia.
7. ¿Qué podrían hacer?

8. ¿Cuánto pagarían?

El profesor de matemáticas escribe un problema difícil en la pizarra.
9. ¿Sabrías resolverlo?

10. ¿A quién podrías pedirle ayuda?

◆ **Actividad 4**

Your class is planning a trip to Spain. There are many places to go and many things to see. Help your classmates by writing about what you would like to do there. (You may add to the list provided.)

Modelo: ir al museo del Prado
        Yo iría al museo del Prado.

1. visitar el palacio de Carlos V

2. pasar mucho tiempo en las plazas famosas

3. sacar fotos del acueducto romano

4. ver la Universidad de Salamanca

5. comer cerca del Alcázar de Segovia

◆ **Actividad 5**

How many questions can you make using the words from each column?
You must use the conditional form of the verb.

A	B	C	D
tú	saber	mentiras	por la tarde
él	acompañarme	a la iglesia	por favor
ella	ir	al concierto	alguna vez
Ud.	venir	conmigo	el sábado
ellos	decirme	la respuesta	siempre
		la verdad	esta noche
		a casa	el domingo

Refrán ▲▲

Have you ever regretted something you said without thinking? For a biblical
parallel to this saying, look up Proverbs 21:23.

En boca cerrada no entran moscas.

9-3 ¿Qué hacemos con el tiempo?

Lectura ▲▲

¿Qué hacemos con el tiempo? ¿Lo aprovechamos o lo malgastamos? Tenemos que comer, dormir y estudiar. ¿Cuánto tiempo pasamos en cada actividad? Sigue leyendo para ver qué parte de tu vida has pasado comiendo, durmiendo, mirando la televisión, asistiendo a la escuela, y participando de otras actividades.

A los 18 años—

Si duermes ocho horas cada noche, habrás dormido 52.596 horas, *o sea, seis años.*

that is

Si tomas dos vasos de leche por día, habrás tomado 822 galones (3.287 litros) de leche.

Si miras dos horas de televisión cada día, habrás mirado la televisión por 13.149 horas, o sea, más de un año y medio.

Si tomas cinco minutos cada día para cepillarte los dientes desde la edad de tres años, habrás pasado más de 456 horas, o sea, más de 19 días *sin parar,* cepillándote los dientes.

nonstop

Si comes dos pedazos de pizza dos veces por semana desde la edad de tres años, habrás comido 416 pizzas de seis pedazos cada una.

¿Cuántos libros habrás leído?

¿Cuántas veces habrás ido a la iglesia?

¿Cuántas veces habrás leído la Biblia entera?

¿Cuánto tiempo habrás pasado con tu familia?

Vocabulario ▲▲

aprovechar	*to take advantage of*
gastar	*to spend*
malgastar	*to waste*

Gramática ▲▲▲

El futuro perfecto

Notice the use of the future perfect in the following sentences.

> Antes del año 2020, yo **habré recibido** mi diploma.
> *Before the year 2020, I will have received my diploma.*

> Dentro de unos seis años, Rosita y Pablo **se habrán casado.**
> *Within about six years, Rosita and Pablo will have gotten married.*

> Dentro de dos años, los González **se habrán ido** a Chile.
> *Within two years, the González family will have gone to Chile.*

Like other perfect tenses, the future perfect tense is a compound tense and is formed as follows:

future of *haber* + past participle

El futuro perfecto			
yo	habré recibido	nosotros(as)	habremos recibido
tú	habrás recibido	vosotros(as)	habréis recibido
Ud., él, ella	habrá recibido	Uds., ellos(as)	habrán recibido

The future perfect tense tells *what will have happened* prior to some time in the future.

◆ Actividad 1

Before the school year is over, the students in Miss Martínez's class will have done many activities. What are those activities?

Modelo: todos los estudiantes / aprender cinco canciones en español
Todos los estudiantes habrán aprendido cinco canciones en español.

1. las chicas / preparar una fiesta para los chicos

2. Carmen / hablar a la clase acerca de la vida en América Central

3. Tomás y Francisco / pasar un fin de semana en un hogar mexicano

4. los chicos / escribir cartas a la embajada de Panamá

5. María y yo / visitar una iglesia hispana

6. la clase entera / comer en un restaurante mexicano

7. la Srta. Martínez / cocinar comida típica de Colombia

8. una señora dominicana / enseñar(nos) a preparar el postre flan

9. Margarita y Pepe / vestir(se) de trajes típicos

10. nosotros / aprender mucho acerca de la cultura hispana

◆ Actividad 2

Set a deadline for doing the following things, and form sentences using the future perfect. You may also find the following prepositions useful: *antes de, después de, dentro de.* Follow the model.

Modelo: tú / decidir a qué universidad quieres asistir
Antes de graduarme, yo habré decidido a qué universidad quiero asistir.

1. tú / ahorrar mil dólares

2. tú / casar(se)

3. tu mejor amigo / graduar(se) de la universidad

4. tú y tu hermano / ir de vacaciones

5. tu equipo de fútbol / ganar el campeonato

6. el presidente de tu clase / llegar a ser abogado

7. el pastor de tu iglesia / jubilar(se) (*to retire*)

8. el capitán de tu equipo de béisbol / jugar en las grandes ligas

El futuro perfecto: para indicar probabilidad

In Spanish the future perfect tense is also used to express probability or to make a guess about a recently completed past event. In a statement it expresses probability.

> Mi hermano no está aquí; **habrá ido** al gimnasio.
> *My brother isn't here; he has probably gone to the gym.*

In the interrogative form it conveys the idea of "I wonder."

> **¿Habrá ganado** nuestro equipo de baloncesto esta tarde?
> *I wonder if our basketball team has won this afternoon.*

◆ Actividad 3

Mónica is asking some questions about people in her school, and María is trying to answer her. Form a question and answer for each situation using the future perfect tense.

Modelo: cuándo conocer Roberto a Diana / este año
> Mónica: *¿Cuándo habrá conocido Roberto a Diana?*
> María: *La habrá conocido este año.*

1. dónde comprar Rosalina su nuevo reloj / en la relojería

2. cuánto costar el reloj / por lo menos $40

3. qué hacer Sarita con el pelo / cortarlo su hermana

4. dónde aprender Margarita a jugar al ténis / tomar clases

5. quién comprarle a Julia el nuevo suéter / comprárselo Marcos

6. quién invitar a Alicia al banquete / invitarle Rodrigo

7. con quién ir Ofelia / ir con Daniel

◆ Actividad 4

Ricardo is at his house waiting for his friends. They were supposed to come to swim in the pool, but they have not arrived yet. He is thinking about things that could have happened. Construct the questions he is thinking.

Modelo: Tomás / ir a jugar al fútbol
> *¿Habrá ido Tomás a jugar al fútbol?*

1. Rafael / ir a la casa de su hermana

2. Jaime y Pedro / decidir ensayar su dúo de trompeta

3. Fernando y Luis / llegar tarde de su viaje

4. Daniel / quedarse dormido

5. Felipe y Mateo / tener que trabajar en la gasolinera esta tarde

6. Rolando / enfermarse después de comer tanta pizza anoche

7. José y Marcos / olvidarse (*to forget*)

La preposición *para*

Notice the use of the preposition *para* in the following sentences.

Compré un reloj **para** mi hermana.

Mi primo trabaja **para** una compañía de computadoras.

Los misioneros salen mañana **para** Lima, Perú.

Estoy ahorrando dinero **para** comprarme un carro.

The preposition *para* may be followed by a noun or an infinitive and usually indicates a purpose or destination. It is often equivalent to the English preposition *for* and is used in questions to ask *for what? (¿para qué?)*.

The purpose or destination indicated by the use of the proposition *para* may be—

- **a person**

  El reloj es **para Sarita.**

- **an object or thing**

  Esta lámpara es **para mi cuarto.**

  Me compré un traje nuevo **para la fiesta.**

- **a place**

  A las diez salgo **para el trabajo.**

- **a point in time**

  Estoy haciendo planes **para el verano.**

- **an action** (infinitive)

  Tengo que estudiar **para aprender** español.

  Voy al restaurante **para comer** una hamburguesa.

When *para* is followed by an infinitive, it may be translated *to* or *in order to.*

◆ **Actividad 5**

What are some of your plans and dreams? Complete the following sentences giving a purpose for each wish. Follow the example in the model.

Modelo: Me gustaría vivir en México para . . . *conocer la civilización de los aztecas; . . . testificar a los mexicanos; . . . ir a Acapulco . . .*

1. Me gustaría tener cien dólares para . . .

2. Me gustaría visitar Granada para . . .

3. Me gustaría conocer al presidente para . . .

4. Me gustaría asistir a la universidad para . . .

5. Me gustaría trabajar en una oficina para . . .

6. Me gustaría hablar mejor el español para . . .

7. Me gustaría ser médico para . . .

◆ **Actividad 6**

Rosa's mother is cleaning her daughter's room and wants to throw things away. Rosa has a reason for keeping each thing. What are her reasons?

Modelo: el diccionario viejo / clase de español
     El diccionario viejo es para la clase de español.

1. la silla rota / Tomás

2. las revistas / mi amiga Carmencita

3. las cartas viejas / leerlas cuando sea mayor

4. las flores desecadas / recordar mi primer banquete de San Valentín

5. las botellas vacías / una colección

6. los animales de peluche / poner en mi cama

7. la caja / mis lápices

8. los zapatos viejos / jugar en el barro (*mud*)

Write as many sentences as you can in five minutes using a word from each column. Use the preposition *para* in each sentence.

A	B	C	D
yo	tener	un examen	una cámara
tú	comprar	unas galletas	el cumpleaños
él	hacer	la guitarra	Rosana
ella	necesitar	la gramática	la fiesta
Ud.	tocar	un vestido	Barcelona
nosotros	estudiar	el cuaderno	el profesor
Uds.	leer	unas flores	el miércoles
ellos	traer	un par de zapatos	por las tardes

Lectura bíblica ▲▲▲▲▲▲▲▲▲▲▲▲▲▲▲▲▲▲▲▲▲▲▲▲▲▲▲▲▲▲▲▲▲▲▲▲▲

I Corintios 13:4-10

El amor es sufrido, es benigno; el amor no tiene envidia, el amor no es jactancioso, no se envanece; no hace nada indebido, no busca lo suyo, no se irrita, no guarda rencor; no se goza de la injusticia, mas se goza de la verdad. Todo lo sufre, todo lo cree, todo lo espera, todo lo soporta. El amor nunca deja de ser; pero las profecías se acabarán, y cesarán las lenguas, y la ciencia acabará. Porque en parte conocemos, y en parte profetizamos; mas cuando venga lo perfecto, entonces lo que es en parte se acabará.

Jesús les dijo: Mi comida es que haga
la voluntad del que me envió, y que
acabe su obra.   Juan 4:34

10-1 Una receta para flan

Lectura ▲▲▲

Flan is the most popular dessert in Hispanic countries. It consists of a custard topped with a caramel syrup. You may want to try the following recipe at home.

Los ingredientes

6 huevos	1/2 cucharadita de sal
3/4 taza de azúcar	1/2 cucharadita de vainilla
3 tazas de leche	

(Para el caramelo:)

3/4 taza de azúcar	2 cucharaditas de agua

over moderate heat

Ponga 3/4 taza de azúcar y 2 cucharaditas de agua en un pequeño sartén *a fuego moderado.* Mueva el sartén al derretir el azúcar para que el caramelo quede **even / melted / withdraw it** *uniforme.* Cuando el azúcar esté *derretido* y sea de color marrón claro, *retírelo* **mold / mixture** del fuego y viértalo en el *molde* del flan, antes de añadir la *mezcla.*

yolks / whites

Bata los huevos lo suficientemente para mezclar las *yemas* y las *claras.* Agregue los demás ingredientes. Mezcle bien y vierta en el molde acara- **shallow container** melado. Coloque el molde dentro de un *recipiente llano* con agua caliente. **enfriar = to cool** Póngalo en el horno a 350° F por una hora. Deje que el flan se *enfríe* y después **refrigerator / upside down** póngalo en la *nevera* por varias horas. Antes de servirlo, viértalo *boca abajo* en un plato. El caramelo quedará por encima.

Vocabulario ▲▲

Los ingredientes

el aceite (*oil*)   el huevo (*egg*)

el azúcar (*sugar*)   la leche (*milk*)

la harina (*flour*)   la levadura en polvo (*baking powder*)

Las fracciones y las medidas

1/2	medio(a)	2/3	dos tercios	cucharada (*tablespoon*)
1/3	un tercio	3/4	tres cuartos	cucharadita (*teaspoon*)
1/4	un cuarto	1/8	un octavo	taza (*cup*)

Verbos relacionados con la cocina

agregar	*to add*	derretir (e→i)	*to melt*
batir	*to beat*	hornear	*to bake*
cernir (e→ie)	*to sift*	medir (e→i)	*to measure*
cocinar	*to cook; to bake*	mezclar	*to mix*
colocar	*to place*	retirar	*to withdraw*
(boca abajo)	(*upside down*)	verter (e→ie)	*to pour*

Gramática ▲▲

El imperativo: las formas afirmativas de *Ud.* y *Uds.*

Compare the verb forms in the following sentences.

¿Compro el libro?	—Sí, **compre** Ud. el libro.
¿Compramos el libro?	—Sí, **compren** Uds. el libro.
¿Cuánto escribo?	—**Escriba** dos párrafos.
¿Cuánto escribimos?	—**Escriban** dos párrafos.

Most *Ud.* (formal) and *Uds.* commands are based on the *yo* form of the present indicative. Drop the *-o* and replace it with the following endings:

	Ud.	*Uds.*
-ar verbs:	**-e**	**-en**
hablar → hablo → habl-	habl**e**	habl**en**
-er and -ir verbs:	**-a**	**-an**
comer → como → com-	com**a**	com**an**
volver → vuelvo → vuelv-	vuelv**a**	vuelv**an**
venir → vengo → veng-	veng**a**	veng**an**

Verbs that have stem changes in the indicative present tense also have stem changes in their imperative forms. Notice the verb *volver* above.

Verbs that end in *-car, -gar,* and *-zar* have a spelling change in the imperative to preserve the sound of the last consonant of the stem:

buscar	**c→qu**	¡**Busque** en la cocina!
jugar	**g→gu**	¡**Jueguen** en el patio, no en la sala!
comenzar	**z→c**	¡Señor, **comience** ahora!

◆ **Actividad 1**

You are the office manager in Mr. Rivera's business firm. Answer the questions below with instructions containing *Ud.* or *Uds.* commands and the elements provided.

Modelo: ¿Está en su oficina el Sr. Marín? (no . . . volver en una hora)
    No, no está ahora. Vuelva Ud. en una hora.

1. ¿Cómo se llega a la oficina 6B? (doblar a la derecha)

2. ¿Dónde ponemos estos informes? (dejar los informes en mi escritorio)

3. ¿Quién puede explicarnos estos documentos? (llamar al Sr. Rivera)

4. ¿Qué hago con estos bocadillos? (llevar los bocadillos al Sr. Ramos)

5. ¿Qué debemos hacer con estos formularios? (completar los formularios ahora, por favor)

6. ¿Contesto el teléfono? (sí, . . . contestar el teléfono)

7. ¿Podemos ver al Sr. Rivera? (esperar un momento)

8. ¿Sabe Ud. dónde está el diccionario? (buscar el diccionario en el estante [*bookshelf*])

◆ **Actividad 2**

You are the guest chef on a television cooking show called *La Cocina Rica.* Describe your favorite meal and tell your viewers how to prepare it. Remember to use the imperative.

El imperativo: las formas irregulares de *Ud. y Uds.*

A few verbs are irregular in the *Ud.* and *Uds.* imperative forms. All are verbs that do not end in *-o* in the first person present indicative.

Infinitive	Present	Command Stem	Command Form
dar	doy	d-	¡**Dé** las gracias por la comida!
estar	estoy	est-	¡**Esté** atento en la clase!
ser	soy	se-	¡**Sea** bueno conmigo!
saber	sé	sep-	¡**Sepan** Uds. el verso mañana!
ir	voy	vay-	¡**Vayan** a la iglesia con Pedro!

◆ **Actividad 3**

Play the role of a business owner by giving instructions to the list of employees below. Use the cues provided along with an *Ud.* or *Uds.* affirmative command.

Modelo: Señor Azuela: comprar más papel para las computadoras
      Señor Azuela, compre más papel para las computadoras.

1. Señor Domingo: dar un informe sobre la distribución de aquel producto

2. Señorita Olivero: ir a la biblioteca para buscar más información

3. Leo y David: estar aquí a tiempo mañana

4. Manolo y Ramonita: ser diligentes en sus responsabilidades

5. Señor Gallegos: ser bueno con el representante del gobierno

6. Señora Blanco: saber de memoria los números telefónicos

7. Lucinda y Marianela: estar presentes para la junta (*meeting*) de las secretarias

8. Francisco y Lorenzo: ir a comer a la una

El imperativo: la forma *tú* afirmativa

Notice the verb forms in the following commands.

¡Miguelito, **toma** la leche!

¡**Come** los vegetales!

Escribe tu nombre en la línea, Ester.

Rafael, **cierra** la puerta, por favor.

The affirmative *tú* imperative form is used to give a command, suggestion, or recommendation to a person you normally address with the *tú* verb form (a close friend, a family member, or someone you address by first name). Thus, this imperative form is also called the familiar command form. For most verbs, this form is the same as the *él* form of the present tense.

The endings for most familiar affirmative commands are as follows:

-ar verbs:	**-a**
-er verbs:	**-e**
-ir verbs:	**-e**

Verbs that have a stem change in the present tense, have the same change in the imperative form: *volver → **vuelve**; recordar → **recuerda**.*

◆ **Actividad 4**

Ana's grandmother is teaching her how to make the family's favorite cake. Play the role of the grandmother as she reads the instructions to Ana.

Modelo: echar una taza de margarina en el recipiente
Echa una taza de margarina en el recipiente.

1. añadir tres tazas de azúcar poco a poco

2. batir bien el azúcar y la margarina

3. añadir cinco huevos, uno a la vez, y batir bien después de cada adición

4. cernir tres tazas de harina con una cucharadita de levadura en polvo y media cucharadita de sal

5. medir una taza de leche

6. añadir la harina poco a poco alternando con la leche

7. mezclar después de cada adición

8. finalmente, echar una cucharada de vainilla y mezclar todo bien

9. vertir la mezcla en un molde bien engrasado

10. cocinar el pastel a 350° F por una hora y quince minutos

◆ Actividad 5

You have been looking after your neighbor's children all afternoon. Before their parents come home, the house needs to be restored to order. What are you going to ask the children to do?

Modelo: María: lavar los platos
   María, lava los platos.

1. Ana: ayudar a María
2. Pedro: limpiar la mesa
3. Rosa: llevar el gato al patio
4. Pedro: recoger los juguetes (*toys*)
5. María: apagar las luces
6. Rosa: dejar de llorar

El imperativo: la forma *tú* irregular

A few verbs are irregular in the affirmative familiar (*tú*) command form.

decir	**di**	¡**Di** lo que vas a hacer!
hacer	**haz**	¡**Haz** tu trabajo!
poner	**pon**	¡**Pon** el flan en el horno!
salir	**sal**	¡**Sal** ahora mismo!
tener	**ten**	¡**Ten** paciencia!
venir	**ven**	¡**Ven** a mi casa!
ir	**ve**	¡**Ve** a la farmacia!
ser	**sé**	¡**Sé** fiel al Señor!

◆ Actividad 6

El pastor les da consejos a los jóvenes. ¿Qué les dice?

Modelo: Juan: hacer el trabajo lo mejor posible
   Juan, haz el trabajo lo mejor posible.

1. Felipe: venir a la iglesia el domingo
2. Samuel: ir a tu padre y hablar con él
3. Rosana: tener paciencia con Roberto
4. Emanuel: ser un ejemplo a los demás
5. Mariana: poner tu Biblia en la mesa
6. Tomasina: hacer tus tareas temprano
7. Pablo: decir la verdad a tu padre
8. Bárbara: salir de tu casa antes de las ocho

◆ **Actividad 7**

The young people at school are very active. The principal always has something for them to do. What are the things he tells them? Put the sentences in the imperative form and join them with a conjunction.

Modelo: Luis: ir al juego esta noche / regresar temprano
Luis, ve al juego esta noche, pero regresa temprano.

1. Mario: salir con los jóvenes mañana / tener cuidado con el auto de tu padre
2. Rafael: venir a mi casa a las siete / llegar a tiempo
3. Felipe: invitar a tus amigos al programa / ser cortés
4. Sergio: traer a tus abuelos al concierto / ponerse el traje negro
5. Juan: ir al trabajo / ser fiel al Señor
6. Marcos: jugar con el equipo de baloncesto / tener cuidado
7. Fernando: pedir permiso a tus padres / ser obediente
8. Paquito: hacer planes de antemano (*in advance*) / tener paciencia

To form the *vosotros* command form, drop the *r* of the infinitive, and add *d:* hablar→hablad; comer→comed; decir → decid. This form is used extensively in the Bible.

Lectura bíblica ▲▲▲▲▲▲▲▲▲▲▲▲▲▲▲▲▲▲▲▲▲▲▲▲▲▲▲▲▲▲▲▲▲▲▲▲▲▲▲

I Tesalonicenses 5:15-24

Mirad que ninguno pague a otro mal por mal; antes seguid siempre lo bueno unos para con otros, y para con todos. Estad siempre gozosos. Orad sin cesar. Dad gracias en todo, porque esta es la voluntad de Dios para con vosotros en Cristo Jesús. No apaguéis al Espíritu. No menospreciéis las profecías. Examinadlo todo; retened lo bueno. Absteneos de toda especie de mal. Y el mismo Dios de paz os santifique por completo; y todo vuestro ser, espíritu, alma y cuerpo, sea guardado irreprensible para la venida de nuestro Señor Jesucristo. Fiel es el que os llama, el cual también lo hará.

CÓRDOBA

CÓRDOBA AND GRANADA

The cities of Córdoba and Granada strikingly illustrate the influence of the Moors in the history of Spain. The Moors, Arabs from North Africa, invaded Spain in A.D. 711. For eight centuries they dominated the country, spreading their Moslem beliefs and enriching Spain's culture, commerce, agriculture, learning, and architecture.

The Moors established their most powerful centers in the southern cities. Córdoba, one of those cities, was the capital of the Moorish Umayyad dynasty. Jewish, Moslem, and Christian scholars gathered there to study languages, law, mathematics, philosophy, music, and medicine. The city remains famous for the Mezquita, a mosque—later turned into a cathedral— with over 1,000 granite, onyx, marble, and jasper pillars.

Granada was the last Arabic stronghold in Spain. It fell to the Spaniards in 1492 as the result of a siege commissioned by the Catholic monarchs Ferdinand and Isabella. Granada's most famous site is the Alhambra, a palace and fortress covering 35 acres and surrounded by 23 red brick towers. The Alhambra's arches and fountains provide an exceptional example of Moorish architecture.

10-2 Las direcciones

Diálogo ▲▲

David necesita unos materiales especiales para un proyecto de arte. Su profesor le ha mandado a una ferretería en el centro de la ciudad. David se baja del autobús en la estación de la Calle Cervantes y la Avenida Borges y decide pedir direcciones.

David: Permiso, señor, estoy buscando una ferretería cerca de aquí. ¿Podría indicarme cómo encontrarla?

dead-end street

Señor: Pues no estoy seguro, pero sí le diré que no siga por esta calle. Esta es una *calle sin salida.* Buenas tardes.

Pobre David no ha recibido mucha ayuda. Él llega a una verdulería y le pregunta a una señora que ve en la esquina.

David: Señora, ¿me podría decir cómo llegar a la ferretería, por favor?

Señora: ¿Cómo dice?

David: Que si sabe Ud. dónde está la ferretería.

traffic signal

Señora: Ah, sí. Siga derecho por la Calle Lope de Vega hasta llegar al segundo *semáforo.* Doble a la izquierda en la Avenida Darío y allí está una frutería en la esquina.

David llega a la frutería y por fin encuentra a un policía.

David: Con permiso, señor, estoy buscando la ferretería. ¿Sabría usted decirme dónde está?

Policia: Sí, cómo no. Doble a la izquierda en la Calle Jiménez y camine una cuadra hasta la Avenida Borges. Allí en la esquina está la ferretería.

David: Gracias, señor. Pase buenas tardes.

◎◎◎◎◎ Vocabulario ◎◎◎◎◎

Hacia allá

caminar dos cuadras
to walk two blocks

cruzar la calle
to cross the street

doblar (a la izquierda, a la derecha)
to turn (to the left, to the right)

ir en dirección contraria
to go in the opposite direction

seguir derecho (de frente)
to go straight ahead

una milla es igual a 1,6 kilómetros
one mile is equal to 1.6 kilometers

AVENIDA BORGES

CALLE LOPE DE VEGA

AVENIDA RUBÉN DARÍO

CALLE CERVANTES

CALLE JIMÉNEZ

AVENIDA OCTAVIO PAZ

A la carnicería	**F** la frutería	**L** la panadería
B la cerrajería	**G** la heladería	**M** la pastelería
C la charcutería	**H** la joyería	**N** la pescadería
D la estación de autobús	**I** la juguetería	**O** la relojería
	J la lechería	**P** la verdulería
E la ferretería	**K** la librería	**Q** la zapatería

Las direcciones

Gramática ▲▲▲

El imperativo: las formas negativas de Ud. y *Uds.*

The negative commands for *Ud.* and *Uds.* just require *no* before the command form.

¡**No cante** tan fuerte!　　　　　¡**No insistan** en salir ahora!

¡**No haga** eso!　　　　　　　　¡**No vayan** lejos!

◆ **Actividad 1**

The students in the Spanish class wrote some rules for the classroom, but they left the verbs in the infinitive. Please write the imperative in the *Uds.* form.

> Modelo: no llegar tarde
> *No lleguen tarde.*

1. no tirar papeles en el piso

2. no masticar chicle (*to chew gum*)

3. no poner los pies en los pupitres

4. no dejar abierta la puerta

5. no escribir en las paredes

6. no interrumpir cuando otra persona habla

7. no hablar inglés en la clase

8. no maltratar (*mistreat*) los libros

El imperativo: las formas negativas de *tú*

To form the negative *tú* commands, begin with the stem of the *yo* form of the present tense and add *-es* to the *-ar* verbs and *-as* to the *-er* and *-ir* verbs. Notice the examples below.

Infinitive	*Yo* form	Command stem	Negative tú command
habl**ar**	no habl**o**	habl-	¡**No hables** con chicle en la boca!
beb**er**	no beb**o**	beb-	¡**No bebas** tantas sodas!
ven**ir**	no veng**o**	veng-	¡**No vengas** tarde a clase!

The negative *tú* commands for the following verbs use the same irregular stem as the *Ud.* and *Uds.* commands.

Infinitive	*Yo* form	Command stem	Negative *tú* command
dar	doy	d-	¡No me **des** tanto helado!
estar	estoy	est-	¡No **estés** triste!
ser	soy	se-	¡No **seas** cruel!
saber	sé	sep-	¡No **sepas** tanto, tonto!
ir	voy	vay-	¡No **vayas** a la iglesia sin Pedro!

◆ **Actividad 2**

Luisa is looking after her neighbor's mischievous daughter. She is becoming impatient with the girl. Play the role of Luisa.

Modelo: no tocar la planta
¡No toques la planta!

1. no jugar en la cocina

2. no gritar (*yell*)

3. no comer tantos dulces

4. no salir al patio

5. no ir a la casa del vecino

6. no entrar en el dormitorio de su hermano

7. no poner los pies en el sofá

8. no beber más refrescos

9. no correr en la casa

El imperativo: la posición de los pronombres

Objective and reflexive pronouns are attached to the end of an affirmative command.

¿Invito a María a la fiesta?	¡Sí, invíta**la**!
¿Invito a Pablo y Rafael?	¡Sí, invíta**los**!
¿Le escribo al presidente?	¡Sí, escríbe**le**!
¿Te doy el libro?	¡Sí, dá**melo**!
¿Me levanto temprano?	¡Sí, levánta**te** temprano!

When the pronoun is attached to the affirmative command, an accent mark is usually needed over the strong vowel of the imperative verb in order to keep the stress on the original syllable. If the command form has only two syllables, the accent mark is not needed.

<blockquote>

¡**Dame** el libro, por favor!

but ¡**Dámelo,** por favor!

</blockquote>

In negative commands, objective and reflexive pronouns precede the verb.

¿Me quedo hasta las nueve?	¡No, no **te** quedes!
¿Te compro una soda?	¡No, no **me la** compres!
¿Le explico el problema?	¡No, no **me lo** explique Ud.!
¿Les leemos el poema?	¡No, no **nos lo** lean Uds.!

◆ **Actividad 3**

You have a house guest who is making many suggestions about things she would like to do while visiting you. Respond to your friend's suggestions in the form of either an affirmative or a negative *tú* command. Do this exercise with a partner and take turns making suggestions and giving commands.

Modelo: llamar por teléfono a Rosita

> *Visitante: Quiero llamar por teléfono a Rosita.*
> *Anfitrión(a) (host): Está bien, llámala. (No, por favor, no la llames.)*

1. leer el periódico ahora

2. invitar a Carlos para cenar

3. escribir una carta a mi amiga

4. decirte el versículo de memoria

5. quedarme en tu casa hasta mañana

6. comerme el dulce de chocolate

7. abrir la ventana

8. prender el televisor

9. tocar el piano

10. apagar el aire acondicionado

Rafael does not like making decisions. He asks his brother Roberto before doing anything. Pretend you are Roberto and answer Rafael according to the situation.

Modelo: ¿Me compro el suéter azul?

Sí, cómpratelo. (No, no te lo compres.)

1. ¿Vendo mi cámara? (sí)

2. ¿Compro las entradas al partido de fútbol? (sí)

3. ¿Hago las tareas antes de la cena? (no)

4. ¿Llamo a Cristina? (no)

5. ¿Invito a Rosita al concierto? (sí)

6. ¿Lavo el auto esta tarde? (no)

7. ¿Me pongo la camisa blanca hoy? (sí)

8. ¿Le escribo al gobernador una carta? (no)

9. ¿Ayudo a Isabel a lavar los platos? (sí)

10. ¿Le pido el auto a papá? (no)

Refrán ▲▲

Success in any area of life never comes easily. It demands the ingredient this proverb emphasizes.

La práctica hace al maestro.

10-3 Las especialidades

Diálogo ▲▲▲

Elena y Margarita, dos estudiantes latinoamericanas, acaban de llegar a España para estudiar algunos cursos de verano. Mientras leen el periódico, encuentran **an ad** *un anuncio* muy interesante.

«**Restaurante La Españolita**
Descubra la gastronomía española: más de 50
especialidades de todas las regiones de España»

Elena y Margarita piden direcciones para el restaurante y descubren que está a dos cuadras del apartamento en donde viven.

Elena: ¡Qué bien! Si vamos un par de veces cada semana, po-
to try; to have a taste dremos *probar* muchos platos diferentes.

Margarita: Sugiero que no vayamos más de una vez por semana.
Tenemos que ahorrar nuestro dinero.

Elena: Está bien. Vamos a ver cómo es el restaurante.

Margarita: Sugiero que leamos el anuncio primero. Veamos las
comidas que anuncian:

Paella valenciana
Cocido madrileño
Caldo gallego
Fabada asturiana
Gazpacho manchego
Gazpacho andaluz

the owners **Elena:** ¡Oye! Hagámonos amigas de *los dueños* y así podremos
about preguntar *sobre* cada plato.

Margarita: No sueñes tanto, Elena. Sugiero que hablemos con uno de los camareros. *Quizás* nos deje leer el menú sin cobrarnos.

perhaps

Elena: ¡Qué graciosa! ¡Comamos allí mañana!

Margarita: No. Sugiero que comamos allí hoy.

◆ Conversación

1. ¿Por qué están Elena y Margarita en España?
2. ¿Está cerca del apartamento el restaurante?
3. ¿Por qué quiere Elena conocer a los dueños?
4. ¿Qué plato te gustaría probar?

Vocabulario ▲▲▲▲▲▲▲▲▲▲▲▲▲▲▲▲▲▲▲▲▲▲▲▲▲▲▲▲▲▲▲▲▲▲▲▲▲▲

Las especialidades culinarias

The following list of food specialties describes popular dishes for each region listed.

España

Paella valenciana: A rice dish made with a variety of seafood or meats (chicken, rabbit, or turkey). It is cooked and served in a round shallow pan called a *paellera*. Originated in the region of Valencia.

Conejo frito con tomate: Fried rabbit in a tomato sauce. Usually served with *tortilla española* (potato omelet) and crusty European bread.

Gazpacho andaluz: A cold vegetable soup. Originated in the region of Andalucía.

Pollo al ajillo: Chunks of chicken fried in olive oil with a whole head of garlic.

México

Chilaquiles: A casserole-type dish made with fried corn tortillas and a sauce consisting of either green or red tomatoes, peppers, sour cream, and cheese.

Mole: A savory sauce made with dark chili peppers, spices, and a hint of chocolate. Served over chicken, turkey, or pork.

Enchiladas: Rolled-up tortillas filled with seasoned chicken or shredded beef and topped with a hot chili sauce.

El Caribe

Plátano (plantain): A special type of cooking banana that may be used green or ripe. Plantains are a popular side dish in the tropical countries and the foundation for many Puerto Rican dishes. Cooking methods vary from deep-frying to baking.

Arroz con pollo: A rice and chicken dish seasoned with tomatoes, onions, garlic, peppers, and fresh herbs. Usually served with seasoned red beans.

Lechón asado: A marinated pig, barbecued on a spit.

Arroz blanco con frijoles negros: White rice and seasoned black beans.

Nicaragua

Nacatamales: A white cornmeal mixture filled with seasoned pork, potatoes, and other fillings, wrapped tightly in a plantain leaf and steamed.

Carne Asada: Marinated beef steak grilled over a charcoal fire. Usually served with rice and beans (called *gallo pinto*), fried plantains, and vinegar slaw.

Tres leches: A rich dessert consisting of a white spongy cake saturated with a mixture of sweet milks and sour cream.

Colombia

Arepa: A thin, flat cake made with either flour or cornmeal and then cooked on a griddle or deep fried.

Papas chorreadas: Boiled potatoes sliced in a sauce consisting of tomatoes, onions, cheese, and cream.

Viuda de pescado: Steamed seasoned fish served with vegetables, potatoes, and yuca.

Argentina / Uruguay

Churrasco: Tenderloin steak usually topped with a spicy garnish called *chimichurri.*

Asado: Seasoned beef or lamb grilled slowly over an open wood fire.

Guiso: A beef stew made with noodles or rice and whole vegetables, such as potatoes, sweet potatoes, carrots, and onions. Prepared in a tomato sauce with green and red peppers, garlic, and hot spices.

Mate: A tealike beverage made from the dried leaves of the *yerba mate.* Usually prepared in a gourd container and sipped through a *bombilla,* a filter straw.

Gramática ▲▲▲

El imperativo: la forma *nosotros* (a softened request)

The *nosotros* command form expresses the idea *Let's . . . (sing, run, leave)!*

¡Escuchemos tu nuevo disco compacto!	*Let's listen to your new CD!*
¡Comamos una pizza!	*Let's eat a pizza!*
¡No salgamos todavía!	*Let's not leave yet!*
¡No volvamos demasiado tarde!	*Let's not return too late!*
¡Vamos al circo!	*Let's go to the circus!*

For most regular verbs and verbs with only an irregularity in the *yo* form, the *nosotros* command form is derived as follows:

	Command Stem	**Command Ending**
-ar verbs:	cantar → canto → cant-	cant**emos**
-er verbs:	correr → corro → corr-	corr**amos**
-ir verbs:	salir → salgo → salg-	salg**amos**

The *-ar* and *-er* stem-changing verbs in the present indicative follow the same pattern in the imperative. Thus, the *nosotros* form has no stem change.

encontrar → encontremos

entender → entendamos

The *-ir* stem-changing verbs, however, do have a stem change in the *nosotros* command form. Notice the examples below.

sentir → sintamos	dormir → durmamos
mentir → mintamos	morir → muramos

The affirmative *nosotros* command form of the verb *ir* is usually *vamos*. The negative command is *vayamos*.

¡Vamos al concierto!	*Let's go to the concert!*
¡Vamos a cantar!	*Let's sing!*
But . . .	
¡No vayamos al parque!	*Let's not go to the park!*

If the affirmative *nosotros* command is a reflexive verb, the final *-s* of the verb is omitted before the pronoun *nos* is added.

irse: vamos + nos = ¡Vámonos!

sentarse: sentemos + nos = ¡Sentémonos!

Verbs that have irregular stems in the *Ud.* and *Uds.* forms, use those same stems in the *nosotros* forms:

dar → demos   saber → sepamos

estar → estemos   ser → seamos

ir → no vayamos

Vamos a + infinitivo como mandato afirmativo

The construction *vamos a + infinitivo* can also be used as an affirmative *nosotros* command.

¡Vamos a comer!   *Let's eat!*
¡Vamos a cantar!   *Let's sing!*
But . . .
¡No comamos!   *Let's not eat!*
¡No cantemos!   *Let's not sing!*

Note that only the imperative form may be used with the negative.

◆ **Actividad 1**

It's Saturday! You and a friend want to get together to do something. When he or she gives a suggestion, you may either accept it or refuse it. Respond with affirmative or negative answers as shown in the model.

Modelo: visitar el museo
      Sí, visitemos el museo. (Sí, visitémoslo.)
      No, no visitemos el museo. (No, no lo visitemos.)

1. organizar un picnic

2. jugar al ténis

3. ir al centro

4. invitar a unos(as) chicos(as) a acompañarnos al centro

5. comprar pollo frito

6. estudiar para el examen

7. caminar por el parque

8. hacer un flan

9. salir con los otros chicos al campo

10. correr en el maratón de la escuela

El modo subjuntivo

All verbs have two characteristics: tense and mood. The **tense** of the verb tells us when the action takes place—in the present, the past, or the future. The **mood** tells us the attitude of the speaker toward the action. In Spanish, as in English, there are three main moods: the indicative, the imperative, and the subjunctive.

The **indicative** mood is used to report facts objectively.

Marisa **tiene** tres hermanos.

Fuimos a la playa para el fin de semana.

The **imperative** mood is used to give direct commands or requests.

Vengan Uds. conmigo, por favor.

¡No **escribas** en las paredes, niño!

The **subjunctive** mood is used to express information in a more subjective manner.

- It can express someone's attitude or will concerning an action or state.

   Queremos que Uds. **vengan** con nosotros.

   (We want you to come with us.)

   Insisto en que Marisa **haga** su tarea.

   (I insist that Marisa do her homework.)

- It can reflect whether one views an action or state as doubtful or unlikely.

   Puede que Tabaré ya **tenga** suficiente dinero.

   (It may be that Tabaré already has enough money.)

   Es imposible que Ud. **sepa** eso.

   (It is impossible for you to know that.)

- It can indicate that one sees an action or state as imaginary or non-existent.

   No conozco ningún libro que **tenga** esa información.

   (I know of no book that has that information.)

   Niego que Ricardo **sea** un estudiante malo.

   (I deny that Ricardo may be a bad student.)

Las especialidades

El presente del subjuntivo: los mandatos indirectos

The subjunctive mood is a verb form that is used in Spanish under certain specific circumstances. The first use we will study is its use in indirect commands.

Indirect commands are the expression of one person's will regarding the actions of another.

Compare the following direct commands with indirect commands.

Direct Commands	Indirect Commands
¡Venga!	Quiero que Ud. **venga.**
(Come!)	*(I want you to come.)*
¡Contésteme!	Deseo que Ud. me **conteste**.
(Answer me!)	*(I want you to answer me.)*
¡No lo **hagas**!	Insisto en que no lo **hagas.**
(Don't do it!)	*(I insist that you not do it.)*
¡Comprémoslo!	Quiero que lo **compremos.**
(Let's buy it!)	*(I want us to buy it.)*

Indirect commands are made by preceding the command with an expression of volition (the will), such as *quiero que, deseo que,* and *insisto que.* The verb form used after such expressions is called the subjunctive verb form.

Note the following regarding indirect commands:

1. The verb in the first clause (the independent clause) expresses some type of volition—a person's will.

2. The verb in the second clause (the subordinate clause) is in the subjunctive. Note that the subordinate clause is introduced by *que.*

You learned the forms of the subjunctive when you studied the imperative, since all but the *tú* and *vosotros* affirmative commands use the present subjunctive.

El presente del subjuntivo: formas regulares

Most verbs derive the present subjunctive forms from the stem of the first person singular (*yo*) of the present indicative. The endings below are added to this stem.

-ar verbs: -e, -es, -e, -emos, -éis, -en
-er, -ir verbs: -a, -as, -a, -amos, -áis, -an

hablar	decir	volver	sentir	dormir
hablo → habl-	digo → dig-	vuelvo → vuelv-	siento → sient-	duermo → duerm-
hable	diga	vuelva	sienta	duerma
hables	digas	vuelvas	sientas	duermas
hable	diga	vuelva	sienta	duerma
hablemos	digamos	volvamos	sintamos	durmamos
habléis	digáis	volváis	sintáis	durmáis
hablen	digan	vuelvan	sientan	duerman

- The *-ar* and *-er* stem-changing verbs have the same stem changes in the subjunctive that they have in the present indicative. See *volver* in the chart above.
- The *e→ie* and *o→ue* *-ir* stem-changing verbs have an additional stem change in *nosotros* and *vosotros*: *e→i* and *o→u*. See *sentir* and *dormir* in the chart above.
- Verbs with the endings *-car, -gar,* and *-zar* have the following spelling changes:
  -car: -que, -ques, -que, -quemos, -quéis, -quen
  -gar: -gue, -gues, -gue, -guemos, -guéis, -guen
  -zar: -ce, -ces, -ce, -cemos, -céis, -cen

El presente del subjuntivo: formas irregulares

The following verbs **do not** derive the form of the present subjunctive from the stem of the *yo* present indicative.

dar	estar	ir	saber	ser
dé	esté	vaya	sepa	sea
des	estés	vayas	sepas	seas
dé	esté	vaya	sepa	sea
demos	estemos	vayamos	sepamos	seamos
deis	estéis	vayáis	sepáis	seáis
den	estén	vayan	sepan	sean

Note: *Haber* is used primarily as the auxiliary verb of the present perfect subjunctive. Its present subjunctive forms are the following: *haya, hayas, haya, hayamos, hayáis, hayan.*

◆ **Actividad 2**

Tell what the teacher wants the students to do.

Modelo: hablar en español
La maestra quiere que hablen en español.

1. llegar a tiempo
2. tomar notas en la clase
3. no hablar en inglés
4. llevar sus libros a la clase
5. aprender las palabras nuevas
6. leer la lección con cuidado
7. no dejar las tareas en casa
8. escribir los verbos correctamente

◆ **Actividad 3**

Role-play a family night conversation. Ask a family member for permission to do the following activities. Your partner should answer according to the information given in parentheses. Follow the model.

Modelo: poner la mesa (sí)
—*¿Pongo la mesa?*
—*Sí, quiero que pongas la mesa.*

1. poner los platos (sí)
2. hacer una lista para las compras (sí)
3. hacer el postre para la cena (sí)
4. poner el flan en la nevera (sí)
5. poner la leche en la cocina (no)
6. hacer el menú (sí)
7. decirle a papá que la cena está lista (no)
8. ir a la iglesia (sí)
9. salir con Pedro (no)
10. volver a casa temprano esta noche (sí)

◆ **Actividad 4**

There is always room for improvement in the things we do. Tell who would want these people to improve their performance. Use the model as a guide.

Modelo: Pablo toca la trompeta. (su profesor de trompeta)
Su profesor de trompeta quiere que la toque mejor.

1. Susana cocina bien. (su padre)

2. Felipe habla español. (su profesora)

3. Tomás juega al fútbol. (su entrenador)

4. Rafael y su hermano cantan. (el director del coro)

5. Tú hablas francés. (tu amiga francesa)

◆ **Actividad 5**

Tell what you would like the following people to do. Be creative!

Modelo: mi hermano
Quiero que mi hermano me preste su radio.

1. mi padre
2. mi abuelo(a)
3. mis amigos(as)

4. mi profesor
5. mi perro
6. el presidente

Expresiones usadas en mandatos indirectos

Some common expressions of volition that are used in indirect commands are listed below. Notice that they are followed by **que** and the subjunctive form of the verb.

Deseo que Ismael **venga** a mi casa mañana.

Exigen que cuatro profesores **asistan** a la reunión.

Mi padre **insiste en que volvamos** antes de la medianoche.

Necesito que ella me **haga** los adornos para la fiesta.

Los profesores **permiten que tengamos** invitados.

Le **pido que traiga** los materiales.

Prefiero que me **llame** temprano.

No **prohiben que comamos** tacos y tostadas.

No **se oponen a que toquemos** música mexicana.

Nos **recomiendan que hablemos** español.

Los jóvenes **ruegan que haya** una fiesta mexicana.

Sugiero que llegues antes de las diez.

El jefe **manda que** sus empleados le **obedezcan.**

◆ Actividad 6

What is your reaction to the following situations? You may use the following phrases to express your reactions: *insisto en que / prohibo que / (no) me opongo a que / (no) permito que / prefiero que / recomiendo que.*

Modelo: Mi hermana usa mi secador de pelo.
  (No) Me opongo a que mi hermana use mi secador de pelo.

1. Mi mejor amigo siempre me dice la verdad.
2. Mi hermano usa mi bicicleta.
3. Mis profesores respetan mis ideas.
4. Mis padres conversan conmigo.
5. Mis amigos me ayudan.
6. El reloj me despierta a las seis de la mañana.
7. Mi pastor me da consejos.
8. Mi madre compra mi ropa.

◆ Actividad 7

The following people are going on vacation. Can you recommend something to them? Start your suggestions with phrases like these: *sugiero que* or *recomiendo que.* You may use verbs such as the following: *llevarse, comprar, aprender, tener cuidado con.*

Modelo: Margarita va a visitar a su primo en España.
  Recomiendo que Margarita se lleve un paraguas.

1. Esteban va a pasar un mes en México.
2. Fernando va a visitar los museos de arte en París.
3. Rolando y su primo van a ver los volcanes en Hawaii.
4. Rosana va a visitar Machu Picchu en el Perú.
5. Tomás va a viajar a Uruguay para ayudar a unos misioneros.
6. Roberto y Carmencita van a Puerto Rico para estar en la playa.
7. Beatriz va a esquiar en Alemania.
8. Rafael va a Madrid para ver una corrida de toros.

Orando también al mismo tiempo
por nosotros, para que el Señor nos
abra puerta para la palabra, a fin de
dar a conocer el misterio de Cristo.
Colosenses 4:3

CAPÍTULO ONCE

11-1 La oración

Lectura bíblica ▲▲▲

Mateo 6:9-13

Padre nuestro que estás en los cielos, santificado sea tu nombre.

Venga tu reino. Hágase tu *voluntad,* como en el cielo, así también en la tierra. El pan nuestro de cada día, dánoslo hoy.

Y perdónanos nuestras deudas, como también nosotros perdonamos a nuestros deudores.

Y no nos metas en tentación, mas *líbranos* del mal; porque tuyo es el reino, y el poder, y la gloria, por todos los *siglos.* Amén.

Vocabulario ▲▲

Cómo orar

Use the following guidelines to help you learn to pray in Spanish.

Opening phrases:

Padre nuestro	*Our Father*
Padre celestial	*Heavenly Father*
Padre amado	*Beloved Father*
Padre santo	*Holy Father*
Señor	*Lord*

will

deliver us
ages

Expressions of thanksgiving:

Gracias por . . .	*Thank You for . . .*
Te agradecemos por . . .	*We thank You for . . .*
Te agradezco por . . .	*I thank You for . . .*
la salvación en Cristo	*salvation in Christ*
tu amor	*your love*
tu protección	*your protection*
la escuela, los maestros	*the school, the teachers*
mis amigos	*my friends*
la comida, el sol, la lluvia	*the food, the sun, the rain*
otro día de vida	*another day of life*
cuidar a mi familia	*taking care of my family*
ayudarme en las clases	*helping me in my classes*
morir por nosotros	*dying for us*
salvar a mi amigo(a)	*saving my friend*

Requests:

Te pido que bendigas a mi madre, a mi amigo(a), a mi pastor.	*I pray that you would bless my mother, my friend, my pastor.*
Bendice a los misioneros, a los maestros, al señor Vargas.	*Bless the missionaries, the teachers, Mr. Vargas.*
Ayuda a (María) para que sane (se mejore) pronto.	*Help (María) to heal (to get better) soon.*
Ayúdame a aprender mucho en las clases.	*Help me to learn much in my classes.*

Closing:

Todo lo pido en el nombre del Señor Jesucristo. Amén.	*I ask all this in the name of the Lord Jesus Christ. Amen.*

◆ **Actividad 1**

1. Using the above phrases as a guide, compose a prayer thanking the Lord for His protection, for your home, for your parents, and for your school and teachers. Ask Him to help you in your schoolwork today.

2. Compose a prayer thanking the Lord for your church and pastor. If a church member is sick, pray that the Lord will heal him or her.

3. Compose a prayer that you might pray before eating your meal.

4. Compose a prayer that you might pray before going to bed at night.

Gramática ▲▲▲

Repaso del subjuntivo en mandatos indirectos

As you learned in Chapter 10, the subjunctive is used after expressions of will regarding the actions of another. In such cases, the independent clause contains the expression of volition (will), and the dependent clause (beginning with *que*) contains the subjunctive verb.

Quiero que lo **hagas** en seguida.	*I want you to do it right away.*
Se oponen a que Carlos **compre** la motocicleta.	*They are opposed to Carlos's buying the motorcycle.*
Preferimos que Ud. **venga** a las ocho.	*We prefer that you come at eight o'clock.*

You may have noticed that English does not always approach statements in quite the same way Spanish does. Of the three English examples given, only the third one shares the same sentence pattern as the Spanish; yet in all three cases, both the Spanish sentences and their English equivalents express the same ideas. In cases such as these, you must learn which patterns express the ideas you wish to communicate.

El presente del subjuntivo: los verbos irregulares

The following verbs do not derive the present subjunctive from the stem of the *yo* present indicative. They are irregular.

dar	estar	haber	ir	saber	ser
dé	esté	haya	vaya	sepa	sea
des	estés	hayas	vayas	sepas	seas
dé	esté	haya	vaya	sepa	sea
demos	estemos	hayamos	vayamos	sepamos	seamos
deis	estéis	hayáis	vayáis	sepáis	seáis
den	estén	hayan	vayan	sepan	sean

CAPÍTULO 11-1

◆ **Actividad 2**

Supply the appropriate present subjunctive form of each verb in parentheses.

Modelo: Tomás quiere que Samuel (estar) _____ en la cafetería a las doce.
Tomás quiere que Samuel esté en la cafetería a las doce.

1. Jorge quiere que Ramón (ir) _____ con él a la iglesia el domingo.

2. Carlos quiere que Benjamín (ser) _____ miembro del cuarteto.

3. El director demanda que los miembros del cuarteto (saber) _____ de memoria las palabras del himno.

4. El profesor quiere que David y yo le (dar) _____ nuestras ideas para el periódico.

5. Los jugadores quieren que Esteban y Pedro (estar) _____ en el equipo de baloncesto.

6. Tomás quiere que Rosa María le (dar) _____ su número de teléfono.

7. Luis quiere que Felipe le (dar) _____ la dirección de Rosita.

8. Jorge quiere que Beatriz y Olga (ir) _____ con él a la pizzería.

◆ **Actividad 3**

Make complete sentences from the elements provided below telling where each person wants the other to go.

Modelo: Samuel / su hermano / a la biblioteca
Samuel quiere que su hermano vaya a la biblioteca.

1. Maribel / nosotros / a España

2. Tomás y Rafael / tú / a Inglaterra

3. Raquel / yo / a Francia durante el verano

4. Roberto y yo / nuestros padres / al Brasil

5. Tú / los jóvenes de la iglesia / a México

6. Yo / Sarita y Carmencita / conmigo a la escuela dominical

7. Usted / yo / a mi próxima clase

8. El médico / Santiago / al hospital

La oración

◆ **Actividad 4**

The youth group is praying. Tell the prayer request of each teenager.

Modelo: David: su hermano / ser / un buen misionero
   David pide que su hermano sea un buen misionero.

1. Rafael: los estudiantes / estudiar / para los exámenes

2. Daniel: los misioneros / tener / buena salud

3. Margarita: su padre / darle / permiso para ir a México en el verano

4. Susana: ella / ser / buen ejemplo a su hermana

5. Rolando: el presidente / saber / gobernar el país

◆ **Actividad 5**

Use words from each of the following columns to form sentences. Your sentences may be affirmative or negative, interrogative or declarative.

A	B	C	D	E
Dios	querer	nosotros	ir	de buen humor
Tabaré	desear	el profesor	estar	dos idiomas
yo	esperar	los estudiantes	saber	el diezmo
nosotros	pedir	mi amigo(a)	tener	a tiempo
mis padres	preferir	tú y yo	dar	feliz
mi profesor(a)	necesitar	yo	ser	el vocabulario
				a la universidad

El subjuntivo: con expresiones de emoción

Spanish speakers also use the subjunctive after verbs or expressions of emotion about a specific situation or about someone else's actions. Note the use of the subjunctive in the following sentences.

Mamá **teme que** yo **vaya** a enfermarme.	*Mother is afraid (that) I am going to get sick.*
Siento que Pablo no **venga**.	*I am sorry (that) Pablo is not coming.*
Me alegro de que estudies español.	*I am glad (that) you are studying Spanish.*

Note: The word *that* may be omitted in English, but *que* is necessary in Spanish.

The following verbs or expressions may be used to express feelings or emotions:

gustar	alegrarse de
lamentar	quejarse de (*to complain about*)
temer (*to fear*)	tener miedo de
sentir	ojalá que

Note: *Ojalá que* (I hope/wish that) is not a verb but is one of the strongest expressions of hope in the Spanish language. It derives from an Arabic expression that once meant "Oh, may Allah grant that . . . ." Any verb following this fixed expression must be in the subjunctive.

> **¡Ojalá que** yo saque una A en el examen! *I hope I get an A on the test!*
>
> **¡Ojalá que** tu padre se mejore pronto! *I hope your father gets well soon!*

◆ **Actividad 6**

Complete each sentence with the correct form of the subjunctive.

Modelo: Me gusta que tú (venir) _____ a visitarnos.
  Me gusta que vengas a visitarnos.

1. Siento que Carolina (estar) _____ enferma.

2. Me alegro de que Patricio y Rafael (querer) _____ venir a la iglesia.

3. Mi pastor teme que yo no (ir) _____ a cantar en el coro.

4. El niño se alegra de que le (llamar) _____ su amiga.

5. Al profesor le gusta que sus alumnos (aprender) _____ a hablar bien el español.

6. Paquito tiene miedo de que su tío le (regañar) _____ .

7. Lamento que tú no (poder) _____ acompañarnos al concierto.

8. Me molesta que Pedro (hablar) _____ durante el servicio en la iglesia.

Vocabulario adicional ▲▲▲▲▲▲▲▲▲▲▲▲▲▲▲▲▲▲▲▲▲▲▲▲▲▲▲▲▲▲▲

The following nouns also double as verbs.

	Noun	**Verb**
(el) amanecer*	*dawn*	*to dawn, to begin the day*
(el) atardecer	*late afternoon, dusk*	*to approach evening*
(el) anochecer	*nightfall*	*to grow dark, to approach nightfall*

*When the subject of the verb *amanecer* is a person, it means *to begin the day*.

Amaneció frío y con lluvia.	*The day dawned cold and rainy.*
Margarita amaneció con dolor de cabeza.	*Margarita began the day with a headache.*

La oración

11-2 Un testimonio

Lectura ▲▲▲

Tomás da su testimonio de cómo llegó a conocer al Señor Jesucristo como su Salvador:

Me crié en un hogar cristiano y siempre quise agradar a mis padres. Por eso, a la edad de seis años, después de un servicio en la iglesia, fui al altar, me arrodillé y oré, mas sin entender lo que en verdad hacía. Yo pensaba que por decir una oración y tomar la mano del pastor había nacido de nuevo.

Después, comprendí lo que significaba de verdad la salvación. Aprendí que todos somos pecadores (Romanos 3:23) y que la paga del pecado es muerte (Romanos 6:23). La Biblia enseña que el infierno es un lugar verdadero y que después de la muerte, si no hemos creído en Jesucristo como nuestro Salvador, pasaremos la eternidad ahí.

Un domingo cuando tenía doce años, mi pastor predicó acerca del infierno. Yo sabía que no había recibido a Jesucristo de verdad y que si moría ese día iría al infierno para siempre. ¡Estaba asustado! Esa noche en mi cama, le pedí a Jesucristo que entrara en mi corazón, que perdonara mis pecados y que fuera mi Salvador. Desde entonces, he tenido la seguridad de que mis pecados han sido perdonados y que un día iré al cielo.

Si tú quieres tener esta misma seguridad, es necesario que te arrepientas y que creas en el hijo de Dios.

1. ¿Cómo era el hogar de Tomás?
2. ¿Cuántos años tenía cuando fue al altar por primera vez?
3. ¿Por qué pensaba que había nacido de nuevo?
4. ¿Qué dice Romanos 3:23?
5. ¿Qué enseña la Biblia acerca del infierno?
6. ¿De qué predicó el pastor cuando Tomás tenía doce años?
7. ¿Por qué estaba asustado Tomás?
8. ¿Qué hizo esa noche ?
9. ¿Tienes tú la seguridad de que vas al cielo? Si la tienes, ¿cómo lo sabes?

Vocabulario ▲▲▲▲▲▲▲▲▲▲▲▲▲▲▲▲▲▲▲▲▲▲▲▲▲▲▲▲▲▲▲▲▲▲▲▲▲

Palabras bíblicas

el cielo (*heaven*)	la gracia (*grace*)	la salvación
la fe (*faith*)	el infierno (*hell*)	la seguridad (*security*)
el gozo (*joy*)	el pecado (*sin*)	

arrepentirse (*to repent*)	convertirse	evangelizar
arrodillarse (*to kneel*)	(*to be converted*)	pecar (*to sin*)
confesar	entregarse	testificar
confiar (*to trust*)	(*to surrender*)	(*to testify; witness*)

Gramática ▲▲▲▲▲▲▲▲▲▲▲▲▲▲▲▲▲▲▲▲▲▲▲▲▲▲▲▲▲▲▲▲▲▲▲▲▲▲

El subjuntivo vs. el infinitivo

In order to express your will or attitude about the actions of another person or about a particular situation, use the sentence pattern as shown in the following examples:

Preferimos que Uds. lo **hagan** ahora.	*We prefer that you do it now.*
Siento que no **vayas** al banquete.	*I am sorry (that) you are not going to the banquet.*

Notice that each sentence above contains two subjects—one for the verb in the first clause, another for the verb in the second clause.

If both verbs refer to the same subject, however, a *verb + infinitive* construction is necessary.

Preferimos hacerlo ahora.	*We prefer to do it now.*
Siento no ir al banquete.	*I'm sorry not to be going to the banquet.*

Complete the following sentences with the correct subjunctive or infinitive form of each verb indicated.

1. Margarita se alegra de (recibir) _____ una carta de Felipe.

2. Felipe tiene miedo de que Margarita no (aceptar) _____ su invitación.

3. Fernando teme (invitar) _____ a Marianela.

4. Marianela no quiere que Fernando le (hablar) _____ .

5. Siento mucho que los chicos (estar) _____ tan temerosos.

6. Me molesta (ver) _____ a las chicas llorar.

7. Todo el mundo se alegra de que el programa (ser) _____ el sábado.

8. Lamento que Víctor no (ir) _____ al programa.

El subjuntivo: con expresiones de duda

The subjunctive is used following expressions of doubt or denial. Notice the following examples.

> **Es posible que** yo **vaya** a España en julio.
>
> **Dudo que** Roberto **venga**.
>
> **No creo que sea** el mejor restaurante.
>
> **No es verdad que** Marta **esté** enferma.
>
> **Negamos que** nuestro hermano **sea** ladrón.

The doubt or denial may range from a slight possibility (*es posible que*) to a confirmed denial (*negar que*).

The following expressions indicate doubt or denial:

Es posible que . . .	Dudo que . . . (*I doubt that . . .*)
Es probable que . . .	No es verdad que . . .
No pienso que . . .	Es imposible que . . .
No creo que . . .	Niego que . . . (*I deny that . . .*)

When the verb *creer* is used in the affirmative, the indicative follows. In this context, *creer* expresses certainty.

> Creo que ella **dice** la verdad.   *I believe (that) she's telling the truth.*

No creer, however, usually expresses doubt and therefore is normally followed by the subjunctive.

> **No creo** que ella **diga** la verdad.   *I don't believe (that) she's telling the truth.*

Creer in questions may express either doubt or certainty according to the intent of the speaker.

¿**Crees** que Ana **diga** la verdad?   *The speaker is indicating doubts about Ana's truthfulness.*

¿**Crees** que Ana **dice** la verdad?   *The speaker either has a neutral opinion or expects the answer to be "yes."*

◆ **Actividad 2**

Supply the appropriate indicative or subjunctive form of each verb in parentheses.

Modelo: Dudo que todos sus parientes (vivir) _____ en Barcelona.
   Dudo que todos sus parientes vivan en Barcelona.

1. Es posible que los estudiantes no (venir) _____ a la clase hoy.

2. Yo sé que Arturo (estudiar) _____ mucho.

3. No creo que su hermana (saber) _____ la respuesta.

4. Es verdad que Miguel (tener) _____ diecinueve años.

5. Creo que todos ellos (estar) _____ contentos hoy.

6. Dudo que Uds. (ir) _____ a España este año.

7. Es probable que Uds. (viajar) _____ a México.

◆ **Actividad 3**

Change the following sentences to make them express a doubt.

Modelo: Pablo dice la verdad.
   ¿Crees que Pablo diga la verdad? OR
   Es posible que Pablo diga la verdad.

1. Margarita quiere ser misionera.

2. Humberto tiene planes de viajar a Colombia.

3. Los jóvenes escuchan las cintas.

4. Felipe y Ana van a llamarse por teléfono.

5. Nosotros compramos los tratados.

6. Tienen el mejor restaurante de toda la ciudad.

7. Pedro y Francisco van a Costa Rica en el verano.

8. Rodolfo no come paella.

◆ **Actividad 4**

With a partner, create as many sentences as you can in five minutes using words from each of the following three columns.

A	B	C
Dudo que . . .	el profesor	comer pizza
Es imposible que . . .	mi hermana	jugar en el torneo
Es probable que . . .	nosotros	decir mentiras
No creo que . . .	los estudiantes	viajar a Barcelona
Niego que . . .	los misioneros	decir la verdad
No pienso que . . .	los españoles	venir a la fiesta
No es verdad que . . .	tú y yo	necesitar ayuda

El subjuntivo: con expresiones impersonales

Impersonal expressions consist of the third-person singular form of *ser* + an adjective. These constructions are called "impersonal" because the subject of the verb *ser* is the implied pronoun *it* rather than a person.

Impersonal expressions, as you learned in Chapter Two, may be followed by an infinitive.

Es necesario **trabajar.**
Es importante **llegar** a tiempo al trabajo.
Es bueno **ser** importante, pero es más importante **ser** bueno.

Such impersonal constructions let the speaker express a value judgment (give an opinion) about an action or state in general without making reference to a person.

Impersonal expressions may also be followed by *que + a clause*. These constructions let the speaker give an opinion about the actions or state of someone specific.

Es necesario que **Ud. trabaje.**
Es importante que **los estudiantes lleguen** a tiempo.
Es probable que **Uds. tengan** un examen.

The impersonal expressions above are followed by a subjunctive clause. Note that the impersonal expressions were used to convey a subjunctive idea: an impersonal command, an emotional attitude, doubt, or uncertainty. Most impersonal expressions fall into one of these categories mentioned.

The following are some common impersonal expressions:

Es bueno (que) . . .	Es malo (que) . . .
Es importante (que) . . .	Es mejor (que) . . .
Es increíble (que) . . .	Es natural (que) . . .
Es indispensable (que) . . .	Es necesario (que) . . .
Es justo (que) . . .	Es peligroso (que) . . .
Es lógico (que) . . .	Es triste (que) . . .

But . . .

Es verdad que él **viene** mañana.
Es cierto que María **está** aquí.
Es evidente que le **gusta** comer.

Impersonal expressions that indicate certainty use the indicative.

◆ **Actividad 5**

Ramonita tells Raúl what she and her friends are going to do. Like a typical brother, Raúl always has a comment in reply. Write Raúl's comments as shown in the model.

Modelo: Margarita y yo vamos a caminar en el parque. (Es peligroso)
Raúl: Es peligroso que caminen en el parque.

1. Pepe y yo vamos a tomar el tren. (Es lógico)

2. Rafael y Pedro van a visitar El Prado. (Es increíble)

3. Yo voy a abrir una cuenta en el banco. (Es bueno)

4. Voy a depositar mi primer cheque en mi cuenta. (Es natural)

5. Voy a dar mi diezmo a la iglesia. (Es justo)

6. Voy a escribirte un cheque. (Es razonable)

7. Voy a comprarme un traje nuevo. (Es ridículo)

8. María y yo vamos a llegar a tiempo a la iglesia. (Es importante)

9. Sandra y Lupita van al parque a pie. (Es mejor / en bicicleta)

◆ **Actividad 6**

There are some things to remember when you have a job. Start each principle with one of the following phrases: *(No) Es bueno que usted / (No) Es necesario que usted / (No) Es importante que usted.*

Modelo: llegar a tiempo
Es importante que Ud. llegue a tiempo.

1. vestirse de ropa limpia

2. ponerse zapatos nuevos

3. cantar siempre en el trabajo

4. llamar a sus amigos por teléfono

5. quejarse de (*complain about*) su trabajo

6. ayudar a un compañero

7. trabajar todo el tiempo sin descanso (*break*)

8. ganar el dinero que le pagan

◆ **Actividad 7**

Write the correct form of each verb indicated. Use either the present indicative or the present subjunctive.

Modelo: Es verdad que nosotros _____ tarde. (llegar)
Es verdad que nosotros llegamos tarde.

1. Es triste que Manolo _____ que trabajar esta noche. (tener)

2. Es mejor que tú _____ las tareas temprano. (terminar)

3. Es posible que _____ visitas a las ocho. (llegar)

4. Es verdad que Marta _____ con su novio. (salir)

5. Es probable que ellos no _____ temprano. (regresar)

6. Es evidente que ellos _____ mucho. (quererse)

7. Es posible que ellos _____ el año próximo. (casarse)

Refrán ▲▲▲

James 4:15 states that in making plans we should say, "If the Lord will, we shall live, and do this, or that." The following proverb also acknowledges that God's purposes overrule our plans.

El hombre propone, pero Dios dispone.
(Man proposes, but God disposes.)

SEVILLA

SEVILLA

Sevilla, the capital of the autonomous community of *Andalucía,* lies on the banks of the Guadalquivir River. This historic city served as the center for the exploration of the New World. As a result of the treasures brought by Columbus and other explorers, Sevilla became the richest Spanish city in the sixteenth century.

Before this time the Arabs occupied the city and left their stamp on its architecture. Sevilla's cathedral is one of the world's largest Gothic buildings. But its beautiful bell tower, the Giralda, originally belonged to a Moslem mosque. The Alcázar, a magnificent palace which at one time housed King Ferdinand and Queen Isabella, is another Moslem contribution to Sevilla.

Sevilla remains influential in Spain's cultural life. In celebration of the 500th anniversary of Columbus's discovery of America, the city hosted the Expo '92 world's fair.

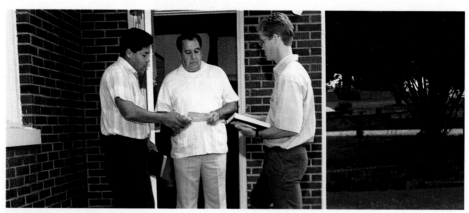

11-3 Testificando

Diálogo ▲▲

Víctor y Tomás, estudiantes del Instituto Bíblico Calvario, salieron una tarde para evangelizar. Víctor tocó a la puerta delantera de una casa grande y el Sr. Andrés lo recibió. Después de conversar un rato, Víctor le habló de Jesucristo:

Víctor: La Biblia dice en Romanos 3:23 que «todos pecaron, y están destituidos de la gloria de Dios». Don Andrés, usted sabe que es pecador, ¿verdad?

Don Andrés: Sí, sé que soy pecador.

in spite of the fact that

Víctor: Pero Dios le ama *a pesar de que* usted es pecador. Jesucristo murió por usted para pagar el precio de su pecado y para que usted pueda tener la vida eterna. Romanos 5:8 dice que «siendo aún pecadores, Cristo murió por nosotros».

Don Andrés: ¿Jesucristo hizo eso por mí?

Víctor: Sí, don Andrés. Dios puede perdonar sus pecados y darle la vida eterna con tal de que crea en su Hijo y le reciba de todo corazón.

Don Andrés: ¡Oh, yo quiero que Dios me perdone antes de que sea demasiado tarde!

knelt down

Don Andrés *se arrodilló* al lado del sillón, oró y recibió a Jesucristo como su Salvador. Después, Víctor le dijo:

— Don Andrés, ya que ha creído en Cristo, quiero que se lo diga a su esposa.

Se dirigieron a la cocina. ¡Qué sorpresa les esperaba! Doña Juana estaba de rodillas orando. Tomás había ido a la otra puerta de la casa donde se encontró con doña Juana. Después de hablar con ella acerca de la salvación en Cristo, ella tambien lo recibió como Salvador.

Gramática ▲▲

El subjuntivo: después de ciertas conjunciones

Certain conjunctions in Spanish are always followed by the subjunctive. These conjunctions point to an event or condition that has not yet taken place or is considered hypothetical (or imaginary).

Iré contigo **con la condición de que** no **lleguemos** tarde.	*I'll go with you on the condition that we don't arrive late.*
Te invito a mi casa **para que pruebes** el flán de mamá.	*I'm inviting you to my house so that you taste Mom's flan.*
Te veré esta noche **a menos que tenga** que estudiar.	*I'll see you tonight unless I have to study.*

Some of these conjunctions include the following:

a menos que	*unless*
antes de que	*before*
con la condición de que	*on the condition that*
con tal de que	*provided that*
en caso de que	*in case*
para que	*in order that; so that*
sin que	*without*

◆ **Actividad 1**

Some of Carolina's friends accept her invitation to a party, but under certain conditions. What are these conditions?

Modelo: Rosa: terminar temprano
   Rosa irá a la fiesta con la condición de que termine temprano.

1. Carlos: tener mucha comida
2. Samuel: Ramona ir con él
3. Felipe: no haber niños pequeños
4. Cándida: invitar a mi hermano también
5. Ernesto: tener juegos interesantes
6. Aida: poder ayudarte a adornar el salón
7. Benito: haber una piñata
8. Fernando y María: ayudarte a limpiar después

◆ **Actividad 2**

The youth group has planned a mission trip to México. Play the part of Benito as he explains to the church congregation the purposes of the trip.

Modelo: los jóvenes: practicar el español
Vamos a ir a México para que los jóvenes practiquen el español.

1. los jóvenes: ayudar a los misioneros

2. los mexicanos: conocer a unos jóvenes americanos

3. los jóvenes: conocer a unos jóvenes mexicanos

4. la iglesia: ser representada en México

5. los mexicanos: recibir el evangelio

6. los jóvenes: tener la oportunidad de enseñar a los niños mexicanos

7. Dios: llamar a algunos jóvenes para ser misioneros

8. Cristo: ser glorificado

◆ **Actividad 3**

Use your imagination to complete the following sentences using a verb in the subjunctive.

Modelo: He traído mi paraguas en caso de que . . . *llueva.*

1. Me levanto temprano a menos que . . .

2. Siempre llevo cinco dólares en mi bolsillo en caso de que . . .

3. Hago mis tareas todos los días para que . . .

4. Puedo salir con mis amigos de noche con la condición de que . . .

5. Llego a mi clase antes de que . . .

6. Debemos orar por nuestro pastor para que . . .

7. Voy a la iglesia todos los domingos a menos que . . .

8. El equipo de baloncesto practica mucho para que . . .

9. Mañana voy a levantarme antes de que . . .

Por + infinitivo

The infinitive is the verb form that usually follows the preposition *por.* Look at the following examples.

Recibimos el trofeo **por ganar** el campeonato.	*We received the trophy for winning the championship.*
Pedro no está en clase hoy **por estar** enfermo.	*Pedro is not in class today because of being sick.*

The Spanish expression *por + infinitive* is equivalent to the English structure *for (because of, for reason of) + -ing verb.*

◆ **Actividad 4**

Combine the two sentences with *por + infinitive.*

Modelo: Margarita gana una medalla. Tiene las notas más altas.
   Margarita gana una medalla por tener las notas más altas.

1. Pedro está en el hospital. Tiene complicaciones.
2. Rolando será el intérprete. Sabe hablar inglés.
3. El Sr. Rivero será nuestro guía (*guide*). Conoce bien Washington D.C.
4. Mateo siempre tiene mucha hambre. Juega al ténis cada mañana.
5. No puedo practicar esta tarde. Tengo que estudiar.
6. Roberto sacó una nota mala. No estudió.
7. Te doy las gracias. Me invitaste a tu iglesia.
8. Le doy gracias a Dios. Me dio la vida eterna.

Testificando

Lectura bíblica ▲▲▲▲▲▲▲▲▲▲▲▲▲▲▲▲▲▲▲▲▲▲▲▲▲▲▲▲▲▲▲▲▲▲▲▲

Efesios 6:13-17

Tomad toda la armadura de Dios, para que podáis resistir en el día malo, y habiendo acabado todo, estar firmes. Estad, pues, firmes, ceñidos vuestros lomos con la verdad, y vestidos con la coraza de justicia, y calzados los pies con el apresto del evangelio de la paz. Sobre todo, tomad el escudo de la fe, con que podáis apagar todos los dardos de fuego del maligno. Y tomad el yelmo de la salvación, y la espada del Espíritu, que es la palabra de Dios.

La mies a la verdad es mucha, mas los obreros pocos; por tanto, rogad al Señor de la mies que envíe obreros a su mies.
Lucas 10:2

12-1 Las misiones

Diálogo ▲▲▲

jungles
amazed

Los estudiantes de la Academia Timoteo acaban de escuchar a un misionero de Colombia relatar algunas de sus experiencias en las *selvas* colombianas. Los jóvenes quedaron *asombrados*. Ellos comparan sus impresiones en la próxima clase.

palm leaves

Anita: El misionero dijo que vive en una casa hecha de palos y barro. Es probable que el techo sea de *hojas de palmera.*

firewood

Rafael: Y recuerden que dijo que cocinan sobre *leña* en el centro de la casa.

hammocks

Susana: Y que duermen en *hamacas.* No creo que yo pueda dormir muy bien en una hamaca.

Anita: Pues yo sí. Me encantan las hamacas. Pero no sé de la comida. Dudo que pueda comer carne de culebra.

Rafael: ¿Carne de culebra? Mmm . . . no debe ser tan mala.

Susana: No creo que sea uno de mis platos favoritos.

Anita: ¿Recuerdan lo que dijo acerca del río?

Rafael: ¡Me gustaría ver esa vaca en la canoa! No me parece posible que haya canoas suficientemente grandes para *aguantar* una vaca.

to hold (to support
the weight of)

Anita: Pero si la canoa es el único modo de transporte de un pueblo a otro y alguien compra una vaca, ¿cómo la va a llevar a su casa si no es por canoa?

Rafael: No sé. Puede ser que hayan canoas grandes.

Susana: Fue interesante escuchar cómo vive la gente en la selva. Algún día me gustaría visitar a esos misioneros en la selva.

Rafael: A mí también me gustaría.

◆ Conversación

1. ¿En qué parte de Colombia trabaja el misionero?

2. ¿Por qué quedaron asombrados los jóvenes?

3. Describa la casa donde vive el misionero.

4. ¿En qué duermen?

5. ¿Qué piensa Rafael de la carne de culebra?

6. ¿Qué quisieran hacer algún día los jóvenes?

Gramática ▲▲▲▲▲▲▲▲▲▲▲▲▲▲▲▲▲▲▲▲▲▲▲▲▲▲▲▲▲▲▲▲▲▲▲▲▲▲

El subjuntivo y el indicativo después de ciertas conjunciones de tiempo

Conjunctions related to time may be followed by either the indicative or the subjunctive. Notice the examples below.

Cuando Cristo **vino** la primera vez, *nació* en Belén.
(Event has already taken place.)

Cuando venga la segunda vez, *vendrá* en las nubes.
(future event)

Miguel no *quiere salir* **mientras** ustedes **están** aquí.
(Event is taking place.)

Miguel *irá* al trabajo **mientras** ustedes **vayan** de compras.
(future event)

If the action or event in the independent clause has actually taken place, is taking place, or regularly takes place, **the indicative** is used in the dependent clause.

If the action or event in the independent clause is still in the future (in relation to the tense of the verb in the other clause), **the subjunctive** is used. The following are some time-related conjunctions:

cuando	*when*	siempre que	*whenever*
después de (que)	*after (that)*	tan pronto como	*as soon as*
hasta que	*until*	una vez que	*once that*
mientras	*while*		

◆ Actividad 1

Some friends are discussing their future plans, but there are some things they have to do before they can actually carry out these plans. Form complete sentences by using the elements provided.

Modelo: Víctor / ir a México / tan pronto como / terminar las clases
Víctor irá a México tan pronto como terminen las clases.

1. Maribel / trabajar en un restaurante / hasta que / ganar $2000
2. Yo / viajar a Canadá / después de que / mis padres comprar un auto nuevo
3. Margarita / pasar una semana en la playa / cuando / su prima invitarla
4. Tú / pintar el auto / una vez que / el mecánico arreglarlo
5. Tomás / estudiar español / cuando / llegar a España
6. Ana María / cuidar a su hermanito / mientras / su mamá estar en el hospital
7. Mi esposa y yo / comprar una cámara de video / tan pronto como / tener suficiente dinero
8. Juan y Pablo / tomar clases de pintura / siempre que / el maestro venir a la escuela.

◆ Actividad 2

Complete the following sentences by using the subjunctive of each verb phrase given in parentheses.

1. Los estudiantes no deben entrar en el salón hasta que . . . (venir la profesora)
2. La profesora va a cerrar la puerta después de que . . . (tocar la campana)
3. Estudiaré el español hasta que . . . (estar cansado)
4. Voy a la universidad cuando . . . (acabar la escuela secundaria)
5. El coro de la iglesia cantará una vez que . . . (saber los himnos)
6. Quiero visitar Barcelona cuando . . . (poder viajar solo)
7. Los misioneros vendrán a nuestra escuela mientras . . . (estar en el país)
8. Quiero hablarles tan pronto como . . . (poder)

♦ **Actividad 3**

Complete the following sentences with the appropriate indicative or subjunctive form of each verb provided.

Modelo: Rafael usa lentes cuando (estudiar) _____ .
Rafael usa lentes cuando estudia. (indicative)
Rafael comprará lentes nuevos cuando (tener) _____ dinero.
Rafael comprará lentes nuevos cuando tenga dinero. (subjunctive)

1. Federico siempre canta mientras (bañarse) _____ .

2. Yo voy a escribir una carta mientras (esperar) _____ a Rolando.

3. Noemí siempre está hablando por teléfono cuando yo (ir) _____ a su casa.

4. Yo te avisaré cuando él (decirme) _____ la fecha.

5. Me gusta leer la Biblia tan pronto como (levantarme) _____ .

6. Quiero estudiar en una universidad cristiana tan pronto como (terminar) _____ la escuela secundaria.

7. Yo estaba nervioso hasta que ella (hablarme) _____ .

8. Maritza va a vivir en Barcelona cuando (tener) _____ 18 años.

El subjuntivo con antecedentes indefinidos o hipotéticos

Look closely at the three sentences below.

Tengo amigos que **son** médicos.

¿Conoces a alguien que **sea** médico?

No hay nadie aquí que **sea** médico.

The *médicos* mentioned in the second part of the first sentence are identified as *amigos* in the first part of the sentence. They are people who exist and whom the speaker knows. The use of the indicative form *son* confirms this fact.

The second example asks about a *médico* whose existence is unknown to the speaker.

¿Conoces a alguien que **sea** médico?

Because his existence is uncertain or hypothetical, the verb (*sea*) that refers to him is in the subjunctive.

In the final example, it is clear that no *médico* exists. The verb *sea* that refers to this non-existent *médico* is again in the subjunctive.

No hay nadie aquí que **sea** médico.

If the speaker refers to something or someone of whose existence he is **sure,** the verb in the clause following *que* is always in the **indicative.**

If the speaker refers to something or someone that **does not exist,** or whose existence **is in question,** the verb in the clause following *que* is always in the **subjunctive.** Examine the pairs of sentences below.

Necesito **un** libro que **tenga**
todos los verbos.
Busco a **alguien** que **sepa**
hablar francés.

Necesito **el** libro que **tiene**
todos los verbos.
Busco **al chico** que **sabe**
hablar francés.

Something as simple as the difference between a definite article (*el, la, los, las*) or an indefinite article (*un, una, unos, unas*) can help you determine whether the verb following *que* should be indicative or subjunctive. Looking for indefinite pronouns such as *alguien, algo, algún, nadie, nada, ningún* can also help.

¿Tienes **un** libro que **tenga**
todos los verbos?

No hay **ningún** libro que **tenga**
todos los verbos.

◆ **Actividad 4**

Supply the appropriate subjunctive form of each verb given in parentheses.

Modelo: Quiero conocer a alguien que (tener) dieciséis años.
Quiero conocer a alguien que tenga dieciséis años.

1. No hay nadie en nuestra clase que (saber) _____ hablar francés.

2. Busco un libro que (ser) _____ interesante.

3. Rafael quiere comprar un auto que (correr) _____ rápido.

4. Prefiero un maestro que (explicar) _____ la materia bien.

5. Quiero tomar mis vacaciones en un país que (tener) _____ playas.

6. No hay nada en el menú que yo (poder) _____ comer.

7. Necesito algo que no (tener) _____ grasa.

8. ¿Quieres pedir algo que te (gustar) _____?

◆ **Actividad 5**

Supply the appropriate indicative or subjunctive form of each verb given in parentheses.

1. Tengo tres hermanos que (llamarse) _____ Beto, Tomás y Rafael.

2. No hay nadie en mi familia que (saber) _____ tocar la guitarra.

3. Tengo una hermana que (saber) _____ tocar el piano.

4. Nos gusta invitar a nuestra iglesia personas que (tener) _____ interés en la música.

5. Cantamos himnos que todos (conocer) _____ .

6. Mi hermana, la que (tocar) el piano _____ , también escribe música.

7. Quiero comprar un himnario que (tener) _____ himnos nuevos.

Resumen de los usos del subjuntivo

The subjunctive mood is used under the following conditions:

- after verbs of volition, as in indirect commands: **Quiero que** venga a mi fiesta.

- after expressions of emotion: **Me alegro de que** conozcas a Cristo.

- after expressions of doubt: Ella **duda que** lleguemos a tiempo.

- after impersonal expressions that express an indirect command, emotion, or doubt: **Es importante que** estudies español.

- after conjunctions followed by unfulfilled conditions: Te acompaño **con tal que** regresemos temprano.

- after conjunctions of time followed by unfulfilled events: Voy al mercado con Carlos **cuando** él venga.

- when referring to a noun that is not definite or may not exist: Quiero una casa **que** tenga piscina.

◆ **Actividad 6**

Complete the sentences with the correct form of each verb indicated.

1. Debemos orar por nuestros amigos para que ellos (pensar) _____ en la necesidad de ser salvos.

2. Dios no quiere que nadie (perderse) _____ .

3. Debemos memorizar la Biblia en caso de que Satanás nos (tentar) _____ a pecar.

4. Dios nos dio su Palabra para que nosotros (poder) _____ vencer la tentación.

5. Todos los creyentes iremos al cielo cuando Cristo (volver) _____ .

◆ **Actividad 7**

Use your imagination and the correct form of each verb indicated to complete the following sentences.

Modelo: Mi maestro quiere que . . . (jugar)
  Mi maestro quiere que (Paco juegue en el torneo.)

1. Un examen es justo con tal de que . . . (probar)

2. Me alegro de que . . . (recordar)

3. Siento mucho que él . . . (no volver)

4. Roberto se queja de que . . . (costar)

5. Todos nos sentamos en la clase tan pronto como . . . (cerrar)

6. Voy a poner los paquetes en la mesa una vez que . . . (mover)

7. Los chicos quieren que las chicas . . . (pensar)

8. Aprendo versículos de memoria para que . . . (poder)

◆ **Actividad 8**

Complete the sentences with the correct form of each verb indicated.

1. Los padres buenos les enseñan a sus hijos a que no (mentir) _____ .

2. Ningún hijo quiere que sus padres (morir) _____ .

3. Los abuelos quieren que sus nietos (sentirse) _____ cómodos con ellos.

4. Papá siempre quiere que nosotros le (pedir) _____ permiso antes de salir.

5. Mi tío quiere que mi primo Roberto le (pedir) _____ permiso también.

6. ¡Ojalá que tú no me (mentir) _____ !

7. Al maestro no le gusta que nosotros (dormir) _____ en la clase.

8. La regla para el equipo de baloncesto es que los jugadores (dormir) _____ ocho horas cada noche.

◆ **Actividad 9**

Form complete sentences using words from each column below. The sentences may be affirmative or negative. Use your imagination!

A	**B**	**C**	**D**
nosotros	querer que	sus hijos	jugar
mis padres	desear que	mis amigos	volver
el Sr. García	alegrarse de que	los estudiantes	mentir
mi amigo(a)	lamentar que	mis padres	dormir
yo	dudar que	los otros	sentir(se)

Vocabulario adicional ▲▲▲▲▲▲▲▲▲▲▲▲▲▲▲▲▲▲▲▲▲▲▲▲▲▲▲▲▲▲▲▲▲▲

In English, the meaning of certain adjectives may be reversed by using a prefix such as *il-, in-, ir-,* or *un-* : for example, necessary/unnecessary. In Spanish, the prefixes *i-, im-,* and *in-* are used to reverse the meanings. Notice that *i-* is used before *l, im-* before *b* and *p,* and *in-* in all other cases.

conveniente	inconveniente
esperado	inesperado
justo	injusto
legal	ilegal
necesario	innecesario
posible	imposible
quieto	inquieto
satisfacción	insatisfacción
tranquilo	intranquilo

La Plaza España con las Torres Venecianas y la plaza de toros en el fondo forma parte de la perspectiva de la ciudad de Barcelona.

BARCELONA

Lying on the shores of the Mediterranean Sea, Barcelona is Spain's most important commercial center. The city produces leather, chemicals, and automobiles, and its busy harbor oversees Spain's imports and exports.

Barcelona serves as the capital of the autonomous community of *Cataluña.* Consequently, Barcelonians are proud of their regional Latin-based language, *Catalán.* Several television and radio stations broadcast completely in *Catalán.*

Barcelona has gained worldwide recognition for its cultural achievements. Among those associated with the city are artist Joan Miró, architect Antonio Gaudí, and cellist Pablo Cassals.

Tourists to Barcelona frequent the old Gothic Quarter, the monument to Christopher Columbus, Gaudí's Temple of the Holy Family, and the Olympic Village which hosted the 1992 Olympic Games.

12-2 El nuevo nacimiento

Lectura bíblica ▲▲▲▲▲▲▲▲▲▲▲▲▲▲▲▲▲▲▲▲▲▲▲▲▲▲▲▲▲▲▲▲▲▲▲▲▲▲▲

Juan 3:1-7

> Había un hombre de los fariseos que se llamaba Nicodemo, un principal entre los judíos. Este vino a Jesús de noche, y le dijo: Rabí, sabemos que has venido de Dios como maestro; porque nadie puede hacer estas señales que tú haces, si no está Dios con él. Respondió Jesús y le dijo: De cierto, de cierto te digo, que el que no naciere de nuevo, no puede ver el reino de Dios. Nicodemo le dijo: ¿Cómo puede un hombre nacer siendo viejo? ¿Puede acaso entrar por segunda vez en el vientre de su madre, y nacer? Respondió Jesús: De cierto, de cierto te digo, que el que no naciere de agua y del Espíritu, no puede entrar en el reino de Dios. Lo que es nacido de la carne, carne es; y lo que es nacido del Espíritu, espíritu es. No te maravilles de que te dije: Os es necesario nacer de nuevo.

Gramática ▲▲▲

El imperfecto del subjuntivo

The simple past tense of the subjunctive, called the imperfect subjunctive, is based on the *ellos* form of the preterite indicative, minus *-ron*. The imperfect subjunctive endings are then added to this stem.

	hablar	comer	salir
(ellos) preterite: Stem:	hablaron habla-	comieron comie-	salieron salie-
yo	hablara	comiera	saliera
tú	hablaras	comieras	salieras
Ud., él, ella	hablara	comiera	saliera
nosotros(as)	habláramos	comiéramos	saliéramos
vosotros(as)	hablarais	comierais	salierais
Uds., ellos(as)	hablaran	comieran	salieran

Since the imperfect subjunctive uses the third-person plural preterite stem, you must have a good working knowledge of the preterite forms. When necessary, refer to previous lessons or consult the Reference Tables in the back of the book.

The following verbs are irregular in the preterite:

Infinitive	*ellos* preterite	*yo* subjunctive
decir	dijeron	dijera
estar	estuvieron	estuviera
ir/ser	fueron	fuera
poner	pusieron	pusiera
tener	tuvieron	tuviera
venir	vinieron	viniera

Note: There is another set of endings for the imperfect subjunctive:

-se	-semos
-ses	-seis
-se	-sen

These endings are commonly used in Spain, in the Bible, and in literature, but are less commonly heard in Latin America. There is no difference in meaning between the two forms.

El empleo del imperfecto del subjuntivo

If the verb in the independent clause is in the past tense, the verb in the
dependent clause is in the imperfect subjunctive tense.

El pastor nos **dijo** que
  habláramos más claro.
Era importante que **estuviera**
  en casa el sábado.
Me alegré de que **se fueran**
  temprano.

*The pastor told us to speak (that
  we should speak) more clearly.
It was important for me to be
  (that I be) at home on Saturday.
I was glad that they left early.*

◆ **Actividad 1**

Ayer la profesora les dio instrucciones a los estudiantes. ¿Qué les dijo?

Modelo: Ana: estudiar más
    Le dijo a Ana que estudiara más.

1. Manolo: aprender los verbos

2. Rafael: preparar un informe

3. Rebeca: pintar un cuadro

4. Margarita: estudiar acerca de Colón

5. tú: leer el capítulo diez

6. Tomás y Pedro: llegar a tiempo

7. María y Rosana: hacer las actividades tres y cuatro

8. Beatriz: ir a la biblioteca

9. Sara y Felipe: no venir mañana

10. todos nosotros: repasar para un examen

◆ **Actividad 2**

Los jóvenes hablan del paseo que hicieron el sábado. ¿Cuáles son sus comentarios?

Modelo: Fuimos de paseo para que los jóvenes (tener) _____ compañerismo.
Fuimos de paseo para que los jóvenes tuvieran compañerismo.

1. Queríamos ir de paseo para que Rita (invitar) _____ a su hermana.

2. Invitamos al pastor para que nos (hablar) _____ antes de salir.

3. Pagamos mil pesetas para que todos (subir) _____ al tren.

4. Llevamos alimentos para que Cecilia y Lourdes no (tener) _____ que cocinar.

5. Tabaré llevó su guitarra para que nosotros (cantar) _____ en la montaña.

6. Tuvimos que regresar temprano para que todos (estar) _____ en la iglesia el domingo.

El subjuntivo después de *si*

You have already seen that *si* (*if*) often introduces a clause that states a condition. This clause is usually followed by another clause that gives a result.

The following sentences use the indicative. The *si* clause is in the present tense, and the result clause is in the future tense.

Si **tengo** tiempo, te **ayudaré.**	*If I have time, I will help you.*
Si **estudias, sacarás** mejores notas.	*If you study, you will get better grades.*
Si **pueden, jugarán** al béisbol esta tarde.	*If they are able, they will play baseball this afternoon.*

Sentences following this pattern make the straightforward statement that if one thing happens, then the other thing will follow. They assume that the event in the result clause will take place if the condition in the *si* clause is met.

The sentences below use the imperfect subjunctive in the *si* clause and the conditional tense in the result clause.

Si tuviera tiempo, escribiría un libro.	*If I had time, I would write a book.* ("If I had time" suggests that I really do not have time.)
Si estudiaras más, sacarías mejores notas.	*If you studied more, you would get better grades.* ("If you studied more" suggests that you do not really study much.)
Si pudieran, jugarían al béisbol esta tarde.	*If they could, they would play baseball this afternoon.* ("If they could" suggests that they really cannot do it.)

Sentences that follow this pattern view the situations in the *si* clause as doubtful or hypothetical, suggesting that the events in the result clause are, therefore, unlikely to take place.

◆ **Actividad 3**

Francisco no está satisfecho con lo que sucede. Quisiera que las circunstancias fueran diferentes.

Modelo: Si yo (tener) _____ mil dólares, (comprar) _____ una computadora nueva.
Si (yo) tuviera mil dólares, compraría una computadora nueva.

1. Si yo (hablar) _____ francés, (ir) _____ a Francia.

2. Si (hacer) _____ mejor tiempo, yo (jugar) _____ al ténis.

3. Si no (estar) _____ lloviendo, nosotros (poder) _____ jugar al béisbol.

4. Si (vivir) _____ en la playa, (estar) _____ en el agua todo el día.

5. Si los estudiantes (escuchar) _____ mejor, el maestro no (tener que) _____ repetir tantas veces.

6. Si nosotros (estudiar) _____ más, (ser) _____ estudiantes más inteligentes.

7. Si yo no (tener) _____ tanta hambre, (esperar) _____ .

8. Si yo no (tener) _____ tanto sueño, (leer) _____ un libro.

◆ **Actividad 4**

¿Qué haría Ud. bajo las siguientes circunstancias? Complete las oraciones según lo que haría.

1. Si yo tuviera dos mil dólares, . . .

2. Si fuera presidente de los Estados Unidos, . . .

3. Si viviera en Nueva York, . . .

4. Si recibiera una C en español, . . .

5. Si mis padres fueran misioneros, . . .

6. Si yo pudiera comer mi comida favorita todos los días, . . .

7. Si fuera director(a) de la escuela, . . .

8. Si tuviera dinero para comprar un automóvil, . . .

9. Si no supiera que Dios me ama, . . .

10. Si no estuviera en esta clase, . . .

Nota Informativa ▲▲▲▲▲▲▲▲▲▲▲▲▲▲▲▲▲▲▲▲▲▲▲▲▲▲▲▲▲▲▲▲▲▲

Did you know that there is a Spanish-speaking country in Africa? The Republic of Equatorial Guinea is located south of Cameroon and includes several small islands off the west coast of Africa. Though most of the people speak tribal languages, Spanish is the official language used in government, commerce, and education. Equatorial Guinea flourished as a colony of Spain, but the nation has suffered much turmoil since it gained its independence in 1968. Its 390,000 inhabitants live in great need of economic and medical assistance. Yet their greatest need is spiritual. Few Protestant missionaries minister in this country dominated by Roman Catholicism and tribal religions.

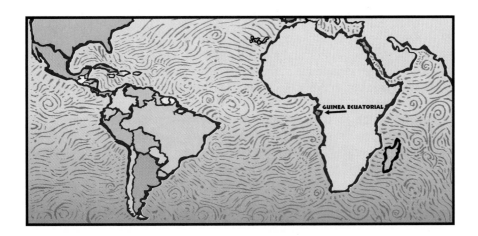

Reference Tables

VERBS

The Indicative Mood

The Present Tense

I speak, am speaking; I eat, am eating; I live, am living

Regular Forms

	First Conjugation -*ar*	Second Conjugation -*er*	Third Conjugation -*ir*
	hablar	**comer**	**vivir**
yo	habl**o**	com**o**	viv**o**
tú	habl**as**	com**es**	viv**es**
él, ella, Ud.	habl**a**	com**e**	viv**e**
nosotros(as)	habl**amos**	com**emos**	viv**imos**
vosotros(as)	habl**áis**	com**éis**	viv**ís**
ellos(as), Uds.	habl**an**	com**en**	viv**en**

Regular Verbs with Spelling Changes

1. Verbs that end in **-*ger*** or **-*gir*** change **g** to **j** before **o**.
   escoger: escojo, escoges, escoge, escogemos, escogéis, escogen
   dirigir: dirijo, diriges, dirige, dirigimos, dirigís, dirigen
   Other examples: *proteger, recoger, ungir*
2. Verbs that end in **-*uir*** add **y** to the end of the stem before adding the ending in all persons of the verb except *nosotros* and *vosotros*.
   construir: construyo, construyes, construye, construimos, construís, construyen
   incluir: incluyo, incluyes, incluye, incluimos, incluís, incluyen
   Other examples: *constituir, destruir, excluir, sustituir*
   oír: *Oír* fits this category but has an irregular first-person singular (*yo*) form (***oigo, oyes, oye, oímos, oís, oyen***). See **Irregular First-Person Verbs.**

Stem-changing Verbs: (-*ar* and -*er* verbs)

1. *e→ie* and *o→ue:* The *e* or *o* closest to the stem is the vowel that changes.

pensar (e→ie)	poder (o→ue)
pienso	puedo
piensas	puedes
piensa	puede
pensamos	podemos
pensáis	podéis
piensan	pueden

2. *u→ue: Jugar* is the only verb with the stem change *u→ue.* It follows the same pattern as the verbs above.

jugar (u→ue)
juego
juegas
juega
jugamos
jugáis
juegan

Stem-changing Verbs: (-*ir* verbs)

1. *e→ie* and *o→ue:* In verbs of this type, the *e* or *o* closest to the stem is the vowel that changes. See *sentir* and *dormir* below.
2. *e→i:* In verbs of this type, the *e* closest to the stem is the vowel that changes. The *e→i* stem change occurs only in -*ir* verbs. See *pedir* below.

sentir (e→ie)	dormir (o→ue)	pedir (e→i)
siento	duermo	pido
sientes	duermes	pides
siente	duerme	pide
sentimos	dormimos	pedimos
sentís	dormís	pedís
sienten	duermen	piden

Irregular First-Person Verbs

1. *Ver, dar, saber,* and *caber* are irregular only in the *yo* form.

ver	dar	saber	caber
veo	**doy**	**sé**	**quepo**
ves	das	sabes	cabes
ve	da	sabe	cabe
vemos	damos	sabemos	cabemos
veis	dais	sabéis	cabéis
ven	dan	saben	caben

2. *-zco* verbs are irregular only in the *yo* form.

conocer	producir
conozco	**produzco**
conoces	produces
conoce	produce
conocemos	producimos
conocéis	producís
conocen	producen

3. *-go* verbs have an irregular *yo* form. Some also have other irregularities.

poner	salir	valer	traer / caer	tener / venir	decir	oír
pon**go**	sal**go**	val**go**	tra**igo** / ca**igo**	ten**go** / ven**go**	d**igo**	o**igo**
pones	sales	vales	traes / caes	**tie**nes / **vie**nes	dices	o**y**es
pone	sale	vale	trae / cae	**tie**ne / **vie**ne	dice	o**y**e
ponemos	salimos	valemos	traemos / caemos	tenemos / venimos	decimos	oímos
ponéis	salís	valéis	traéis / caéis	tenéis / venís	decís	oís
ponen	salen	valen	traen / caen	**tie**nen / **vie**nen	dicen	o**y**en

Irregular Verbs: *ser, ir, estar, haber*

ser	ir	estar	haber
soy	voy	estoy	he
eres	vas	estás	has
es	va	está	ha
somos	vamos	estamos	hemos
sois	vais	estáis	habéis
son	van	están	han

The Preterite Tense

I spoke; I ate; I lived

Regular Forms

	First Conjugation -ar **hablar**	Second Conjugation -er **comer**	Third Conjugation -ir **vivir**
yo	habl**é**	com**í**	viv**í**
tú	habl**aste**	com**iste**	viv**iste**
él, ella, Ud.	habl**ó**	com**ió**	viv**ió**
nosotros(as)	habl**amos**	com**imos**	viv**imos**
vosotros(as)	habl**asteis**	com**isteis**	viv**isteis**
ellos(as), Uds.	habl**aron**	com**ieron**	viv**ieron**

Verbs with Spelling Changes

1. In first-person singular (*yo*) form only:

   Verbs ending in *-car:* The *c* changes to *qu* before *é.*

   sacar: sa**qué,** sacaste, sacó, sacamos, sacasteis, sacaron

   Verbs ending in *-gar*: The *g* changes to *gu* before *é.*

   jugar: ju**gué,** jugaste, jugó, jugamos, jugasteis, jugaron

   Verbs ending in *-zar:* The *z* changes to *c* before *é.*

   comenzar: comen**cé,** comenzaste, comenzó, comenzamos, comenzasteis, comenzaron

2. In third-person singular and plural (*él, ella, Ud., ellos(as), Uds.*) only:

   Verbs ending in *-eer, -uir,* and the verbs *caer* and *oír:**

   ió→yó, ieron→yeron

   creer: creí, creíste, cre**yó,** creímos, creísteis, cre**yeron**

   influir: influí, influiste, influ**yó,** influimos, influisteis, influ**yeron**

   * For *caer* and *oír*, see **Ready-reference Verb Charts.**

Verbs with Stem Changes

In third-person singular and plural only:

1. **-ir** verbs whose only irregularity is the stem change *e→ie* or *e→i* in the present tense: *e→i*

   sentir: sentí, sentiste, s**i**ntió, sentimos, sentisteis, s**i**ntieron

   pedir: pedí, pediste, p**i**dió, pedimos, pedisteis, p**i**dieron

2. *-ir* verbs with the stem change $o \rightarrow ue$ in the present tense: $o \rightarrow u$

    morir: morí, moriste, murió, morimos, moristeis, murieron

    dormir: dormí, dormiste, durmió, dormimos, dormisteis, durmieron

Irregular Verbs

Irregular endings: *-e, -iste, -o, -imos, -isteis, -ieron*

1. *hacer, querer, venir*

hacer	➡ hic.-*
querer	➡ quis-
venir	➡ vin-

*The *c* changes to *z* before *o*.

2. *andar, estar, haber, poder*

andar	➡ anduv-
estar	➡ estuv-
haber	➡ hub-
poder	➡ pud-

3. *poner, saber, tener*

poner	➡ pus-
saber	➡ sup-
tener	➡ tuv-

4. *decir, traer, producir, bendecir**

    Endings: *-e, -iste, -o, -imos-, -isteis, -eron***

decir	➡ dij-
traer	➡ traj-
producir	➡ produj-
bendecir	➡ bendij-

*Most verbs ending in *-cir* follow the above conjugation pattern.
**Notice that the *j-* at the end of the stem of these verbs replaces the *i* of the third-person plural ending.

Ir and ser

These two verbs share the same irregular forms in the preterite.

ir	ser
fui	fui
fuiste	fuiste
fue	fue
fuimos	fuimos
fuisteis	fuisteis
fueron	fueron

The Imperfect Tense

I used to speak, I used to eat, I used to live

Regular Forms

Most verbs are regular in the imperfect tense.

hablar	comer	vivir
hablaba	comía	vivía
hablabas	comías	vivías
hablaba	comía	vivía
hablábamos	comíamos	vivíamos
hablabais	comíais	vivíais
hablaban	comían	vivían

Irregular Forms

Only three verbs are irregular in the imperfect tense.

ser	ir	ver
era	iba	veía
eras	ibas	veías
era	iba	veía
éramos	íbamos	veíamos
erais	ibais	veíais
eran	iban	veían

The Future Tense

I will (shall) speak; I will (shall) eat; I will (shall) live

Regular Forms:

Infinitive + *-é, -ás, -á, -emos, -éis, -án*

hablar	comer	vivir
hablar**é**	comer**é**	vivir**é**
hablar**ás**	comer**ás**	vivir**ás**
hablar**á**	comer**á**	vivir**á**
hablar**emos**	comer**emos**	vivir**emos**
hablar**éis**	comer**éis**	vivir**éis**
hablar**án**	comer**án**	vivir**án**

Irregular Forms

The irregular verbs attach the future tense endings (listed above under **Regular Forms**) to an irregular stem instead of to the infinitive. The irregular future tense verbs and their stems are listed below:

decir	→ dir-	querer	→ querr-
haber	→ habr-	saber	→ sabr-
hacer	→ har-	salir	→ saldr-
poder	→ podr-	tener	→ tendr-
poner	→ pondr-	venir	→ vendr-

The Conditional Tense

I would speak; I would eat; I would live

Regular Forms:

Infinitive + *-ía, -ías, -ía, -íamos, -íais, -ían*

hablar	comer	vivir
hablar**ía**	comer**ía**	vivir**ía**
hablar**ías**	comer**ías**	vivir**ías**
hablar**ía**	comer**ía**	vivir**ía**
hablar**íamos**	comer**íamos**	vivir**íamos**
hablar**íais**	comer**íais**	vivir**íais**
hablar**ían**	comer**ían**	vivir**ían**

Most verbs are regular in the conditional tense.

Irregular Forms

The irregular verbs attach the conditional tense endings (listed under **Regular Forms**) to an irregular stem instead of to the infinitive. The irregular conditional tense verbs and their stems are the same as for the irregular future tense. (See: **The Future Tense—Irregular Forms.**)

The Present Perfect

I have spoken; I have eaten; I have lived
Tense formation: *haber* in present tense + past participle

The Pluperfect

I had spoken; I had eaten; I had lived
Tense formation: *haber* in imperfect tense + past participle

The Future Perfect

I will have spoken; I will have eaten; I will have lived
Tense formation: *haber* in future tense + past participle

The Conditional Perfect

I would have spoken; I would have eaten; I would have lived
Tense formation: *haber* in conditional tense + past participle

Present Perfect	Pluperfect	Future Perfect	Conditional Perfect
hablar	**comer**	**vivir**	**tomar**
he hablado	**había** comido	**habré** vivido	**habría** tomado
has hablado	**habías** comido	**habrás** vivido	**habrías** tomado
ha hablado	**había** comido	**habrá** vivido	**habría** tomado
hemos hablado	**habíamos** comido	**habremos** vivido	**habríamos** tomado
habéis hablado	**habíais** comido	**habréis** vivido	**habríais** tomado
han hablado	**habían** comido	**habrán** vivido	**habrían** tomado

See also: **Irregular Past Participles**

Present Participles

Speaking; eating; living

Regular Forms

The participial ending attaches to the stem of the infinitive.
>   *-ar* verbs: *-ando*
>   *-er, -ir* verbs: *-iendo*
>
>   *hablar → hablando*
>   *comer → comiendo*
>   *vivir → viviendo*

Irregular Forms

1. Verbs ending in **-aer, -eer, -uir,** and the verb **oír: -iendo → yendo.**

   traer → trayendo
   leer → leyendo
   construir → construyendo
   oír → oyendo

2. All three types of stem-change **-ir** verbs (*e→ie, o→ue, e→i*) have an extra stem change in the present participle: *e→i, o→u.*

   sentir → sintiendo
   pedir → pidiendo
   dormir → durmiendo

Progressive Forms

The present participles may combine with the verb **estar** to form the **present progressive form:**

estoy hablando
estás comiendo
estamos viviendo

Past Participles

Spoken; eaten; lived

Regular Forms

The participial ending attaches to the stem of the infinitive.

-ar verbs: **-ado**
-er, -ir verbs: **-ido**

hablar → hablado
entender → entendido
pedir → pedido

Irregular Forms

The following verbs have irregular past participles.

abrir	→ abierto	morir	→ muerto
cubrir	→ cubierto	poner	→ puesto
decir	→ dicho	romper	→ roto
escribir	→ escrito	ver	→ visto
hacer	→ hecho	volver	→ vuelto

Past Participles as Adjectives

When a past participle combines with *ser* or *estar,* it has four forms (*-o, -os, -a, -as*) and agrees in number and gender with the noun it describes.

> *La ventana está **rota**.*
> *Los libros fueron **escritos** por Octavio Paz.*

Past Participles and the Compound Tenses

When a past participle combines with *haber,* it forms part of a compound verb tense and has only one form ending in **-o.**

> *Nosotras no **hemos comprado** la casa.*

The Subjunctive Mood

The Present Subjunctive

(that) I (may) speak; (that) I (may) think; (that) I (may) return; (that) I (may) feel; (that) I (may) sleep

Regular Forms

Most verbs derive their present subjunctive forms from the stem of the first-person singular (*yo*) form of the present indicative. (See: **The Indicative Mood—The Present Tense.**) Note *hablar* in the following chart.

Verbs with Spelling Changes

Verbs with the endings *-car, -gar,* and *-zar* have the following spelling changes:

> **-car:** *-que, -ques, -que, -quemos, -quéis, -quen*
> **-gar:** *-gue, -gues, -gue, -guemos, -guéis, -guen*
> **-zar:** *-ce, -ces, -ce, -cemos, -céis, -cen*

Stem-changing Verbs (*-ar* and *-er* verbs)

-ar and *-er* stem-changing verbs have the same stem changes in the subjunctive that they have in the indicative. Note *pensar* and *volver* in the following chart.

Stem-changing Verbs (*-ir* verbs)

e→ie and *o→ue* verbs have an additional stem change in the *nosotros* and *vosotros* forms: *e→ie → i* and *o→ue → u.* Note *sentir* and *dormir* below.

hablar →	pensar →	volver →	sentir →	dormir →
hablo → habl-	pienso → piens-	vuelvo → vuelv-	siento → sient-	duermo → duerm-
hable	piense	vuelva	sienta	duerma
hables	pienses	vuelvas	sientas	duermas
hable	piense	vuelva	sienta	duerma
hablemos	pensemos	volvamos	sintamos	durmamos
habléis	penséis	volváis	sintáis	durmáis
hablen	piensen	vuelvan	sientan	duerman

Irregular Forms

The following verbs **do not** derive the form of the present subjunctive from the stem of the *yo* present indicative:

ser	ir	dar	estar	haber	saber
sea	vaya	dé	esté	haya	sepa
seas	vayas	des	estés	hayas	sepas
sea	vaya	dé	esté	haya	sepa
seamos	vayamos	demos	estemos	hayamos	sepamos
seáis	vayáis	deis	estéis	hayáis	sepáis
sean	vayan	den	estén	hayan	sepan

The Imperfect Subjunctive

(that) I might speak; (that) I might say; (that) I might return; (that) I might feel; (that) I might sleep

All verbs in the imperfect subjunctive are based on the third-person plural form of the preterite tense. (See: **The Indicative Mood—The Preterite Tense.**) The last three letters of the verb (*-ron*) are removed and the subjunctive endings are added.

hablar→	decir→	volver→	sentir→	dormir→
hablaron→ habla-	dijeron→ dije-	volvieron→ volvie-	sintieron→ sintie-	durmieron→ durmie-
hablara (hablase)	dijera (dijese)	volviera (volviese)	sintiera (sintiese)	durmiera (durmiese)
hablaras (hablases)	dijeras (dijeses)	volvieras (volvieses)	sintieras (sintieses)	durmieras (durmieses)
hablara (hablase)	dijera (dijese)	volviera (volviese)	sintiera (sintiese)	durmiera (durmiese)
habláramos (hablásemos)	dijéramos (dijésemos)	volviéramos (volviésemos)	sintiéramos (sintiésemos)	durmiéramos (durmiésemos)
hablarais (hablaseis)	dijerais (dijeseis)	volvierais (volvieseis)	sintierais (sintieseis)	durmierais (durmieseis)
hablaran (hablasen)	dijeran (dijesen)	volvieran (volviesen)	sintieran (sintiesen)	durmieran (durmiesen)

Note: The first person plural (*nosotros*) form of the imperfect subjunctive takes an accent mark on the second-to-last syllable.

The Imperative Mood (Command Forms)

Regular forms

Speak!, Eat!, Write!

Most command forms are derived from the present subjunctive forms. (See: **The Subjunctive Mood—The Present Subjunctive.**) The regular *tú* affirmative command uses the same form as the third-person singular (*él, ella*) form of the present indicative. (See: **The Indicative Mood—The Present Tense.**)

	Affirmative Commands	Negative Commands
	third-person indicative	present subjunctive
Tú	habla come escribe	no hables no comas no escribas
	present subjunctive	present subjunctive
Ud. / Uds.	hable / hablen coma / coman escriba / escriban	no hable / no hablen no coma / no coman no escriba / no escriban
	present subjunctive (or) *vamos a* + infinitive	present subjunctive
Nosotros (Let's)	hablemos / vamos a hablar comamos / vamos a comer escribamos / vamos a escribir	no hablemos no comamos no escribamos

Irregular Affirmative *tú* Forms

Eight verbs are irregular in the *tú* affirmative command in that they do not use the third-person singular form of the present indicative. In the negative all use the present subjunctive form.

decir	di		**salir**	sal
hacer	haz		**ser**	sé
ir	ve		**tener**	ten
poner	pon		**venir**	ven

Ready-reference Verb Charts

andar	to walk			Present progressive andando Past participle andado			
Present	Preterite	Imperfect	Future	Conditional	Present Subjunctive	Imperative (familiar)
ando	**anduve**	andaba	andaré	andaría	ande	anda
andas	**anduviste**	andabas	andarás	andarías	andes	no andes
anda	**anduvo**	andaba	andará	andaría	ande	
andamos	**anduvimos**	andábamos	andaremos	andaríamos	andemos	
andáis	**anduvisteis**	andabais	andarás	andaríais	andeis	
andan	**anduvieron**	andaban	andarán	andarían	anden	

caber	to fit			Present progressive cabiendo Past participle cabido			
Present	Preterite	Imperfect	Future	Conditional	Present Subjunctive	Imperative (familiar)
quepo	**cupe**	cabía	cab**ré**	cab**ría**	**quepa**	cabe
cabes	**cupiste**	cabías	cab**rás**	cab**rías**	**quepas**	no quepes
cabe	**cupo**	cabía	cab**rá**	cab**ría**	**quepa**	
cabemos	**cupimos**	cabíamos	cab**remos**	cab**ríamos**	**quepamos**	
cabéis	**cupisteis**	cabíais	cab**réis**	cab**ríais**	**quepáis**	
caben	**cupieron**	cabían	cab**rán**	cab**rían**	**quepan**	

caer	to fall			Present progressive cayendo Past participle caído			
Present	Preterite	Imperfect	Future	Conditional	Present Subjunctive	Imperitive (familiar)
ca**igo**	caí	caía	caeré	caería	ca**iga**	cae
caes	caíste	caías	caerás	caerías	ca**igas**	no caigas
cae	ca**yó**	caía	caerá	caería	ca**iga**	
caemos	caímos	caíamos	caeremos	caeríamos	ca**igamos**	
caéis	caísteis	caíais	caeréis	caeríais	ca**igáis**	
caen	ca**yeron**	caían	caerán	caerían	ca**igan**	

conocer	to know			Present progressive	conociendo	Past participle	conocido

Present	Preterite	Imperfect	Future	Conditional	Present Subjunctive	Imperative (familiar)
cono**zco**	conocí	conocía	conoceré	conocería	cono**zca**	conoce
conoces	conociste	conocías	conocerás	conocerías	cono**zcas**	no conozcas
conoce	conoció	conocía	conocerá	conocería	cono**zca**	
conocemos	conocimos	conocíamos	conoceremos	conoceríamos	cono**zcamos**	
conocéis	conocisteis	conocíais	conoceréis	conoceríais	cono**zcáis**	
conocen	conocieron	conocían	conocerán	conocerían	cono**zcan**	

dar	to give			Present progressive	dando	Past participle	dado

Present	Preterite	Imperfect	Future	Conditional	Present Subjunctive	Imperative (familiar)
doy	**di**	daba	daré	daría	**dé**	da
das	**diste**	dabas	darás	darías	**des**	no des
da	**dio**	daba	dará	daría	**dé**	
damos	**dimos**	dábamos	daremos	daríamos	**demos**	
dais	**disteis**	dabais	daréis	daríais	**deis**	
dan	**dieron**	daban	darán	darían	**den**	

decir	to say			Present progressive	diciendo	Past participle	dicho

Present	Preterite	Imperfect	Future	Conditional	Present Subjunctive	Imperative (familiar)
digo	**dije**	decía	**diré**	**diría**	**diga**	di
dices	**dijiste**	decías	**dirás**	**dirías**	**digas**	no digas
dice	**dijo**	decía	**dirá**	**diría**	**diga**	
decimos	**dijimos**	decíamos	**diremos**	**diríamos**	**digamos**	
decís	**dijisteis**	decíais	**diréis**	**diríais**	**digáis**	
dicen	**dijeron**	decían	**dirán**	**dirían**	**digan**	

estar — *to be*

Present progressive estando **Past participle** estado

Present	Preterite	Imperfect	Future	Conditional	Present Subjunctive	Imperative (familiar)
est**oy**	**estuve**	estaba	estaré	estaría	est**é**	está
estás	**estuviste**	estabas	estarás	estarías	est**és**	no estés
está	**estuvo**	estaba	estará	estaría	est**é**	
estamos	**estuvimos**	estábamos	estaremos	estaríamos	est**emos**	
estáis	**estuvisteis**	estabais	estaréis	estaríais	est**éis**	
están	**estuvieron**	estaban	estarán	estarían	est**én**	

haber — *to have* (auxiliary)

Present progressive habiendo **Past participle** habido

Present	Preterite	Imperfect	Future	Conditional	Present Subjunctive
he	**hube**	había	hab**ré**	hab**ría**	**haya**
has	**hubiste**	habías	hab**rás**	hab**rías**	**hayas**
ha	**hubo**	había	hab**rá**	hab**ría**	**haya**
hemos	**hubimos**	habíamos	hab**remos**	hab**ríamos**	**hayamos**
habéis	**hubisteis**	habíais	hab**réis**	hab**ríais**	**hayáis**
han	**hubieron**	habían	hab**rán**	hab**rían**	**hayan**

hacer — *to make, to do*

Present progressive haciendo **Past participle** hecho

Present	Preterite	Imperfect	Future	Conditional	Present Subjunctive	Imperative (familiar)
hago	**hice**	hacía	har**é**	har**ía**	**haga**	haz
haces	**hiciste**	hacías	har**ás**	har**ías**	**hagas**	no hagas
hace	**hizo**	hacía	har**á**	har**ía**	**haga**	
hacemos	**hicimos**	hacíamos	har**emos**	har**íamos**	**hagamos**	
hacéis	**hicisteis**	hacíais	har**éis**	har**íais**	**hagáis**	
hacen	**hicieron**	hacían	har**án**	har**ían**	**hagan**	

| ir | to go | | | | Present progressive | yendo | Past participle | ido |

Present	Preterite	Imperfect	Future	Conditional	Present Subjunctive	Imperative (familiar)
voy	fui	iba	iré	iría	vaya	ve
vas	fuiste	ibas	irás	irías	vayas	no vayas
va	fue	iba	irá	iría	vaya	
vamos	fuimos	íbamos	iremos	iríamos	vayamos	
vais	fuisteis	ibais	iréis	iríais	vayáis	
van	fueron	iban	irán	irían	vayan	

| oír | to hear | | | | Present progressive | oyendo | Past participle | oído |

Present	Preterite	Imperfect	Future	Conditional	Present Subjunctive	Imperative (familiar)
oigo	oí	oía	oiré	oiría	oiga	oye
oyes	oíste	oías	oirás	oirías	oigas	no oigas
oye	oyó	oía	oirá	oiría	oiga	
oímos	oímos	oíamos	oiremos	oiríamos	oigamos	
oís	oísteis	oíais	oiréis	oiríais	oigáis	
oyen	oyeron	oían	oirán	oirían	oigan	

| poder | to be able | | | | Present progressive | pudiendo | Past participle | podido |

Present	Preterite	Imperfect	Future	Conditional	Present Subjunctive
puedo	pude	podía	podré	podría	pueda
puedes	pudiste	podías	podrás	podrías	puedas
puede	pudo	podía	podrá	podría	pueda
podemos	pudimos	podíamos	podremos	podríamos	podamos
podéis	pudisteis	podíais	podréis	podríais	podáis
pueden	pudieron	podían	podrán	podrían	puedan

poner	to put			Present progressive	poniendo	Past participle	puesto

Present	Preterite	Imperfect	Future	Conditional	Present Subjunctive	Imperative (familiar)
pon**go**	**puse**	ponía	pon**dré**	pon**dría**	pon**ga**	pon
pones	**pusiste**	ponías	pon**drás**	pon**drías**	pon**gas**	no pongas
pone	**puso**	ponía	pon**drá**	pon**dría**	pon**ga**	
ponemos	**pusimos**	poníamos	pon**dremos**	pon**dríamos**	pon**gamos**	
ponéis	**pusisteis**	poníais	pon**dréis**	pon**dríais**	pon**gáis**	
ponen	**pusieron**	ponían	pon**drán**	pon**drían**	pon**gan**	

producir	to produce			Present progressive	produciendo	Past participle	producido

Present	Preterite	Imperfect	Future	Conditional	Present Subjunctive	Imperative (familiar)
produ**zco**	**produje**	producía	produciré	produciría	produ**zca**	produce
produces	**produjiste**	producías	producirás	producirías	produ**zcas**	no produzcas
produce	**produjo**	producía	producirá	produciría	produ**zca**	
producimos	**produjimos**	producíamos	produciremos	produciríamos	produ**zcamos**	
producís	**produjisteis**	producíais	produciréis	produciríais	produ**zcáis**	
producen	**produjeron**	producían	producirán	producirían	produ**zcan**	

querer	to want			Present progressive	queriendo	Past participle	querido

Present	Preterite	Imperfect	Future	Conditional	Present Subjunctive	Imperative (familiar)
qu**ie**ro	**quise**	quería	quer**ré**	quer**ría**	**quiera**	quiere
qu**ie**res	**quisiste**	querías	quer**rás**	quer**rías**	**quieras**	no quieras
qu**ie**re	**quiso**	quería	quer**rá**	quer**ría**	**quiera**	
queremos	**quisimos**	queríamos	quer**remos**	quer**ríamos**	**queramos**	
queréis	**quisisteis**	queríais	quer**réis**	quer**ríais**	**queráis**	
qu**ie**ren	**quisieron**	querían	quer**rán**	quer**rían**	**quieran**	

saber	to know			Present progressive	sabiendo	Past participle	sabido

Present	Preterite	Imperfect	Future	Conditional	Present Subjunctive	Imperative (familiar)
sé	**supe**	sabía	sab**ré**	sab**ría**	**sepa**	sabe
sabes	**supiste**	sabías	sab**rás**	sab**rías**	**sepas**	no sepas
sabe	**supo**	sabía	sab**rá**	sab**ría**	**sepa**	
sabemos	**supimos**	sabíamos	sab**remos**	sab**ríamos**	**sepamos**	
sabéis	**supisteis**	sabíais	sab**réis**	sab**ríais**	**sepáis**	
saben	**supieron**	sabían	sab**rán**	sab**rían**	**sepan**	

salir	to go out			Present progressive	saliendo	Past participle	salido

Present	Preterite	Imperfect	Future	Conditional	Present Subjunctive	Imperative (familiar)
sal**go**	salí	salía	sal**dré**	sal**dría**	sal**ga**	sal
sales	saliste	salías	sal**drás**	sal**drías**	sal**gas**	no salgas
sale	salió	salía	sal**drá**	sal**dría**	sal**ga**	
salimos	salimos	salíamos	sal**dremos**	sal**dríamos**	sal**gamos**	
salís	salisteis	salíais	sal**dréis**	sal**dríais**	sal**gáis**	
salen	salieron	salían	sal**drán**	sal**drían**	sal**gan**	

seguir	to follow			Present progressive	siguiendo	Past participle	seguido

Present	Preterite	Imperfect	Future	Conditional	Present Subjunctive	Imperative (familiar)
sigo	seguí	seguía	seguiré	seguiría	**siga**	sigue
si**gues**	seguiste	seguías	seguirás	seguirías	**sigas**	no sigas
si**gue**	siguió	seguía	seguirá	seguiría	**siga**	
seguimos	seguimos	seguíamos	seguiremos	seguiríamos	**sigamos**	
seguís	seguisteis	seguíais	seguiréis	seguiríais	**sigáis**	
si**guen**	siguieron	seguían	seguirán	seguirían	**sigan**	

Reference Tables

ser — to be

Present progressive: siendo   Past participle: sido

Present	Preterite	Imperfect	Future	Conditional	Present Subjunctive	Imperative (familiar)
soy	fui	era	seré	sería	sea	sé
eres	fuiste	eras	serás	serías	seas	no seas
es	fue	era	será	sería	sea	
somos	fuimos	éramos	seremos	seríamos	seamos	
sois	fuisteis	erais	seréis	seríais	seáis	
son	fueron	eran	serán	serían	sean	

tener — to have

Present progressive: teniendo   Past participle: tenido

Present	Preterite	Imperfect	Future	Conditional	Present Subjunctive	Imperative (familiar)
tengo	tuve	tenía	tendré	tendría	tenga	ten
tienes	tuviste	tenías	tendrás	tendrías	tengas	no tengas
tiene	tuvo	tenía	tendrá	tendría	tenga	
tenemos	tuvimos	teníamos	tendremos	tendríamos	tengamos	
tenéis	tuvisteis	teníais	tendréis	tendríais	tengáis	
tienen	tuvieron	tenían	tendrán	tendrían	tengan	

traer — to bring

Present progressive: trayendo   Past participle: traído

Present	Preterite	Imperfect	Future	Conditional	Present Subjunctive	Imperative (familiar)
traigo	traje	traía	traeré	traería	traiga	trae
traes	trajiste	traías	traerás	traerías	traigas	no traigas
trae	trajo	traía	traerá	traería	traiga	
traemos	trajimos	traíamos	traeremos	traeríamos	traigamos	
traéis	trajisteis	traíais	traeréis	traeríais	traigáis	
traen	trajeron	traían	traerán	traerían	traigan	

valer	to be worth			Present progressive	valiendo	Past participle	valido

Present	Preterite	Imperfect	Future	Conditional	Present Subjunctive	Imperative (familiar)
val**go**	valí	valía	val**dré**	val**dría**	val**ga**	val
vales	valiste	valías	val**drás**	val**drías**	val**gas**	no valgas
vale	valió	valía	val**drá**	val**dría**	val**ga**	
valemos	valimos	valíamos	val**dremos**	val**dríamos**	val**gamos**	
valéis	valisteis	valíais	val**dréis**	val**dríais**	val**gáis**	
valen	valieron	valían	val**drán**	val**drían**	val**gan**	

venir	to come			Present progressive	viniendo	Past participle	venido

Present	Preterite	Imperfect	Future	Conditional	Present Subjunctive	Imperative (familiar)
ven**go**	**vine**	venía	ven**dré**	ven**dría**	ven**ga**	ven
vienes	**viniste**	venías	ven**drás**	ven**drías**	ven**gas**	no vengas
viene	**vino**	venía	ven**drá**	ven**dría**	ven**ga**	
venimos	**vinimos**	veníamos	ven**dremos**	ven**dríamos**	ven**gamos**	
venís	**vinisteis**	veníais	ven**dréis**	ven**dríais**	ven**gáis**	
vienen	**vinieron**	venían	ven**drán**	ven**drían**	ven**gan**	

ver	to see			Present progressive	viendo	Past participle	visto

Present	Preterite	Imperfect	Future	Conditional	Present Subjunctive	Imperitive (familiar)
veo	vi	veía	veré	vería	**vea**	ve
ves	viste	veías	verás	verías	**veas**	no veas
ve	vio	veía	verá	vería	**vea**	
vemos	vimos	veíamos	veremos	veríamos	**veamos**	
veis	visteis	veíais	veréis	veríais	**veáis**	
ven	vieron	veían	verán	verían	**vean**	

volver	to return				Present progressive volviendo	Past participle vuelto
Present	**Preterite**	**Imperfect**	**Future**	**Conditional**	**Present Subjunctive**	**Imperitive (familiar)**
vuelvo	volví	volvía	volveré	volvería	**vuelva**	vuelve
vuelves	volviste	volvías	volverás	volverías	**vuelvas**	no vuelvas
vuelve	volvió	volvía	volverá	volvería	**vuelva**	
volvemos	volvimos	volvíamos	volveremos	volveríamos	**volvamos**	
volvéis	volvisteis	volvíais	volveréis	volveríais	**volváis**	
vuelven	volvieron	volvían	volverán	volverían	**vuelvan**	

Nouns

Gender

All nouns are either masculine or feminine.
1. Most nouns ending in *-a, -d, -ción,* or *-sión* are feminine.
   la mesa, la niña, la amiga, la verdad, la libertad, la nación, la decisión
   Exceptions: *el mapa, el día, el cesped,* and words that end in *-ama* or *-ema*: *el programa, el problema*
2. Most nouns ending in *-o, -l, -n* or *-r* are masculine.
   el niño, el perro, el himno, el papel, el avión, el profesor
   Exceptions: *la mano, la radio*
3. Nouns ending in *-e* or *-z* may be either masculine or feminine.
   el sobre, la fuente; el lápiz, la cruz

Number

All nouns are either singular or plural.
1. Nouns ending in a vowel form the plural by adding *-s*.
   las niñas, los himnos, las llaves
2. Nouns ending in a consonant form the plural by adding *-es*.
   las libertades, los papeles, los aviones
3. Nouns ending in *-z* change the *z* to *c* before adding *-es*.
   los lápices, las cruces

Determiners

Articles

	Masculine Singular	Masculine Plural	Feminine Singular	Feminine Plural
Definite Articles *(the)*	el	los	la	las
Indefinite Articles *(a, an; some)*	un	unos	una	unas
Demonstrative Adjectives *(this / these that / those)*	este ese aquel	estos esos aquellos	esta esa aquella	estas esas aquellas
Possessive Adjectives *(my, your, his, her, our, your, their)*	mi tu su nuestro su	mis tus sus nuestros sus	mi tu su nuestra su	mis tus sus nuestras sus

Contractions

a + el = al
de + el = del

Adjectives

Agreement

Adjectives must agree in number and gender with the noun they modify.
  1. Adjectives that end in *-o* have four forms: *-o, -a, -os, -as*.

el niño bueno	*los niños buenos*
la niña buena	*las niñas buenas*

  2. Adjectives that end in *-e* or **a consonant** have only two forms, singular and plural. They do not have separate gender forms.

chico inteligente	*chicas inteligentes*
libro azul	*plumas azules*

  3. Adjectives that end in *-ista* or *-ócrata* also have only two forms, singular and plural. They do not have separate gender forms.

pastor bautista	*iglesias bautistas*
diputado demócrata	*legislaturas demócratas*

  4. Unlike other adjectives that end in a consonant, adjectives of nationality that end in a consonant have four forms.

un chico español	*unos señores españoles*
una familia española	*unas ciudades españolas*

Special Forms

Certain adjectives drop the final *-o* before a masculine singular noun:

alguno → algún muchacho	malo → mal muchacho
ninguno → ningún muchacho	primero → primer muchacho
bueno → buen muchacho	tercero → tercer muchacho

Pronouns

Subject	Direct Object	Indirect Object	Reflexive	Object of Preposition
yo	me	me	me	(a) mí*
tú	te	te	te	(a) ti*
usted	lo, la	le	se	(a) usted [*reflexive*: (a) sí*]
él, ella	lo, la	le	se	(a) él, (a) ella [*reflexive*: (a) sí*]
nosotros, nosotras	nos	nos	nos	(a) nosotros, nosotras
vosotros, vosotras	os	os	os	(a) vosotros, vosotras
ustedes	los, las	les	se	(a) ustedes [*reflexive*: (a) sí*]
ellos, ellas	los, las	les	se	(a) ellos, ellas [*reflexive*: (a) sí*]

*Con + mí = conmigo; con + ti = contigo; con + sí = consigo

Pronoun Position in Relation to the Verb

1. The object pronoun (whether direct, indirect, or reflexive) always precedes a single conjugated verb.

   Leo **la Biblia.** → **La** leo.
   No he visto **al Sr. Rivera**. → No **lo** he visto.

2. In a sentence containing a verb + infinitive construction, the object pronoun (direct, indirect, or reflexive) may either precede the conjugated verb or be attached to the end of the infinitive.

   Voy a aprender **el canto.** → **Lo** voy a aprender.
   Voy a aprender**lo.**
   Quiero aprender **el canto.** → **Lo** quiero aprender.
   Quiero aprender**lo.**
   Tengo que aprender **el canto.** → **Lo** tengo que aprender.
   Tengo que aprender**lo.**

3. In a sentence containing *estar* + present participle, the object pronoun (direct, indirect, or reflexive) may either precede the verb *estar* or be attached to the end of the present participle.

   Estoy escuchando **la cinta** ahora. → **La** estoy escuchando ahora.
   Estoy escuchándo**la** ahora.

4. The object pronoun is attached to the end of an affirmative command, but it precedes a negative command.

Pon **los platos** en la mesa. → Pon**los** en la mesa.
No pongas **los platos** en la mesa. → No **los** pongas en la mesa.

Order of Multiple Object Pronouns

1. The reflexive pronoun precedes all other object pronouns.
2. The indirect object pronoun always precedes the direct object pronoun.
3. When the indirect object pronoun *le* or *les* is followed by *lo, la, los,* or *las* it is replaced by *se.* (*le lo* → *se lo*)

Position of Multiple Object Pronouns in Relation to the Verb

The rules that govern the position of multiple object pronouns in relation to the verb are the same as those that govern the position of single object pronouns.

Doy las buenas noticias a todos. → **Se las** doy (a todos).
Voy a dar las buenas noticias a todos. → **Se las** voy a dar (a todos).
Voy a dár**selas** (a todos).
Preste su libro a Enrique. → Préste**selo.**
No preste su libro a Enrique. → No **se lo** preste.

Demonstrative Pronouns

This one, these, that one, those

Masculine Singular	Masculine Plural	Feminine Singular	Feminine Plural	Neuter
éste	éstos	ésta	éstas	esto
ése	ésos	ésa	ésas	eso
aquél	aquéllos	aquélla	aquéllas	aquello

Affirmative and Negative words

Affirmatives		Negatives*	
sí	*yes*	no	*no*
algo	*something*	nada	*nothing*
alguien	*somebody*	nadie	*nobody*
algún	*some, any*	ningún	*none, not any*
algunos	*some, any*	ningunos	*none, not any*
alguna	*some, any*	ninguna	*none, not any*

Affirmatives		Negatives*	
algunas	some, any	ningunas	none, not any
a veces	at times	nunca	never
algunas veces	sometimes		
siempre	always	nunca jamás	never (emphatic)
o . . . o	either . . . or	ni . . . ni	neither . . . nor

*A negative word may precede the verb: *Nadie habló.* Or, it may follow the verb if another negative word such as *no* precedes the verb: *No habló **nadie.***

Prepositions

a	to, at	en medio de	in the middle of
ante	before (standing in front of)	entre	between, among
antes de	before (in time)	enfrente de	in front of, across from
bajo	under, beneath	frente a	in front of, facing
con	with	hacia	toward
contra	against	hasta	until
de	of, from	para	for (in order to), in the direction of, compared to
debajo de	under	por	for, by, through, for the sake of
desde	from, since	por debajo de	passing beneath
después de	after (in time)	según	according to
detrás de	behind	sin	without
delante de	in front of	sobre	above, over, on top of
durante	during	tras	after (following behind)
en	in, on, at		

Days of the Week

lunes	Monday	viernes	Friday
martes	Tuesday	sábado	Saturday
miércoles	Wednesday	domingo	Sunday
jueves	Thursday		

Months of the Year

enero	*January*	julio	*July*
febrero	*February*	agosto	*August*
marzo	*March*	septiembre	*September*
abril	*April*	octubre	*October*
mayo	*May*	noviembre	*November*
junio	*June*	diciembre	*December*

Numbers

Cardinal numbers

0	cero	10	diez	20	veinte	30	treinta
1	uno	11	once	21	veintiuno	31	treinta y uno
2	dos	12	doce	22	veintidós	32	treinta y dos
3	tres	13	trece	23	veintitrés	40	cuarenta
4	cuatro	14	catorce	24	veinticuatro	50	cincuenta
5	cinco	15	quince	25	veinticinco	60	sesenta
6	seis	16	dieciséis	26	veintiséis	70	setenta
7	siete	17	diecisiete	27	veintisiete	80	ochenta
8	ocho	18	dieciocho	28	veintiocho	90	noventa
9	nueve	19	diecinueve	29	veintinueve	100	cien

101	ciento uno	199	ciento noventa y nueve	800	ochocientos
102	ciento dos	200	doscientos	900	novecientos
103	ciento tres	201	doscientos uno	1.000	mil
114	ciento catorce	300	trescientos	2.000	dos mil
120	ciento veinte	400	cuatrocientos	2.500	dos mil quinientos
121	ciento veintiuno	500	quinientos	10.000	diez mil
131	ciento treinta y uno	600	seiscientos	100.000	cien mil
145	ciento cuarenta y cinco	700	setecientos	1.000.000	un millón

Ordinal numbers

Ordinal numbers up to ten are the most commonly used. Ordinal numbers agree in gender and number with the noun they modify.

1º, 1ª, 1ᵉ͏ʳ*	primero, primera, primer
2º, 2ª	segundo, segunda
3º, 3ª, 3ᵉ͏ʳ*	tercero, tercera, tercer
4º, 4ª	cuarto, cuarta
5º, 5ª	quinto, quinta
6º, 6ª	sexto, sexta
7º, 7ª	séptimo, séptima
8º, 8ª	octavo, octava
9º, 9ª	noveno, novena
10º, 10ª	décimo, décima

Primero and *tercero* are shortened to *primer* and *tercer* before a masculine singular noun.

Some Facts About Syllables, Vowels, and Accent Marks:

About syllables:

Syllable division in Spanish follows these rules:

1. If a consonant comes between two vowels, divide after the first vowel (*pa-pel*).

ca-pa	be-né-fi-co	ca-rro
jó-ven	to-car	mu-cha-cha
A-mé-ri-ca	e-lla	re-loj

   Note: The consonant pairs *ll*, *rr*, and *ch* may never be divided.

2. Always divide between two consonants unless the second consonant is *l* or *r* (*has-ta*, *ár-bol*; but *ta-bla*, *Pe-dro*).

e-le-gan-te	cua-der-no	no-so-**tros**
pas-tor	ven-ta-nas	im-po-si-**ble**
ser-vir	co-mu-ni-can-do	des-cu-**br**ir
e-le-men-to	ac-ce-so	re-**gla**

3. Always divide a cluster of three consonants between the last two unless the final consonant is *l* or *r*.

pers-**p**ec-ti-va	e-jem-**pl**o
ins-**t**an-te	ex-**pl**o-rar
cons-**t**ar	es-**cr**i-bir
ins-**p**i-rar	es-**tr**uc-tu-ra

About vowels:

The nucleus of any syllable is either a single vowel or a diphthong. The vowels *a, e, i, o, u* are divided into two categories:

Strong vowels	Weak vowels
a, e, o	i, u

A **diphthong** is a pair of vowels, at least one of which **must** be an *i* or a *u*. In other words, a diphthong consists of either a pair of weak vowels or one weak vowel and one strong vowel. The two elements of a diphthong blend together to form a single syllable. A pair of strong vowels divides into separate syllables.

Words with single-vowel syllables	Words with diphthongs
im-po-si-ble	**cuo**-ta
e-le-gan-te	**ciu**-dad
can-tan-te	**dia**-**rio**
fe-o	m**ie**-do
ja-le-o	**dei**-dad
ca-e-mos	co-lo-n**ia**
e-le-men-to	v**io**
i-de-a	p**ie**
a-é-re-o	p**ue**r-ta

False diphthongs:

If the *i* or the *u* has a written accent, it is not considered a weak vowel; therefore, it cannot form part of a diphthong. It belongs to one syllable, and the other vowel beside it belongs to another. Notice the difference between these words:

Ma-rio, Ma-rí-a   con-ti-nuo, con-ti-nú-o   rio, rí-o

The accent over the weak vowel makes it into the strongest vowel of the word and also creates an extra syllable.

About written accent marks:

In Spanish, written accent marks usually appear over words to indicate which syllable receives the greater stress. Not all words have written accent marks over them because they conform to certain predictable rules. Most words with written accent marks have them because they fail to conform to those rules. You must be able to apply the rules of accentuation for words that you see in print as well as words that you hear and must write down for yourself.

Reading words you see:

1. If a word ends in **a vowel, or -n or -s** and has no written accent mark, stress the next to last syllable as you read it aloud.

   ca-sa   **can**-tan   a-**mi**-gos

   co-ro   **jo**-ven   pa-**ra**-guas

2. If a word ends in **a consonant other than -n or -s** and has no written accent, stress the last syllable as you read it aloud.

   a-**mor**   a-**bril**   a-**zul**

   can-**tar**   doc-**tor**   sa-**lud**

3. If a word in print has a written accent mark, stress the syllable that has the accent mark over it.

   lá-piz   ca-**pí**-tu-lo   **Á**-fri-ca

   na-**ción**   bo-**lí**-gra-fo   **sí**-la-ba

Writing down words you hear:

If you must write down a word you hear, you can determine whether it needs a written accent mark by listening for the stressed syllable, as well as paying attention to the last letter of the word.

1. If a word you hear ends in **a vowel or -n or -s,** it needs a written accent mark over the stressed syllable **only** if the stressed syllable is the last syllable of the word.
   /ca-**jon**/ → cajón
   /to-ca-**ra**/ → tocará

2. If a word you hear ends in **a consonant other than -n or -s,** it needs a written accent mark over the stressed syllable **only** if the stressed syllable is the next to last syllable of the word.
   /**ces**-ped/ → césped
   /**la**-piz/ → lápiz

3. Any word you hear that is stressed on a syllable **other than** the last, or next to last syllable always has a written accent mark over the stressed syllable.

/ca-***ta***-lo-go/ → *catálogo*

/***cuen***-ta-me-lo/ → *cuéntamelo*

Exceptions:

Certain words carry accent marks to distinguish one meaning or usage from another in homophones (words that are pronounced alike but have different meanings).

el	*the*	él	*he*
tu	*your*	tú	*you*
mi	*my*	mí	*me*
se	*one's self (reflexive pron.)*	sé	*I know*
de	*of, from*	dé	*give (formal command)*
este	*this (demonstrative adj.)*	éste	*this one (demonstrative pron.)*
si	*if*	sí	*yes*

All interrogatives *(quién, qué, dónde, cuándo, por qué, cómo, etc.)*, whether in a direct question or in a statement that contains a question, and all exclamation words carry written accent marks over the stressed syllable.

¿Qué tienes en la mano?   *¡Qué interesante!*

¿Dónde está Enrique?   *No sabemos quién lo hizo, ni por qué.*

Note: Some words that have accent marks in the singular do not have accent marks in the plural, and viceversa.

canción → canciones   *lección → lecciones*

joven → jóvenes   *examen → exámenes*

Por vs. para

Por + sustantivo

The preposition *por* followed by a noun is used to express various ideas. The English equivalent of *por* is not always "for." Note the ideas expressed by *por*:

- **in exchange for** (*for, in place of*)

  Compré un traje nuevo **por** treinta dólares.

  Cambiaré mi bicicleta **por** una motocicleta.

  Cristo murió en la cruz **por** mí.

- **manner or means** (*by*)

    Mandaré el paquete a Uruguay **por** correo aéreo.

    Me dieron las noticias **por** teléfono.

- **duration of time** (*for, during, in*)

    Voy a viajar **por** tres semanas.

    Me gusta estudiar **por** la mañana.

- **cause or motive** (*for, because of, on behalf of, for the sake of*)

    ¿Se casó con él **por** amor o **por** dinero?

    ¿A qué hora vienes **por** mí?

    Estoy muy preocupada **por** ti.

    Rafael le hablará al director técnico **por** todo el equipo.

    Los padres se sacrifican **por** sus hijos.

- **movement** (*along, through, by, around*)

    El pobre perrito estaba caminando **por** la calle cuando lo vi.

    La carretera Panamericana pasa **por** los países de América Central.

    El cartero pasará **por** nuestra casa a la una.

    Los jóvenes paseaban **por** el parque.

- **other expressions that use** *por:*

    cien **por ciento** (*one hundred percent*)

    ochenta kilómetros **por hora** (*eighty kilometers per hour*)

La preposición *para*

The preposition *para* may be followed by a noun or an infinitive and usually indicates a purpose or a destination. It is often equivalent to the English preposition *for* and is used in questions to ask *for what?* (*¿para qué?*).

The purpose or destination indicated by the use of the preposition *para* may be any of the following:

- **a person**

    El mate y la bombilla son **para Tabita.**

    Compré una revista deportiva **para Tabaré.**

- **an object or thing**

    Esta lámpara es **para mi cuarto.**

    Me compré un traje nuevo **para la fiesta.**

- **a place**

    A las siete y media salgo **para el trabajo.**

    Los misioneros salen mañana **para Montevideo.**

- **a point in time**

> Estoy haciendo planes **para el verano.**
>
> Esperamos ir a Uruguay **para la Navidad.**

- **an action** (infinitive)

> Tengo que estudiar **para aprender** español.
>
> Estoy ahorrando dinero **para viajar** a Uruguay.

When *para* is followed by an infinitive, it may be translated *to* or *in order to.*

Por + infinitivo

The preposition *por* may also be followed by an infinitive. The Spanish expression *por + infinitivo* is equivalent to the English structure *for + -ing verb.*

> Recibimos el trofeo **por ganar** el campeonato de fútbol.
>
> Pablo Martín no está en clase hoy **por estar** enfermo.

When *por* is followed by an infinitive, it may be translated *for, because of,* or *for reason of.*

GLOSSARY

Spanish/English

abierto(adj.) open

abogado(a)(noun) lawyer

abrigo(m.) coat

abrir(regular *-ir* verb) to open

abrochar(regular *-ar* verb) to hook; to button or fasten

abuelo(a)(noun) grandfather; grandmother; **abuelos** grandparents

aburrido(adj.) boring

aburrir(regular *-ir* verb) to bore; **aburrirse** to be bored

acabar (de)(regular *-ar* verb) to have just (done something)

acariciar(regular *-ar* verb) to caress; pet

accidente(m.) accident

aceite(m.) oil

aceptable(adj.) acceptable

aceptar(regular *-ar* verb) to accept

acerca de(prep.) about; concerning

acero(m.) steel

acompañar(regular *-ar* verb) to accompany; to go along with

acordeón(m.) accordion

acostarse(stem-changing verb, *o→ue*) to lie down; to go to bed

acostumbrarse a(regular *-ar* verb) to get used to; grow accustomed to

adelantar(regular *-ar* verb) to advance; pass

administrador(a)(noun) administrator

adoración(f.) adoration; worship

adorar(regular *-ar* verb) to adore; worship

aduana(f.) customs

aeromozo(a)(noun) airline attendant

aeropuerto(m.) airport

afeitar(se)(regular *-ar* verb) to shave (oneself)

aficionado(a)(noun) amateur; fan

agregar(regular *-ar* verb) to add

agua(f.) water (preceded by *el* in the singular)

ahora(adv.) now

ahorros(m. pl.) savings

aire(m.) air; **aire libre** outdoors

alabar(regular *-ar* verb) to praise

al lado de(prep.) beside

alegrarse (de)(regular *-ar* verb) to rejoice; to be glad

alegre(adj.) happy; glad

alegría(f.) happiness; cheer

alfombra(f.) rug; carpet

algo(indef. pron.) something

algodón(m.) cotton

alguien(indef. pron.) someone

algún(adj.) = alguno (before a singular m. noun)

algunas veces(adv.) sometimes

alguno(adj.) any; some; (pron.) someone; something

alineación(f.) alignment

alma(f.) soul (preceded by the article *el* in the singular)

almacén(m.) 1. department store; 2. warehouse

almohada(f.) pillow

almorzar(stem-changing verb, *o→ue*) to have lunch

almuerzo(m.) lunch

aló hello (telephone greeting)

alrededor de(prep.) around

alto(adj.) tall; ¡alto! stop!

allí(adv.) there

ama de casa(f.) homemaker

amar(regular *-ar* verb) to love

amarillo(adj.) yellow

a menos que(conj.) unless

amo(m.) master

amparo(m.) shelter; protection

anaranjado(adj.) orange

ancho(adj.) wide

andar(regular *-ar* verb) to walk (around)

andén(m.) station platform

anillo(m.) ring

anoche(adv.) last night

anochecer 1. (verb) to grow dark; 2. (m.) nightfall

antes (de)(prep.) before

antibiótico(m.) antibiotic

antiguamente(adv.) formerly; long ago

antipatía(f.) dislike

antipático(adj.) unfriendly

anuncio(m.) advertisement; announcement

aparecer(irregular first-person verb, like *conocer*) to appear

aparente(adj.) apparent

aparición (f.) apparition

apariencia(f.) appearance

apartamento(m.) apartment

apenas(adv.) scarcely; hardly

apio(m.) celery

aprender(regular -er verb) to learn

aprovechar(regular -ar verb) to take advantage of

aquí(adv.) here

arañar(regular -ar verb) to scratch; claw

árbitro(m.) referee; umpire

árbol(m.) tree

arete(m.) earring

arma de fuego(m.) firearm

arpa(f.) harp (preceded by the article *el* in the singular)

arquero(m.) goalie (soccer)

arquitecto(a)(noun) architect

arrepentirse(stem-changing verb, *e→ie*) to repent

arriba de(prep.) above; on top of

arrodillarse(regular -ar verb) to kneel

arroz(m.) rice; **arroz con leche** rice milk pudding

artista(noun) artist

ascensor(m.) elevator

así(adv.) thus; so; **así que** and so

asiento(m.) seat; **asiento delantero** front seat; **asiento trasero** back seat

asistente de vuelo(noun) flight attendant

asistir (a)(regular -ir verb) to attend; to go to

asno(m.) donkey

asombrarse(regular -ar verb) to be amazed

aspirina(f.) aspirin

astilla(f.) splinter

asunto(m.) a matter; **asuntos legales** legal matters

asustado(adj.) frightened

asustar(regular -ar verb) to frighten

atender(stem-changing verb, *e→ie*) to take care of; pay attention to

atentamente(adv.) a closing remark in a business letter

aterrizar(regular -ar verb) to land (an airplane)

atleta(noun) athlete

atrás(prep.) behind

atrasado(adj.) 1. late, delayed; 2. backward

atún(m.) tuna fish

audiencia(f.) audience

aula(f.) classroom (preceded by the article *el* in the singular)

aún(adv.) yet; still

aunque(conj.) although

autobús(m.) bus

automóvil(m.) automobile; car

auxilio(m.) aid; help

ave(f.) bird (preceded by the article *el* in the singular)

a veces(adv.) sometimes

ayer(adv.) (m.) yesterday

ayudar(regular -ar verb) to help

azafata(f.) stewardess; flight attendant

azúcar(m. or f.) sugar

azul(adj.) blue

bajar(regular -ar verb) to descend; **bajar (de)** to come down from; get off of (a vehicle)

bajo(adj.) 1. short (in stature); 2. low

bala(f.) bullet

balazo(m.) shot; bullet wound

balón(m.) ball

baloncesto(m.) basketball

ballena(f.) whale

banco(m.) 1. bank; 2. bench

banda(f.) 1. musical band; 2. edge; border

bandera(f.) banner; flag

bandido(m.) bandit; outlaw

banquete(m.) banquet; feast

bañar(se)(regular -ar verb) to bathe (oneself)

bañera(f.) bathtub

baño(m.) 1. bath; 2. bathroom

barato(adj.) cheap

barba(f.) beard

barbero(m.) barber

barca(f.) small boat

barco(m.) boat; ship

barro(m.) mud; clay

bate(m.) baseball bat

bateador(m.) batter (baseball)

batear(regular -ar verb) to bat

batería(f.) battery (of a car)

batir(regular -ir verb) to beat; to mix or stir

batuta(f.) baton

baúl(m.) trunk (of an automobile)

beber(regular -er verb) to drink

bebida(f.) drink; beverage

béisbol(m.) baseball

belleza(f.) beauty

bello(adj.) fair; beautiful

bendecir(irregular verb, like *decir*) to bless

besar(regular -ar verb) to kiss

Biblia(f.) Bible

biblioteca(f.) library

bigote(m.) mustache

billete(m.) bill; ticket

biología(f.) biology

biólogo(a)(noun) biologist

bisabuelo(a)(noun) great grandfather; great grandmother

bizcocho(m.) cake

blanco(adj.) white

blando(adj.) 1. bland, soft; 2. weak, delicate

blusa(f.) blouse

boca(f.) mouth; **boca abajo** face down

bocadillo(m.) sandwich

boda(f.) wedding

bodas de oro(f.) fiftieth wedding anniversary

boleto(m.) ticket (railroad, theater, etc.)

bolsa(f.) bag

bolsillo(m.) pocket

bonito(adj.) good-looking; pretty

bosque(m.) forest

bota(f.) boot

botar el balón(regular -*ar* verb) to bounce the ball

botella(f.) bottle

botiquín(m.) medicine chest

botón(m.) button

brazo(m.) arm

brécol(m.) broccoli

brincar(regular -*ar* verb) to jump; leap

bruja(f.) witch

bueno(adj.) good

bufanda(f.) scarf

búho(m.) owl

burro(m.) donkey; **burrito** little donkey

buscar(regular -*ar* verb) to look for; to seek

buzón(m.) mailbox

caballo(m.) horse

cabello(m.) hair of the head

cabeza(f.) head

cabina(f.) cabin; compartment

cabra(f.) goat

cadena(f.) chain

caer(irregular first-person verb, like *traer*) to fall

café(m.) coffee; **café con leche** coffee with milk; **café negro** black coffee

cafetería (f.) cafeteria

caja(f.) 1. box; 2. cash register

calcetín(m.) sock

calentar(regular -*ar* verb) to warm; heat

calmar(regular -*ar* verb) to calm; to quiet

calor(m.) heat; **Hace calor.** It is hot.

callarse(regular -*ar* verb) to be quiet

calle(f.) street

calleja(f.) alley; lane

cama(f.) bed

camarero(a)(noun) waiter; waitress

camarón(m.) shrimp

cambiar(regular -*ar* verb) to change; **cambiar dinero** to exchange money

cambio(m.) change; exchange; **cambio de velocidades** gear shift

caminar(regular -*ar* verb) to walk

camisa(f.) shirt; **camisa de vestir** dress shirt

camiseta(f.) undershirt; T-shirt

campamento(m.) camp

campana(f.) bell

campo(m.) 1. field; 2. country; rural area

canas(f.) gray hair

cancha(f.) ball court

canoa(f.) canoe

cansado(adj.) tired

cansarse de(regular -*ar* verb) to grow tired of

cantante(m. or f.) singer

cantar(regular -*ar* verb) to sing

cantidad(f.) quantity

cañón(m.) cannon

capa(f.) cape; cloak

capitán(m.) captain

capó(m.) hood (of a car)

cápsula(f.) capsule

cara(f.) face

carbón(m.) charcoal

cárcel(f.) jail; prison

cargar(regular -*ar* verb) to load; to burden

carne(f.) meat; **carne de res** beef

carnicería(f.) butcher store; meat market

caro(adj.) expensive

carrera(f.) 1. race; 2. career

carretera(f.) highway

carro(m.) car; **carro de equipaje** luggage cart

carta(f.) letter

cartera(f.) purse; billfold

cartero(m.) postman

casa(f.) house **en casa** at home

casarse (con)(regular -*ar* verb) to get married (to)

casero(adj.) 1. of the home; domestic; 2. homemade

castaño(adj.) brown

castillo(m.) castle

catedral(f.) cathedral

cebolla(f.) onion

cebra(f.) zebra

cementerio(m.) cemetery

cena(f.) supper; dinner

cenar(regular -*ar* verb) to have supper; to dine

cenizas(f.) ashes

centro(m.) downtown; **centro comercial** (m.) shopping center

cepillar(se)(regular -*ar* verb) to brush (oneself)

cepillo(m.) brush; **cepillo de dientes** (m.) toothbrush

cerca de(prep.) near to

cercano(adj.) near

cerdo(m.) hog; pig

cerebro(m.) brain

cerilla(f.) match

cerner(stem-changing verb, *e→ie*) (also **cernir**) to sift

cerrado(adj.) closed

cerrajería(f.) locksmith's store

cerrar(stem-changing verb, *e→ie*) to close

cesto(m.) basket

ciego(a)(noun.) a blind person

cielo(m.) sky; heaven

ciencia(f.) science

científico(a)(noun) scientist

cintura(f.) waist; waistline

cinturón(m.) belt; **cinturón de seguridad** seat belt

cirujano(a)(noun) surgeon

ciudadano(a)(noun) citizen

claras(f.) egg whites

clarinete(m.) clarinet

cobija(f.) blanket

cobrar(regular *-ar* verb) 1. to collect; 2. to charge; **cobrar un cheque** to cash a check

cobrador conductor (R.R.)

cocer(stem-changing verb, *o→ue*) to cook; bake

cocina(f.) kitchen

cocinar(regular *-ar* verb) to cook

cocinero(a)(noun) cook

coche(m.) car

codo(m.) elbow

colgar(stem-changing verb, *o→ue*) to hang up **colgar el teléfono** to hang up the telephone

colmado 1. (m.) grocery store; 2. (adj.) full

colocar(regular *-ar* verb) to arrange; set

colonizar(regular *-ar* verb) to colonize; **colonizador** (m.) colonizer; **colono** colonist

collar(m.) necklace

comedor(m.) dining room

comentador(a)(noun) commentator

comentar(regular *-ar* verb) to comment

comenzar(stem-changing verb, *e→ ie*) to begin

comer(regular *-er* verb) to eat

comisaría(f.) police headquarters

como 1. (conj.) as (in comparisons); 2. (adv.) ¿**Cómo?** how

compañero(a)(noun) companion; friend; **compañero de clase** classmate

compartir(regular *-ir* verb) to divide; to share

compositor(a)(noun) composer

comprar(regular *-ar* verb) to buy

comprender(regular *-er* verb) to understand

comprometerse (con)(regular *-er* verb) 1. to commit oneself; 2. become engaged (to)

computadora(f.) computer

comunismo(m.) communism

con(prep.) with **con destino a** with a destination of

con permiso Excuse me. (lit. *with your permission*)

con tal que(conj.) provided that

concierto(m.) concert

conducir(irregular first-person verb, like *conocer*) to drive

conductor engineer (R.R.)

confesar(regular *-ar* verb) to confess

confiar(regular *-ar* verb) to trust; to confide

congregación(f.) congregation

congreso(m.) congress

conjunto(m.) ensemble

conocer(irregular first-person verb) to know; to be acquainted with people or places

conocido(adj.) known

conquistador(a)(noun) conqueror

conquistar(regular *-ar* verb) to conquer

consistente(adj.) consistent

consistir en(regular *-ir* verb) to consist of

consolar(stem-changing verb, *o→ue*) to console; comfort

constante(adj.) constant

constantemente(adv.) constantly

contador(a)(noun) accountant

contar(stem-changing verb, *o→ue*) 1. to count; 2. to tell; 3. to relate

contento(adj.) happy; satisfied

contestador automático(m.) answering machine

contestar(regular *-ar* verb) to answer

contrabajo(m.) bass; double bass

conveniente(adj.) convenient

conversar(regular *-ar* verb) to talk

convertir(regular *-ir* verb) to convert

corazón(m.) heart

corbata(f.) necktie

cordero(m.) lamb

cordón(m.) shoelace

coro(m.) choir

coronel(m.) colonel

correcto(adj.) correct

correo(m.) 1. mail; 2. post office

correr(regular *-er* verb) to run

corriente 1. (f.) electrical current; 2. (adj.) current; up-to-date; **cuenta corriente** checking account (bank)

corrupto(adj.) corrupt

corte 1. (m.) cut; **corte de pelo** haircut; 2. (f.) court of justice

cortés(adj.) courteous; gracious; polite

cortina(f.) curtain

corto(adj.) short (in length)

cosa(f.) thing

costado(m.) side

costar(stem-changing verb, *o→ue*) to cost; ¿**Cuánto cuesta?** How much does it cost?

costilla(f.) rib

costumbre(f.) 1. custom; 2. habit

coz(f.) kick

crecer(irregular first-person verb, like *conocer*) to grow

creer(regular -*er* verb) to believe

crema(f.) 1. cream; **crema de afeitar** shaving cream; 2. lotion; 3. sour cream

creyente(noun) believer

criarse(regular -*ar* verb) to grow up

cruz roja(f.) the Red Cross

cruzar(regular -*ar* verb) to cross

cuadra(f.) city block

cuadrado(adj.) 1. square; 2. checkered

cuadro(m.) painting; picture

cuál(es)(interrog. adj., pron.) which one(s); what

cualquier(indef. adj., pron.) anyone; whichever; any

cuando(conj.) when; **¿cuándo?** (adv.) when

cuánto(-os;-a;-as)(interrog. adj., pron.) how much; how many

cuarto(m.) room; bedroom

cubrir(regular -*ir* verb) to cover

cucaracha(f.) cockroach

cuchara(f.) spoon; teaspoon

cucharada(f.) tablespoon

cuchillo(m.) knife

cuello(m.) 1. collar (on a shirt); 2. neck

cuenta(f.) bill

cuento(m.) story; tale

cuerno(m.) horn (of an animal)

cuero(m.) 1. hide; 2. leather

cuidar(regular -*ar* verb) to take care of

culebra(f.) snake

cumplir(regular -*ir* verb) to complete; to fulfill

cuñado(a)(noun) brother-in-law; sister-in-law

chaleco(m.) vest

chaqueta(f.) jacket

charcutería(f.) pork butchery

cheque(m.) check; **cheques de viajero** traveler's checks

chocar(regular -*ar* verb) 1. to wreck; 2. have an accident

choclo(m.) ear of corn

chofer(noun) chauffeur

chuleta(f.) cutlet; chop

churrasco(m.) roasted meat; barbecue

dar(irregular first-person verb, like *estar*) to give; **dar de comer** to feed; **dar la mano** to shake hands

de buen humor in a good mood

de estación a estación station to station (telephone call)

de frente straight ahead

de mal humor in a bad mood; upset

de persona a persona person to person (telephone call)

de pronto(adv.) suddenly

¿de quién? whose?

de repente(adv.) suddenly

¿de veras? Is that true? Really?

debajo de(prep.) under

deber(regular -*er* verb) to owe; **deber + infinitive** to ought to; to be supposed to

débil(adj.) weak

decir(stem-changing verb *e→i;* irregular first-person verb) to say; to tell

dedo(m.) finger

defensa(f.) defense

dejar(regular -*ar* verb) 1. to leave; 2. to cease; **dejar (de)** to stop (doing something); **dejar suelto** to leave loose

delante de(prep.) in front of

delantero(m.) forward (sports)

delgado(adj.) thin; slim

demasiado(adv.) too (much)

democracia(f.) democracy

demora(f.) delay

dentista(noun) dentist

dentro de(prep.) inside of

depender (de)(regular -*er* verb) to depend (on)

dependiente(noun) sales person

deportes(m.) sports

deportista(noun) one who is active in sports

deportivo(adj.) sporting; having to do with sports

depositar(regular -*ar* verb) to deposit

depósito de gasolina(m.) gas tank

derecha(f.) right; right side; right hand

derecho(adj.) straight

derretir(regular -*ir* verb) to melt

derrota(f.) defeat

derrotar(regular -*ar* verb) to defeat

desayunar(regular -*ar* verb) to have breakfast

desayuno(m.) breakfast

descolgar el teléfono(stem-changing verb, *o→ue*) to pick up the telephone

descubrir(regular -*ir* verb) to discover; **descubridor(a)** (noun) discoverer

desde(prep.) from; since; **desde entonces** since then

desembarcar(regular -*ar* verb) to unload; to disembark

desfile(m.) parade

deshacer(irregular first-person verb, like *hacer*) to undo; destroy

desierto(m.) desert

despachar(regular -*ar* verb) to dispatch

despedida(f.) farewell

despegar(regular -*ar* verb) to take off; to detach

despertador(m.) alarm clock

despertar(se)(stem-changing verb, *e→ie*) to wake up (oneself)

despistado(adj.) confused

después (de)(prep.) after

destino(m.) destination

detenerse(irregular first-person verb, like *tener*) to detain; stop

detrás (de)(prep.) behind

deuda(f.) debt

deudor(a)(noun) debtor

devolver(stem-changing verb, *o→ue*) to return; restore

dientes(m.) teeth

diezmo(m.) tithe

digno(adj.) worthy

dinero(m.) currency; money

diputado(m.) deputy; representative

dirección(f.) 1. address; 2. direction; **dirección opuesta** the opposite direction

director(a)(noun) principal; director; conductor (in music)

dirigir(irregular first-person verb, like *escoger*) to direct; guide; **dirigirse a** to address (someone)

discutir(regular -*ir* verb) to discuss; argue

disfrutar(regular -*ar* verb) to enjoy

diversión(f.) amusement

divertido(adj.) amusing; fun-loving

divertir(se)(stem-changing verb, *e→ie*) to amuse; to have fun; to enjoy oneself

doblar(regular -*ar* verb) to turn

docena(f.) dozen

dolor(m.) pain; **dolor de espalda** backache; **dolor de cabeza** headache; **dolor de estómago** stomachache

¿dónde?(adv.) where?; **¿dónde está?** where is it?

dorado(adj.) golden

dormir(stem-changing verb, *o→ue*) to sleep; **dormirse** to go to sleep

dormitorio(m.) bedroom

dosis(f.) dose; dosage

ducha(f.) shower

duchar(se)(regular -*ar* verb) to shower

dueño(a)(noun) owner; landlord

dulce 1. (m.) candy; 2. (adj.) sweet

dúo(m.) duet

durante(adv.) during

durazno(m.) peach

duro(adj.) hard

e (conj.) and (before words that begin with *i* or *hi*)

economía(f.) economy

echar(regular -*ar* verb) to cast; throw; **echar de menos (a alguien)** to miss (someone); **echar una carta** to mail a letter

educación física(f.) physical education

efectivo(m.) cash

ejemplo(m.) example

ejército(m.) army

elección(f.) election

embarcar(regular -*ar* verb) to embark

embestir(stem-changing verb, *e→i*) to assail; attack

empatar(regular -*ar* verb) to tie (in a game or competition)

empezar(stem-changing verb, *e→ie*) to begin

empleado(a) 1. (noun) employee; 2. (adj.) employed

emplear(regular -*ar* verb) to employ

empleo(m.) employment; business

empresa(f.) company; business

empresario(a)(noun) entrepreneur

en(prep.) on; in; inside of; **en medio de** in the middle of; **en frente de** in front of; **en seguida** immediately

enamorarse (de)(regular -*ar* verb) to fall in love with

encantar(regular -*ar* verb) to delight

encarcelado(adj.) imprisoned

encima de(prep.) on top of

encontrar(stem-changing verb, *o→ue*) to find; to meet; to run into

endosar un cheque(regular -*ar* verb) to endorse a check

enfermarse(regular -*ar* verb) to become sick

enfermera(o)(noun) nurse

enfermo(adj.) sick

enfriarse(regular -*ar* verb) to become cold

enojado(adj.) annoyed; angry

enojarse (con)(regular -*ar* verb) to be or become angry with

ensalada(f.) salad

ensayar(regular -*ar* verb) to rehearse; to practice

enseñar(regular -*ar* verb) 1. to teach; 2. to show

entender(stem-changing verb, *e→ie*) to understand

entrada(f.) 1. entrance; door; 2. ticket of admission

entrar(regular -*ar* verb) to enter

entre(prep.) among; between

entregarse(regular -*ar* verb) to submit; surrender

época(f.) epoch; age

equipaje(m.) luggage

equipo(m.) team

equivocado(adj.) mistaken; wrong

errar(regular -*ar* verb) 1. to err; miss; mistake; 2. to roam

esclavitud(f.) slavery

escoger(irregular first-person verb) to choose

escorpión(m.) scorpion

escribir(regular -*ir* verb) to write

escritor(a)(noun) writer; author

escuchar(regular -*ar* verb) to listen (to)

escudero(noun) shield-bearer; squire

escuela(f.) school

esmeralda(f.) emerald

espacio(m.) space

espalda(f.) back

espejo(m.) mirror; **espejo retrovisor** rear view mirror

esperar(regular -*ar* verb) to wait (for)

espinaca(f.) spinach

esposo(a)(noun) spouse; husband or wife

espumoso(adj.) frothy; foamy

esquí(m.) ski

esquiar(regular -*ar* verb) to ski

esquina(f.) corner

estación de autobús(f.) bus station

estadio(m.) stadium

estancia(f.) 1. cattle ranch; 2. stay; sojourn

estante(m.) bookshelf

estar(irregular verb) to be

estilo(m.) style

estómago(m.) stomach

estornudar(regular -*ar* verb) to sneeze

estrecho(adj.) narrow

estrella(f.) star

estudiante(noun) student

estudiar(regular -*ar* verb) to study

estufa(f.) stove

eternidad(f.) eternity

evangelizar(regular -*ar* verb) to evangelize

examinar(regular -*ar* verb) to examine

exigente(adj.) demanding

exigir(regular -*ir* verb) to demand; require

éxito(m.) success

explicación(f.) explanation

explicar(regular -*ar* verb) to explain

explorador(a)(noun) explorer

explorar(regular -*ar* verb) to explore

expresión(f.) expression

extraño(adj.) strange

fácil(adj.) easy

facturar(regular -*ar* verb) to invoice; bill

falda(f.) skirt

farmacéutico(a)(noun) pharmacist

fascinar(regular -*ar* verb) to fascinate

fauna(f.) fauna; animals collectively

fe(f.) faith

fecha(f.) date; **¿Qué fecha es hoy?** What is today's date?

felicitar(regular -*ar* verb) to congratulate

feo(adj.) ugly

ferretería(f.) hardware store

ferrocarril(m.) railroad

festejo(m.) celebration; festivities

fiebre(f.) fever

filete(m.) fillet

fin de semana(m.) weekend

finca(f.) farm; ranch

firma(f.) signature

flaco(adj.) slim; skinny

flan(m.) custard

flauta(f.) flute

flor(f.) flower

florero(a)(noun) florist

foca(f.) seal

formulario(m.) blank form

fortaleza(f.) 1. fortress; 2. fortitude; strength

fósforo(m.) 1. phosphorus; 2. match

frecuente(adj.) frequent

freno(m.) brake

frente(f.) forehead; **frente a** (prep.) in front of

fresco(adj.) cool

frijoles(m.) beans; **frijoles negros** black beans

frío(adj.) cold; **Hace frío.** It is cold. **Tengo frío.** I am cold.

fruta(f.) fruit

frutería(f.) fruit shop

fuego(m.) fire; **fuego moderado** moderate heat (cooking)

fuera de(prep.) outside of

fuerte(adj.) strong

fusilar(regular -*ar* verb) to shoot

fútbol(m.) soccer

fútbol americano football

gallina(f.) hen; chicken

gallo(m.) rooster; cock

ganadero(m.) rancher

ganado(m.) livestock; cattle

ganar(regular -*ar* verb) to win; gain

ganga(f.) bargain

gasolinera(f.) gas station

gastar(regular -*ar* verb) to spend; use up; **gastar la batería** to run down the battery

gasto(m.) expenditure; consumption

gato(m.) 1. cat; 2. jack of a car

generoso(adj.) generous

gerente(m.) manager

gigante(m.) giant

gimnasia(f.) gymnastics

gimnasio(m.) gymnasium

gobierno(m.) government

golosinas(f. pl.) candy

golpear(regular -*ar* verb) to strike; hit

gordo(adj.) fat

gracia(f.) grace

gramo(m.) gram (metric unit of weight)

grande(adj.) big

grandeza(f.) greatness; grandeur

gris(adj.) gray

grúa(f.) tow truck

guante(m.) glove

guapo(adj.) handsome; beautiful

guardafango(m.) fender (of an automobile)

guerra(f.) war

guerrillero(m.) guerrilla

guineo(m.) banana

habichuelas(f.) beans; **habichuelas verdes** green beans

hablar(regular -*ar* verb) to speak

hacer(irregular first-person verb) to do; to make; **hacer daño** to do damage; **hacer escala** to make a stop (R.R.); to have a layover (plane); **hacer trasbordo** to change (train, plane, or boat); **hacerse el tonto** to play dumb

hacienda(f.) large ranch; estate

hamaca(f.) hammock

hamburguesa(f.) hamburger

harina(f.) flour

hasta que(conj.) until

hay(adv. expression) there is; there are

hazaña(f.) deed; feat

heladería(f.) ice-cream parlor

hembra(f.) female

herencia(f.) inheritance

herida(f.) wound

hermano(a)(noun) brother; sister

hermoso(adj.) beautiful

hermosura(f.) beauty

hierba(f.) grass; weed

hígado(m.) liver

higo(m.) fig

hijo(a)(noun) son; daughter; **hijos** children

himnario(m.) hymnal

himno(m.) hymn

hipopótamo(m.) hippopotamus

historia(f.) history

hogar(m.) home

hoja(f.) 1. leaf; 2. sheet (of paper)

hombro(m.) shoulder

hora(f.) hour; time; **hora de llegada** time of arrival; **hora de salida** time of departure

horario(m.) schedule

horno(m.) oven

hoy(adv.) today **hoy día**(adv.) nowadays

huelga(f.) strike

huerto(m.) garden

hueso(m.) bone

huésped(m.) guest

huevo(m.) egg; **huevos fritos** fried eggs; **huevos revueltos** scrambled eggs

huir(irregular verb) to flee

humear(regular -*ar* verb) to emit smoke

ida y vuelta round trip

idioma(m.) language

iglesia(f.) church

igual(adj.) equal

imaginación(f.) imagination

imaginar(regular -*ar* verb) to imagine

incluir(irregular verb) to include

independencia(f.) independence

infierno(m.) hell

ingeniero(a)(noun) engineer

inglés(m.) English

ingrato(adj.) ungrateful

inmigración(f.) immigration

inodoro(m.) toilet

insecto(m.) insect

insistentemente(adv.) insistently

insistir (en)(regular -*ir* verb) to insist (on)

interés(m.) interest

interesante(adj.) interesting

intermitente(m.) turn signal

intestino(m.) intestine

invierno(m.) winter

invitar(regular -*ar* verb) to invite

ir (irregular verb) to go; **ir de compras** to go shopping; **irse** to leave; **¿A cuánto van?** What's the score?

isla(f.) island

izquierda(f.) left

jabón(m.) soap

jamás(adv.) never

jamón(m.) ham; **jamón y queso** ham and cheese (sandwich)

jarabe(m.) syrup

jonrón(m.) homerun (baseball)

joven 1. (noun) young person; 2. (adj.) young

joya(f.) jewel

joyería(f.) jewelry shop

juez(noun) judge **juez de línea** line judge (sports)

jugador(a)(noun) player

jugar(stem-changing verb, *u→ue*) to play (games or sports)

jugo(m.) juice; **jugo de naranja** orange juice; **jugo de piña** pineapple juice

juguete(m.) toy

juguetería(f.) toy store

jungla(f.) jungle

junto a(prep.) beside

justo(adj.) 1. just; fair; 2. correct; exact

kilogramo(m.) kilogram (metric unit of weight); 2.2 lbs.

kilómetro(m.) kilometer (metric unit of distance); 0.62 miles

labio(m.) lip

laboratorio(m.) laboratory

lago(m.) lake

lámpara(f.) lamp

lana(f.) wool

langosta(f.) lobster

lanzador(m.) pitcher (baseball)

lápiz(m.) pencil

largo(adj.) long

largura(f.) extent; length

lata(f.) can **lata de refresco** can of soft drink

lavabo(m.) lavatory

lavamanos(m.) sink

lavar(regular *-ar* verb) to wash; **lavar la ropa** to do the laundry; **lavar los platos** to do the dishes; **lavarse** to wash oneself

leche(f.) milk

lechería(f.) dairy

lechero(m.) milkman

lechuga(f.) lettuce

leer(regular *-er* verb) to read

legal(adj.) legal

legumbre(f.) vegetable

lejos de(prep.) far from

lentamente(adv.) slowly

lenteja(f.) lentil

lento(adj.) slow

leña(f.) firewood; kindling

león(m.) lion

leopardo(m.) leopard

levadura(f.) yeast; leaven

levantar(regular *-ar* verb) to pick up; to raise; **levantarse** to get up

leve(adj.) light (in weight); of little importance

libertad(f.) liberty

librar(regular *-ar* verb) to free; liberate

librería(f.) bookstore

limón(m.) lemon

limpiaparabrisas(m.) windshield wipers

limpiar(regular *-ar* verb) to clean

limpio(adj.) clean

lindo(adj.) pretty

línea(f.) line **línea ocupada** busy line (telephone)

liso(adj.) smooth; plain

listo(adj.) ready

lobo(m.) wolf

loco(adj.) crazy; insane; mad

locura(f.) madness; insanity

lodo(m.) mud

lomo(m.) loin; back

lucha(f.) strife; struggle

luchar(regular *-ar* verb) to wrestle

luego(adv.) later

luna(f.) moon **luna creciente** crescent moon

luz(f.) light (pl. *luces*)

llamada(f.) call; **llamada a larga distancia** long-distance call; **llamada a cobro revertido/por cobrar** collect call

llamar(regular *-ar* verb) to call

llanta(f.) tire; wheel rim; **La llanta se reventó.** The tire blew.

llave(f.) key

llegada(f.) arrival

llegar(regular *-ar* verb) to arrive

llevar(regular *-ar* verb) to take; to carry; **llevar puesto** to have on; wear

lluvia(f.) rain

macho(adj. *and* noun) male

madera(f.) wood

maestro(a)(noun) teacher

mago(a)(noun) magician

maíz(m.) corn

malestar(m.) uneasiness; discomfort

maleta(f.) suitcase

malgastar(regular *-ar* verb) to waste; squander

malo(adj.) mean; bad

malla(f.) net (volleyball)

mandar(regular *-ar* verb) to send

manga(f.) sleeve

mano(f.) hand

manta(f.) blanket

mantel(m.) tablecloth

manzana(f.) apple

mañana 1. (f.) morning 2. (adv.) tomorrow

manifestaciones(f.) public demonstrations

máquina(f.) machine; **máquina de escribir** typewriter

mar(m., sometimes f.) sea

marca(f.) brand name

marcar(regular *-ar* verb) to mark; to dial; **marcar el número equivocado** to dial the wrong number; **marcar un gol** to score a goal

marimba(f.) musical instrument similar to a xylophone

marinero(m.) sailor

mariposa(f.) butterfly

marisco(m.) shellfish

marrón(adj.) brown

mártir(noun) martyr

más(adv.) 1. more; 2. most; 3. plus; **más que** more than

matar(regular -ar verb) to kill

matemáticas(f. pl.) mathematics

mayor(adj.) older; greater

mayoría(f.) majority

mecánico(m.) mechanic

medias(f.) socks; stockings; **medias de seda** silk stockings

medicina(f.) medicine

médico(noun) medical doctor

medio(adj.) half; **a medio camino** half way

medir(stem-changing verb, *e→i*) to measure

mejor 1. (adj.) comp. of *bueno;* better; superl. of *bueno;* best; 2. (adv.) comp. of *bien;* better; well; superl. of *bien;* best

mejorarse(regular -ar verb) to improve; recover

mencionar(regular -ar verb) to mention

menor(adj.) younger; smaller

menoría(f.) minority

menos(adv.) less

mentir(stem-changing verb, *e→ie*) to tell a lie

menú(m.) menu

mercado(m.) market; **mercado común** the common market

mermelada(f.) jam

mesero(a)(noun) waiter; waitress

meter(regular -er verb) to put in; insert; **meter un punto** to score a point

metralleta(f.) automatic rifle; machine gun

mezclar(regular -ar verb) to mix

mientras(conj.) while

milla(f.) mile

mimado(adj.) spoiled

mirada(f.) look; glance

mirar(regular -ar verb) to look at

misionero(a)(noun) missionary

mismo(adj.) 1. same; 2. self

mochila(f.) backpack

molestar(regular -ar verb) to bother

molino(m.) mill; windmill

moneda(f.) currency; coin

mono(m.) monkey

monotonía(f.) monotony

monótono(adj.) monotonous

montaña(f.) mountain

morder(stem-changing verb, *e→ie*) to bite

moreno(adj.) brown; brunette

morir(stem-changing verb, *o→ue*) to die

mosca(f.) fly

mostaza(f.) mustard

muchacho(a)(noun) boy; girl

mucho(adj., adv.) much; many; a lot; **muchas veces** many times

muñequitos(m.) cartoons

músculo(m.) muscle

museo(m.) museum

música(f.) music

músico(a)(noun) musician

nacer(irregular first-person verb, like *conocer*) to be born; **nacer de nuevo** to be born again

nada(indef. pron.) nothing (not anything)

nadar(regular -ar verb) to swim

nadie(indef. pron.) no one (not anyone)

naranja(f.) an orange

nariz(f.) nose

natación(f.) swimming

natural(adj.) natural

naturaleza(f.) nature

navaja(f.) knife

Navidad(f.) Christmas

necesario(adj.) necessary

necesitar(regular -ar verb) to need

negar(stem-changing verb, *e→ie*) to refuse; deny; prohibit

negro(adj.) black

nervioso(adj.) nervous

neumático(m.) tire

ni(conj.) neither; nor **ni siquiera** not even

nieto(a)(noun) grandson; granddaughter

nieve(f.) snow

ningún(adj.) = ninguno (before a singular m. noun)

ninguno 1. (adj.) not any; no; 2. (indef. pron.) none; no one; nobody

nobleza(f.) nobility

noticias(f.) news

novela(f.) novel

nube(f.) cloud

nuca(f.) nape of the neck

nuera(f.) daughter-in-law

nuevo(adj.) new

número(m.) 1. number; 2. size

nunca(adv.) never; **nunca jamás** never ever

o (conj.) or; **o sea** that is

obedecer(irregular first-person verb, like *conocer*) to obey

obra(f.) work; labor; musical work

obrero(a)(noun) laborer; blue-collar worker

ocupar(regular -*ar* verb) to occupy; **ocuparse (de)** to be in charge of

ocurrir(regular -*ir* verb) to occur; to happen

oficina del director(f.) principal's office

oficinista(noun) office clerk

ofrecer(irregular first-person verb, like *conocer*) to offer

oír(irregular first-person verb) to hear

¡ojalá!(interj.) I hope so!

ojo(m.) eye

olvidar(se)(regular -*ar* verb) to forget

olla(f.) pot

ópera(f.) opera

oponerse (a)(irregular verb, like *poner*) to oppose

oración(f.) prayer

orar(regular -*ar* verb) to pray

oratoria(f.) (study of) speech

ordenar(regular -*ar* verb) 1. to put in order; 2. to command

orgulloso(adj.) proud

originalmente(adv.) originally

oro(m.) gold

orquesta(f.) orchestra

oso(a)(noun) bear

ostra(f.) oyster

otro(adj., pron.) other **otra vez** again; another time

oveja(f.) sheep

paciente 1. (noun) patient; 2. (adj.) patient

padre(m.) father

pagar(regular -*ar* verb) to pay

página(f.) page

país(m.) country

palo(m.) stick; piece of wood

pan(m.) bread; **pan dulce** sweet bread; danish; **pan tostado** toast

panadería(f.) bakery

panecillo(m.) bun

pantalones(m.) pants; trousers **pantalones cortos** shorts

pañuelo(m.) handkerchief

papa(f.) potato; **papas fritas** french fries; **puré de papas** mashed potatoes

papel (m.) paper; **papel higiénico** toilet paper

paquete(m.) package

para(prep.) for; **para siempre** forever; **para que;** (conj.) that; in order that; so that

parabrisas(m.) windshield

paraguas(m.) umbrella

parar(regular -*ar* verb) to stop

parecer(irregular first-person verb, like *conocer*) 1. to appear; seem; 2. appear to be; **parecerse (a)** to look alike; resemble each other

párpado(m.) eyelid

parque(m.) park

párrafo(m.) paragraph

participante(noun) participant

participar(regular -*ar* verb) to participate

partido(m.) game; match; **partido político** political party

pasado mañana the day after tomorrow

pasaje(m.) ticket

pasajero(a)(noun) passenger

pasaporte(m.) passport

pasar(regular -*ar* verb) to pass

pasta de dientes(f.) toothpaste

pastel(m.) cake; pie

pastelería(f.) pastry shop

pastilla(f.) pill

pata(f.) leg or paw of an animal

patear(regular -*ar* verb) to kick **patear el balón** to kick the ball

pato(a)(noun) duck

patria(f.) fatherland; native land

patriotismo(m.) patriotism

patrón(a)(noun) employer; boss

pavo(a)(noun) turkey

pecado(m.) sin

pecador(a)(noun) sinner

pecar(regular -*ar* verb) to sin

pedal de aceleración(m.) gas pedal; accelerator

pedido(m.) request; order (in a restaurant)

pedir(stem-changing verb, $e \rightarrow i$) to ask (for); request **pedir un préstamo** to ask for a loan

peinado(m.) hair style

peinar(se)(regular -*ar* verb) to comb one's hair

peine(m.) comb

peligro(m.) danger

pelirrojo(adj.) redheaded

pelo(m.) hair

pelota(f.) ball

pelotero(m.) baseball player

peludo(adj.) hairy

peluquería(f.) beauty shop

pensar(stem-changing verb, $e \rightarrow ie$) to think

peor(adj.; adv.) worse; worst

pequeño(adj.) small

perder(stem-changing verb, $e \rightarrow ie$) to lose

perfectamente(adv.) perfectly

perfecto(adj.) perfect

periódico(m.) newspaper

perla(f.) pearl

permitir(regular -*ir* verb) to permit; allow; let

pero(conj.) but

perro(a)(noun) dog; **perro de caza** hunting dog

pertenecer(irregular first-person verb, like *conocer*) to belong to

pescadería(f.) fish market

pescado(m.) fish

pesebre(m.) manger

petición(f.) request; petition

pez(m.) fish (pl. *peces*)

pie(m.) foot; **a pie** on foot

piedra(f.) stone

pimienta(f.) pepper

pingüino(m.) penguin

pintor(a)(noun) painter

piscina(f.) pool

planchar(regular *-ar* verb) to iron (clothes)

planeta(m.) planet

planta(f.) plant

plata(f.) silver

plataforma(f.) platform

platillo(m.) cymbal

playa(f.) beach

plaza(f.) plaza; square

plomero(m.) plumber

pobre(adj.) poor

pobreza(f.) poverty

poco small amount (of)

poder(stem-changing verb, *o→ue*) to be able to; can; may

poesía(f.) poetry

policía(noun) police officer; (f.) police force

político(a)(noun) politician; (f.) politics

polvo(m.) dust; powder

pollito(m.) chick

pollo(m.) chicken **pollo frito** fried chicken

pomada(f.) ointment; cream

poner(irregular first-person verb, like *hacer*) to place; to put; **poner la mesa** to set the table; **ponerse** to put (clothes) on

por cierto(adv.) surely

por dentro(adv.) on the inside

por fin(adv.) finally

por fuera(adv.) on the outside

por la mañana(adv.) in the morning

por la noche(adv.) at night

por la tarde(adv.) in the afternoon

por lo menos at least

¿por qué? why?; **porque** (conj.) because

por supuesto of course

portería(f.) goal (soccer)

portero(m.) goalie (soccer)

posada(f.) inn; lodge

postre(m.) dessert

pozo(m.) well

practicar(regular *-ar* verb) to practice

prado(m.) field; meadow

precio(m.) price

predicador(m.) preacher

predicar(regular *-ar* verb) to preach

preferir(stem-changing verb, *e→ie*) to prefer

preguntar(regular *-ar* verb) to ask a question

prenda(f.) pledge; token

preocupación(f.) preoccupation; concern

preocuparse(regular *-ar* verb) to worry; be concerned

preparar(regular *-ar* verb) to prepare; **preparar la comida** to prepare a meal; **preparar(se)** to get (oneself) ready

presentar(regular *-ar* verb) to present; to introduce

presidente(noun) president

presión(f.) tension; pressure

prestar(regular *-ar* verb) to loan

pretexto(m.) pretext

primero(adj.) first (in order); **primeros auxilios** first aid

primo(a)(noun) cousin

principio(m.) 1. the beginning; origin; 2. principle

probar(stem-changing verb, *o→ue*) to try; taste; **probarse** to try (clothes) on

procedente de originating from

producir(irregular first-person verb, like *conocer*) to produce

prometer(regular *-er* verb) to promise

promover(stem-changing verb, *o→ue*) to promote

pronto(adv.) immediately; **de pronto** (adv.) suddenly

propina(f.) tip

propio(adj.) one's own

proteger(irregular first-person verb, like *escoger*) to protect

protestar(regular *-ar* verb) to protest

próximo(adj.) next

pueblo(m.) 1. small town; village; 2. people; populace

puerta(f.) door; gate; **puerta de embarque** boarding gate; **puerta de salida** exit

pulmón(m.) lung

pulpo(m.) octopus

pulsera(f.) bracelet

pulso(m.) pulse

punto(m.) point; **punto de vista** point of view

pureza(f.) purity

puro(adj.) pure

quedarse(regular *-ar* verb) to stay

¿Qué pasa? What's up? What's happening?

¡Qué pena! What a shame! How sad!

¡Qué va! No way!

querer(stem-changing verb, *e→ie*) to want; to like

¿Qué te parece? What do you think?

¿quién? who? whom?; **¿a quién?** to whom?

quieto(adj.) quiet; still; calm

quinceañera(f.) fifteenth birthday girl

quitarse(regular -ar verb) to take (clothes) off

quizás(adv.) perhaps

radiador(m.) radiator

rápidamente(adv.) rapidly

rápido(adj.) rapid

ratón(m.) mouse

raya(f.) stripe; stroke; dash; **rayado/de rayas** (adj.) striped

rayo(m.) beam; ray

real(adj.) 1. real; 2. royal

rebasar(regular -ar verb) to go beyond; pass (a vehicle)

rebote(m.) rebound

recado(m.) message

recalentar(stem-changing verb, *e→ie*) to overheat (car); to reheat

recepción(f.) reception

recepcionista(noun) receptionist

receptor(m.) catcher (baseball); receiver

receta(f.) 1. prescription; 2. recipe

recetar(regular -ar verb) to prescribe

recibir(regular -ir verb) to receive

recipiente(m.) recipient

reclamación de equipaje(f.) baggage claim

recomendar(stem-changing verb, *e→ie*) to recommend

recordar(stem-changing verb, *o→ue*) to remember

redacción(f.) writing; composition

reducir(irregular first-person verb, like *conocer*) to reduce

refresco(m.) soft drink

regalo(m.) gift

regresar(regular -ar verb) to return

regularmente(adv.) regularly

reír(stem-changing verb, *e→i*) to laugh

reloj(m.) clock; watch

relojería(f.) watchmaker's shop

remo(m.) oar; paddle

repartir(regular -ir verb) to divide; distribute

repetir(stem-changing verb, *e→i*) to repeat

repleto(adj.) replete; full

repollo(m.) cabbage; coleslaw

república(f.) republic

rescatar(regular -ar verb) to rescue; ransom

reservar(regular -ar verb) to reserve

restaurante(m.) restaurant

retirar(regular -ar verb) to withdraw; **retirar dinero** to withdraw money from a bank account

retraso(m.) delay

reunir (dinero)(regular -ir verb) to gather (money)

revisar(regular -ar verb) 1. to review; examine; check; 2. to revise

revisor(a)(noun) inspector; examiner; auditor

revista(f.) magazine

revolución(f.) revolution

revólver(m.) revolver

rico(adj.) 1. rich; 2. delicious (food)

rifle(m.) rifle

rincón(m.) corner

riñón(m.) kidney

río(m.) river

riqueza(f.) riches; wealth

rizado(adj.) curly

roca(f.) rock

rodar(stem-changing verb, *o→ue*) to roll; run on wheels

rodilla(f.) knee

rogar(stem-changing verb, *o→ue*) to ask; beg

rojo(adj.) red

romper(regular -er verb) to break

rozar(regular -ar verb) to touch or brush lightly

rubio(adj.) blond(e)

rueda de repuesto(f.) spare tire

ruido(m.) noise

sábana(f.) sheet

saber(irregular first-person verb) to know

sabio(adj.) wise

sacar(regular -ar verb) to take (away or off) **sacar fotos** to take pictures

sal(f.) salt

sala(f.) living room; **sala de clase** classroom; **sala de espera** waiting room

salida(f.) exit; departure

salir(irregular first-person verb, like *hacer*) to go out; **salir bien (mal)** to turn out well (poorly)

salón de belleza(m.) beauty parlor

saltar(regular -ar verb) to jump

salvación(f.) salvation

sanar(regular -ar verb) to heal

sandalia(f.) sandal

sangre(f.) blood

sano(adj.) in good health; well

santo(adj.) holy

sargento(a)(noun) sergeant

sartén(m.) frying pan

satisfacción(f.) satisfaction

satisfecho(adj.) satisfied

secador de pelo(m.) hair dryer

secarse(regular -*ar* verb) to dry oneself

seco(adj.) dry

secretario(a)(noun) secretary

seguir(stem-changing verb, *e→i*) to follow; to keep on going

segundo(adj.) second (in order)

seguridad(f.) security

selva(f.) jungle

sello(m.) stamp

semáforo(m.) traffic light

senador(m.) senator

sensación(f.) sensation

sensible(adj.) perceptible; sensitive

sentar(se)(stem-changing verb, *e→ie*) to seat (oneself)

sentimientos(m. pl.) feelings

sentir(stem-changing verb, *e→ie*) to feel; to regret; **sentirse** to feel (physical or emotional state)

señalar(regular -*ar* verb) to point out; to indicate with signals

sepultura(f.) grave

ser(irregular verb) to be (identification; characteristic)

serio(adj.) serious

serpiente(f.) serpent; snake

servilleta(f.) napkin

servir(stem-changing verb, *e→i*) to serve

siempre(adv.) always

siempre que(conj.) whenever

siglo(m.) century; age

sillón(m.) upholstered chair

simpatía(f.) sympathy

simpático(adj.) friendly; nice

sin que(conj.) without

sistema solar(m.) solar system

sobre 1. (m.) envelope; 2. (prep.) on; upon; on top of

sobrino(a)(noun) nephew; niece

socialismo(m.) socialism

sofá(m.) sofa

sol(m.) sun

solapa(f.) lapel

soldado(m.) soldier

sombrero(m.) hat

sonar(stem-changing verb, *o→ue*) to sound; to ring

sonreír(stem-changing verb, *e→i*) to smile

soñar(stem-changing verb, *o→ue*) to dream

sopa(f.) soup

subir(regular -*ir* verb) to go up; **subir (a)** to board (a vehicle)

suceder(regular -*er* verb) to happen; occur

suegro(a)(noun) father-in-law; mother-in-law

sueño(m.) 1. dream; 2. sleep

suéter(m.) sweater

sugerir(stem-changing verb, *e→i*) to suggest

suplir(regular -*ir* verb) to supply

tacaño(adj.) stingy

tacón alto(m.) high heel

talonario(m.) checkbook

talla(f.) size

también(adv.) also

tambor(m.) drum

tampoco(adv.) neither

tan(adv.) as; so

tan pronto como(conj.) as soon as

tardar (en)(regular -*ar* verb) to delay (in)

tarde 1. (f.) afternoon; 2. (adj.) late

tarea(f.) homework; assignment; job

tarjeta(f.) card; **tarjeta postal** postcard; **tarjeta de embarque** boarding pass; **tarjeta amarilla** yellow card (soccer); **tarjeta de crédito** credit card

tasa(f.) rate; price

taza(f.) cup

teatro(m.) theater

teléfono(m.) telephone; **teléfono público** public telephone

televisor(m.) television set

temperatura(f.) temperature

temprano(adj.) early

tenaz(adj.) tenacious

tenedor(m.) fork

tener(irregular verb) to have; **tener éxito** to be successful; **tener como meta** to have as a goal

tensión(f.) tension

tentar(stem-changing verb, *e→ie*) to tempt

tercero(adj.) third (in order); **tercera base** third base (baseball)

terminal(m.) terminal

terminar(regular -*ar* verb) to finish

ternera(f.) veal

terreno(m.) ground; terrain

testificar(regular -*ar* verb) to witness

testuz(m.) 1. nape; 2. forehead (of animals)

tiburón(m.) shark

tienda(f.) store

tierno(adj.) tender

tigre(m.) tiger

tijeras(f. pl.) scissors

tío(a)(noun) uncle; aunt

tirar(regular -*ar* verb) 1. to throw; 2. to pull

toalla(f.) towel

tobillo(m.) ankle

tocadiscos(m.) record player

tocador(m.) dresser

tocar(regular -*ar* verb) 1. to touch; 2. to play (an instrument) **tocar a la puerta** to knock

tocino(m.) bacon

todavía(adv.) yet; still

tomar(regular -*ar* verb) 1. to take; 2. to drink; **tomar asiento** to take a seat; **tomar café** to have coffee; **tomar un paseo** to go for a walk or drive

tomate(m.) tomato

tono(m.) tone

tonto(adj.) dumb; foolish

toro(m.) bull

toser(regular -*er* verb) to cough

trabajar(regular -*ar* verb) to work

traducir(irregular first-person verb, like *conocer*) to translate

traer(irregular first-person verb) to bring

traje(m.) suit; outfit

tranquilizante(m.) tranquilizer

tranquilo(adj.) calm; easy-going

trasero(adj.) back; rear

tratar (de)(regular -*ar* verb) to try (to)

tren(m.) train

triste(adj.) sad

tristeza(f.) sadness

trombón(m.) trombone

trompeta(f.) trumpet

u (conj.) or (used instead of *o* before words that begin with *o* or *ho*)

último(adj.) last

una tras otra one after another

una vez one time; once **una vez que** (conj.) once that

unido(adj.) united

uniforme 1. (m.) uniform; 2. (adj.) uniform; consistent

unión(f.) union

unir(regular -*ir* verb) unite

usar(regular -*ar* verb) to use; **uso propio** one's own use

uva(f.) grape

vaca(f.) cow

vacaciones(f. pl.) vacation

valentía(f.) bravery

vaso(m.) drinking glass

vecino(a)(noun) neighbor

vegetal(m.) vegetable

venado(m.) deer; stag

vendedor(a)(noun) seller; salesperson

vender(regular -*er* verb) to sell

venir(stem-changing verb *e→ie*; irregular first-person verb) to come

venta especial(f.) special sale

ventana(f.) window

ver(irregular first-person verb) to see; look; **¿Cómo me veo?** How do I look?

verdad(f.) truth; **¿Verdad?** Isn't that right?

verde(adj.) green

verdulería(f.) vegetable shop

verdura(f.) vegetable

verter(stem-changing verb, *e→ie*) to pour; spill; shed

vestido(m.) dress

vestir(se)(stem-changing verb, *e→i*) to dress (oneself)

vez(f.) time; turn; **a la vez** at the same time; **a veces** sometimes; **cada vez** each time; **de una vez** at once; once and for all; **esta vez** this time

vía(f.) way; train tracks

viajar(regular -*ar* verb) to travel

victoria(f.) victory

viejo(adj.) old

viento(m.) wind

violín(m.) violin

violoncelo(m.) cello

visado(m.) visa

visitar(regular -*ar* verb) to visit

vivir(regular -*ir* verb) to live

volante(m.) steering wheel

volar(stem-changing verb, *o→ue*) to fly

volibol(m.) volleyball

voluntad(f.) will

volver(stem-changing verb, *o→ue*) to return; to go back

votar(regular -*ar* verb) to vote

y (conj.) and

ya(adv.) already

ya no no longer

yema(f.) egg yolk

yerno(m.) son-in-law

zanahoria(f.) carrot

zancudo(m.) mosquito

zapatería(f.) shoe shop

zapatero(m.) shoemaker; cobbler

zapato(m.) shoe; **zapatos deportivos** tennis shoes

INDEX

Acknowledgments

A careful effort has been made to trace the ownership of selections included in this textbook in order to secure permission to reprint copyright material and to make full acknowledgment of their use. If any error or omission has occurred, it is purely inadvertent and will be corrected in subsequent editions, provided written notification is made to the publisher.

Alianza Editorial S.A. "Los músicos de Bremen" from *Jacob y Wilhelm Grimm: Cuentos* by Jacob and Wilhelm Grimm, translated by Pedro Gálvez. Copyright © 1976. Used by permission.

American Bible Society Excerpts from *La Santa Biblia: Antiguo y Nuevo Testamento* Versión Reina-Valera, copyright © 1960. Used by permission.

"Bolívar" first published in *Sonetos Sinfónicos,* 1914.

Herederos de Juan Ramón Jiménez "El viaje definitivo" and excerpts from *Platero y yo* used by permission of Carmen Hernández-Pinzón Moreno.

Holt, Rinehart and Winston, Inc. "Lo fatal" by Rubén Darío from *Literatura Hispanoamericana: Antología e Introducción Histórica* Vol. 2 edited by Enrique A. Imbert and Eugenio Florit, copyright © 1970. Used by permission.

Photograph Credits

The following agencies and individuals have furnished materials to meet the photographic needs of this textbook. We wish to express our gratitude to them for their important contribution.

David Bell
Kathy Bell
Bob Jones University Collection of Sacred Art
Jaime Bonilla
Kenneth G. Casillas
Mike Dodgens
Eastman Chemicals Division
Embassy of Spain

Embassy of Uruguay
James Gardner
Déborah D. Garwood
Beulah E. Hager
Inter-American Development Bank
George Jensen
Ken Jensen
Barbara Lewis
Library of Congress

Bruce Martin
Bryan Martin
National Gallery of Art, Washington, D.C.
Ed Richards
George Rogier
United States Dept. of Agriculture
Unusual Films
Ward's Natural Science Est.
World Bank Photo

Cover
Courtesy of Mike Dodgens
Title pages
Unusual Films ii; Kenneth G. Casillas ii-iii; George Jensen iii; Déborah D. Garwood iii; World Bank Photo, Huffman xvi
Chapter 1
Unusual Films 1, 27; George Rogier 7; Ward's Natural Science Est. 12; Mike Dodgens 23; Beulah E. Hager 29
Chapter 2
Mike Dodgens 33, 41; Ken Jensen 45 (top), 60; Embassy of Uruguay 45 (bottom); James Gardner 51; Beulah E. Hager 65; David Bell 70
Chapter 3
Unusual Films 71, 91; Bruce Martin 82 (l); World Bank Photo, I. Andrews 82 (r)

Chapter 4
Beulah E. Hager 103, 116; Eastman Chemicals Division 108; Jaime Bonilla 119, 128
Chapter 5
Mike Dodgens 131, 142; Beulah E. Hager 137; Inter-American Development Bank 138, 149; David Bell 143; Ed Richards 148; James Gardner 157; Unusual Films 158
Chapter 6
Unusual Films 159; Bryan Martin 176; World Bank Photo, G. Franchini 177; Library of Congress 179; Bob Jones University Collection of Sacred Art 181; Beulah E. Hager 183
Chapter 7
U.S. Dept. of Agriculture 187; Embassy of Spain 202; Mike Dodgens 207

Chapter 8
Unusual Films 209; Barbara Lewis 215; David Bell 219, 224
Chapter 9
National Gallery of Art 229; Unusual Films 241; Mike Dodgens 247
Chapter 10
Unusual Films 253, 254, 267, 270; Kathy Bell 268; Beulah E. Hager 274
Chapter 11
Unusual Films 279, 280, 294; Mike Dodgens 286
Chapter 12
Unusual Films 299; George Rogier 305; Mike Dodgens 307